Content COUNTS!

Developing Disciplinary Literacy Skills, K–6

Jennifer L. Altieri

INTERNATIONAL
Reading Association
800 BARKSDALE ROAD, PO BOX 8139
NEWARK, DE 19714-8139, USA
www.reading.org

The International Reading Association attempts, through its publications, to provide a forum for a wide spectrum of opinions on reading. This policy permits divergent viewpoints without implying the endorsement of the Association.

Executive Editor, Publications   Shannon Fortner

Managing Editor   Christina M. Terranova

Editorial Associate   Wendy Logan

Design and Composition Manager   Anette Schuetz

Design and Composition Associate   Lisa Kochel

Cover   Design, Alissa Jones; Photographs (clockwise from top left): © Shutterstock Images, © Shutterstock Images, © nyul/123RF.com, © Dmitriy Shironosov/123RF.com, © Shutterstock Images

The publisher would appreciate notification where errors occur so that they may be corrected in subsequent printings and/or editions.

Library of Congress Cataloging-in-Publication Data

Altieri, Jennifer L.

  Content counts! : developing disciplinary literacy skills, K-6 / Jennifer L. Altieri.

     p. cm.

  Includes bibliographical references and index.

  ISBN 978-0-87207-838-3

  1. Language arts (Elementary) 2. Content area reading. I. Title.

  LB1576.A61573 2011

  372.6--dc22

                                        2011004799

Suggested APA Reference

Altieri, J.L. (2011). *Content counts! Developing disciplinary literacy skills, K–6*. Newark, DE: International Reading Association.

For English learners Aklilu and Ashenafi as they embark
on their literacy journey.

CONTENTS

PART I

Making Content Count: Getting Started in the Elementary Grades

Trying It Out: Activities for Fostering Disciplinary Literacy Skills in Math, Science, and Social Studies

ABOUT THE AUTHOR

 **Jennifer L. Altieri** is an associate professor and coordinator of the Division of Literacy Education in the School of Education at The Citadel in Charleston, South Carolina, USA. She is the author of *Literacy + Math = Creative Connections in the Elementary Classroom* (International Reading Association [IRA], 2010) and coauthor of *Moving Toward an Integrated Curriculum in Early Childhood Education* (National Education Association, 1996). She has also published articles in *Teaching Children Mathematics*, *Teaching Exceptional Children*, *Reading Psychology*, *Reading Research and Instruction*, and other professional journals.

After completing her BS in elementary education at Bowling Green State University, Ohio, USA, she moved to Houston, Texas, USA. There she taught in the Aldine and Spring independent school districts. Jennifer has served as a reading consultant for elementary and middle schools in the St. Louis Public and University City school districts in St. Louis, Missouri, USA, and at Port Royal Elementary in Beaufort, South Carolina. She has conducted workshops at the elementary and middle school levels on a variety of literacy topics and is known for her enthusiasm and sense of humor.

Jennifer earned her MEd from the University of Houston and her PhD from Texas A&M University. Along with serving on *The Reading Teacher*'s and *Reading Horizons*'s editorial boards, she is on the Board of Directors for Charleston Community of Readers and recently served on IRA's 2010 Standards Committee.

She resides in Mt. Pleasant, South Carolina, and is excited to be a new mom to biological brothers adopted from Africa.

Author Information for Correspondence

Jennifer welcomes your questions and comments. Please feel free to contact her at jennifer.altieri@citadel.edu.

PREFACE

"What did you do today?" is a question many of us hear every day, a question so common that we may not even give it much thought, but what *did* you do today? As an elementary teacher, have you ever attempted to actually summarize everything you try to accomplish with your students in an ordinary school day? It truly is mind-boggling how many things we try to accomplish each and every day when working with students. Along with fostering and strengthening the literacy skills students bring to our classrooms, we as elementary educators must help students develop a solid foundation of knowledge and skills in science, social studies, and math. As we seek to introduce, expand, and reinforce our elementary students' content knowledge, we begin to realize the complexity of the task at hand. Although secondary teachers focus on only one or two content areas, elementary teachers are expected to be able to develop students' knowledge of many content areas.

Let's look at some of the common content area expectations often experienced in elementary school as articulated in standards created by state and professional organizations, the increasingly high-stakes testing, and the demands made through the large amount of information available with technology. In math, students are expected not only to understand the order of operations but also to learn and be able to apply a great deal of other mathematical information before they complete the elementary grades. Students must become knowledgeable about their community, the United States as a nation, and the world through the social studies curriculum, but they are also expected to develop civic competence. Then, there is the large body of scientific knowledge that students must be able to comprehend. Although all of this content information is important, we must also ensure that students possess the literacy skills necessary to communicate their understanding. They must be able to read and comprehend informative texts; orally articulate their knowledge; convey information about social studies, science, and math topics through writing; and be able to not only view content area information but also visually represent knowledge. As Wood (2003) emphasizes, content literacy is no longer just for secondary classrooms.

Although elementary teachers are expected to develop math, science, and social studies skills while fostering literacy development, there are very few literacy texts written to assist elementary teachers with developing content area knowledge. Content literacy texts are written primarily for middle and high school teachers, and even then the books often focus on science and social studies and provide minimal attention to the field of mathematics. Chall, Jacobs, and Baldwin (1990) have written about the fourth-grade slump, which occurs when students are suddenly expected to read to learn, so we must do everything we can to prepare students at the very earliest levels in developing what Shanahan and Shanahan (2008) refer to as "disciplinary literacy skills." Disciplinary literacy refers to "literacy skills specialized to history, science, mathematics, literature, or other subject matter" (p. 44). Therefore, this text is written to fill a void in the content area textbooks currently available by providing ideas to strengthen disciplinary literacy at even the youngest of ages. Each content area has unique demands that students must be familiar with to navigate the math, science, and social studies text they will encounter at the upper grades and later in life. This book seeks to focus on activities that relate to the specific demands of math, science, and social studies text.

This text is also designed to assist elementary teachers in shifting from an emphasis on narrative texts to more informative types of materials. To do this, we must provide appropriate literacy activities and introduce students to informative texts as early as possible. Many phenomenal teachers tell me that they have to make a conscious choice to use informative texts because their inclination is to select fiction to connect with content areas; they grew up enjoying many wonderful storybooks, and those are the ones they automatically try to connect to topics and themes their students are learning.

Duke (2000) surprised many people in the field when her research revealed that students experience only 3.6 minutes of informative text per day. However, when I share her research with practicing teachers, many are not surprised. As children, they were exposed to a great deal of fiction, and they often believe that students enjoy and will be more engaged with make-believe stories; yet, a great deal of writing in the educational field shows that students enjoy informative texts (e.g., Caswell & Duke, 1998; Pappas, 1993). Informative trade books have improved greatly over the years, and although textbooks may be thought of for teaching content area material, they are far from the only choice for the math,

science, and social studies classroom. There are many great trade books available with amazing pictures, fascinating information, and linguistic features designed to help the reader get the most from the text. *Content Counts! Developing Disciplinary Literacy Skills, K–6* will help teachers as they seek to strengthen the use of informative texts in their classrooms by providing ideas for selecting and using the texts, as well as sharing available children's texts.

In the chapters that follow, the term *text* is used in the broadest sense. Many of our students are what Prensky (2005) calls "digital natives." Unlike some of us, including myself, who are "digital immigrants," our students were born in a time when technology was already playing an important part in their world. Therefore, using nonprint media helps us make learning relevant and applicable to students' lives outside the classroom, and this type of text is used in many activities in this book. Also, creating and comprehending text viewed through technological means is necessary for students to be viewed as literate and be prepared to be productive citizens in the continually more technologically oriented world.

Beginning at the earliest of grades, elementary teachers must see themselves as content area teachers. Teachers must incorporate strategies and activities with diverse informative texts to strengthen students' math, science, and social studies learning.

Chapter by Chapter: Let's Look at the Content

This book is divided into two parts. In Part I, "Making Content Count: Getting Started in the Elementary Grades," we examine the rationale for strengthening content learning in the elementary grades and explore how to infuse meaningful informative texts into the classroom. Chapter 1, "Why Content Counts: Rethinking Content Literacy Instruction With K–6 Learners," begins by briefly examining how our vision of literacy has changed and how this change has led to an increased emphasis on content area literacy. This chapter reflects on our literacy goals for the students in our classrooms. Whereas the ability to read print often was the focus of literacy learning in the past, it is no longer enough. In order for our students to develop into adults who are considered truly literate, students must know so much more. Our literacy vision must be broad enough so that *communicating* means more than reading and writing, and *text* refers to more than traditional printed pages that students can hold in their hands.

By exploring the changing view of literacy, we see why content literacy must be focused on in the early grades.

This chapter also explores how a content area focus allows us to work within the time constraints we already experience as elementary educators and enables us to better meet the standards for the different content areas. There are not enough hours in the day to focus specific periods of time on reading, writing, oral language, math, science, and social studies content. Even if the time were available, creating barriers between the different areas will not prepare students to develop the knowledge that they need. Therefore, it is imperative that literacy learning be embedded within the content knowledge we strive to develop with our students. As Chapter 1 continues, we examine the increasing pressure on the educational system to ensure that students have a solid understanding of math, science, and social studies. We look at how disciplinary literacy involves skills unique to the various content areas. Finally, key components of a strong content area focus are shared with readers as the background is set for the rest of the text.

Chapter 2, "Selecting Materials for Content Area Connections," encourages teachers to look at the wide variety of materials that can be incorporated into math, science, and social studies lessons. Although research shows that the textbook continues to play a large role in classrooms, many educators believe that it should be used as only one type of resource. In general, students have a great deal of difficulty comprehending textbooks. Therefore, teachers must take a closer look at other forms of imported texts, local texts, and nonprint media that might be used with our students. Each type of text is discussed in depth, and specific guidelines for selecting diverse forms of text are shared. Finally, the chapter ends by looking at the most important link between texts and students: the teacher. Educators can select the materials and strategies that will best meet the needs of their students. By doing so, teachers will enhance students' content knowledge, but students will also be able to communicate their understanding. The materials in this chapter are encouraged throughout the activities discussed in Chapters 3–6. Found throughout Chapters 1 and 2, the "Try It Out" and "Discussion Point" features are designed to provide readers with the opportunity to apply and discuss some of the ideas shared in these chapters.

After building the foundation through the first part of this book, the second part translates ideas into classroom experiences, with specific

activities for math, science, and social studies. The chapters in Part II, "Trying It Out: Activities for Fostering Disciplinary Literacy Skills in Math, Science, and Social Studies," progress from helping students read content area texts to assisting them in viewing and visually representing content area information. As each chapter focuses on an aspect of literacy (i.e., reading, oral communication, writing, viewing and visually representing), activities that enhance specific disciplinary literacy skills necessary in math, science, and social studies are provided. Along with explaining the steps for each activity in the "How It Works" sections, many of the activities also contain a section called "A Look Inside One Classroom," which explains how an elementary teacher implemented the strategy. Accompanying samples range from kindergarten through grade 6, often including student work. Although pseudonyms are used in lieu of actual names for all student work included in the figures and the text, no changes were made to the students' original writing and spelling.

Additionally, after many of the suggestions and activities, the reader will find a section entitled, "Additional Ways to Try It Out." This section is a continuation of the "Try It Out" feature seen in Part I of this text. "Additional Ways to Try It Out" provides suggestions on modifying specific activities or strategies. All of the activities included in Chapters 3–6 were chosen because they can be modified to work with a range of ages.

Chapter 3, "Meeting the Reading Comprehension Demands of Each Content Area," focuses on the specific requirements of comprehending extended text in math, science, and social studies and how we might best focus students' attention on those requirements through reading-focused activities. Shanahan and Shanahan's (2008) work focuses our attention on the fact that students must read math texts very differently from social studies texts to gain the necessary understanding from print. Students must closely focus on each word and understand math symbols. Furthermore, focusing on visuals and text, and the relationship between the two, is often a key issue with science texts. Conversely, social studies texts often require students to try to analyze author bias and understand the main idea. These and other differences are noted, and the engaging activities within this book introduce the reading demands for math, science, and social studies.

Although getting students to talk in a classroom is rarely difficult, we need to transform that talk into meaningful oral communications. In Chapter 4, "Orally Communicating Content Area Knowledge," ideas are

shared for developing oral language skills and meeting disciplinary literacy needs. The chapter begins with a brief discussion of research supporting the importance of enhancing listening and speaking skills in the content areas. Then, specific activities that can develop the technical vocabulary required for math and science, as well as suggestions for discussing cause and effect and other broad concepts related to social studies, are shared. Each of the activities in this chapter enhances oral communication. Although some of these activities can be used with various content areas, they are discussed within the context of specific subjects so that the reader can understand the demands of those types of text.

In Chapter 5, "Creating Content Connections Through Writing to Learn," we examine ideas to strengthen the unique writing expectations of each content area and share writing strategies that can enhance math, science, and social studies learning. Shanahan and Shanahan (2008) show us many ways that the writing demands differ for these content areas. For instance, in math, students must be taught how to translate symbols into words and vice versa. Likewise, scientists must be able to write articles and take lab notes, which require two very different types of writing. Therefore, it is important that students experience the wide range of writing demands necessary for scientific literacy. Finally, students can develop a better understanding of others' perspectives through writing about social studies content. Therefore, students become even more proficient at understanding the content they encounter in social studies. By providing a variety of ideas for cultivating writing skills, teachers are able to help sustain interest in the writing process. The goal of this chapter is to use writing as a tool to deepen content area understanding and strengthen the skills needed to develop disciplinary literacy.

As our vision of literacy changes, the ability to view and visually represent information is even more important. Chapter 6, "Creating Meaningful Visuals and Developing Viewing Skills in the Content Areas," emphasizes the importance of strengthening students' viewing and visual representation skills in the elementary classroom while enabling students to expand their math, social studies, and science knowledge. Many of the activities in this chapter discuss ways to incorporate viewing and visually representing information through the use of technology. The chapter begins by explaining the necessity for developing such skills, and similar to the other chapters included in Part II, it includes a wide variety of specific activities for math, science, and social studies.

As we strive to create literate individuals who can thrive in the world, we must shift our focus on content literacy to the elementary grades. Developing students with strong literacy skills is an admirable goal. We all want our students to be excellent readers and writers and be able to communicate their ideas through oral communication and visuals, but we must also seek to strengthen content knowledge with young students. Therefore, we must focus on developing the disciplinary literacy skills necessary for our students to continue to be successful with future texts. My hope is that by reading and reflecting on the ideas, activities, and research presented within this text, we can enhance the teaching of math, science, and social studies in the elementary grades and enable students to become more effective communicators. As knowledgeable educators, we continually strive to improve our own understanding and teaching, and my hope is that this book will play a small part in that process.

Acknowledgments

I have been influenced by many great leaders in the field of literacy, such as James Hoffman, Nell Duke, and Timothy and Cynthia Shanahan, whose writing constantly makes me want to learn more and better meet the literacy needs of my students.

All of the teachers who walk through my classroom doors also play an important role in the way I think. I especially want to thank Shannon Thornhill, Lindsay Egloff, Shannon Bassett, Kelly Lozier, Sara Buckley, Charles Manning Blakely, Sarah Coyne, Ashley Pfeffer, Brooke Irimescu, and all of the other teachers who took time out of their busy schedules to work with me and listen to my ideas. Alice Hambright, with all of her technological expertise, makes my job easier on a daily basis so that I have time to write, and my colleagues help me keep life in perspective.

Of course, no book is possible without the feedback and guidance of others. Therefore, I appreciate all of the assistance I received from editor Stacey Reid, as well as the assistance of Anne Fullerton, Corinne Mooney, and Shannon Fortner at the International Reading Association. I also look forward to receiving even more feedback from the readers of this text as they work toward developing disciplinary literacy skills and knowledge with elementary students.

Making Content Count: Getting Started in the Elementary Grades

Why Content Counts: Rethinking Content Literacy Instruction With K–6 Learners

....

Ms. B. is a third-grade teacher. Like many teachers, she puts in a great deal of time outside of her classroom to ensure that her students are involved with meaningful and engaging activities. She is also well aware of the importance of developing fluent readers and strong writers and works hard to help her students develop the necessary literacy skills. Each day, her class schedule has an allocated time for shared reading, guided reading, math, reading aloud, writing, working with words, science, and social studies.

Today, like most days, she starts with 20 minutes of shared reading. After the class finishes that, it is time for guided reading. Due to some interruptions and several students returning from receiving special services, it is slightly later than expected when the students finish guided reading. Therefore, the time allotted for math is modified, and once Ms. B. knows the students have a thorough understanding of the mathematical operation they are learning through the use of manipulatives, she lets them complete the remaining math problems at home. After lunch, there is time allocated for reading aloud, so her students see fluent reading demonstrated and develop an interest in books, and then the students have 40 minutes of writing. Because the class loves the books of Tomie dePaola, Ms. B. is sharing *Adelita: A Mexican Cinderella Story* (2004), in an effort to broaden her students' experiences with multiethnic literature.

As the afternoon continues, the students spend 20 minutes working with words during a time designated for word study. Unfortunately, by now it is 1:45 P.M. instead of 1:25 P.M., and instead of the 50 minutes planned for science today (science is taught three days a week and social studies two days a week during this time), Ms. B. only has 40 minutes to introduce nutrition, the next topic the class will study. She takes out the pop-up book she planned to use today, *The Very Hungry Caterpillar* by Eric Carle (2009), and does a modified lesson focusing on healthy

eating habits. Halfway through the book, the fire alarm sounds, and she promises the students the science lesson will be continued on Wednesday when they have science again. The students prepare for recess and then dismissal.

....

Does this classroom scenario sound familiar? The content areas and allocated time frames described here are from an actual, current elementary teacher's schedule. When looking at a variety of other elementary teachers' classroom schedules, the subjects are often the same with minor variations. For instance, writer's workshop, independent reading, and self-selected reading are a few other areas that sometimes replace some of the ones listed in Ms. B.'s schedule. Trying to maintain a schedule such as the one in this vignette is exhausting for the teacher and the students.

Clearly, the teacher is spending as much time as possible developing literacy skills with the students, and if things work out ideally during the school day—which we know rarely happens—students will have 70 minutes of math and 50 minutes of either science or social studies. It is also evident that the teacher is working hard to expose her students to quality children's books. However, we have to ask ourselves if there is a way to modify this schedule to better support disciplinary literacy skills in math, science, and social studies. Is there a way to dedicate more time to these subjects without decreasing the time spent on nurturing literacy development? Are there modifications that can be made to ensure that students will have not only the necessary reading and language arts skills to be considered literate as adults but also the essential content area knowledge and experiences that will prepare them for life?

DISCUSSION POINT

Think about your own goals in developing strong content-literate students. Do you believe there is adequate time in your daily schedule for math, science, and social studies? What opportunities do students have to incorporate the skills they develop during reading and language arts into the content areas? Are they developing the literacy skills they need that are specific to each of those areas? How might your own schedule be changed to better meet that goal?

The Changing View of Literacy

Before we talk about current content literacy expectations, let's begin by looking at how literacy skills and content area knowledge have traditionally been developed in the elementary classroom. For many years, developing literacy skills meant specifically focusing efforts on teaching reading and writing. Many students already knew how to speak and hear when they entered formal schooling, so oral language skills were expected to develop naturally. Therefore, reading and writing were the focus of the school day, and those were the skills heavily tested on standardized tests. As Flood and Lapp (1997) clearly state, there was an almost irrational loyalty to reading and writing. Literacy was viewed as a set of skills to be developed, and during the time of day reserved for reading and language arts, the focus was on teaching students to read narrative stories and create well-written sentences.

Then, the rest of the classroom day was divided into segments allocated for science, math, social studies, and other content areas. Math, similar to reading, was an emphasized area, and therefore, there was little time left to teach science or social studies. Unfortunately, it was often hit-or-miss with the other content areas, and the majority of efforts were focused on those subjects that were tested.

There were also minimal materials provided to achieve educational goals. The term *texts* referred solely to printed words on paper, and often that meant teaching with a basal series for reading and using district-adopted content area textbooks for science, social studies, and math. Incorporating technology into the classroom referred to turning on the overhead projector, watching a video, or taking students to the computer lab during a brief designated time each week. Computers were primarily used to reinforce isolated skills through repetitive drill and games.

It is easy to look back at that time period and shudder. However, we have to realize that the view of literacy has changed a great deal since that time, and it will continue to change. The idea of what it takes to be considered literate today is not the same as it was even 10 years ago. The view of literacy is continually changing because the skills students must develop to thrive in society are constantly expanding and becoming more complex. For instance, according to Alvermann (2001b), "Everyday literacy practices are changing at an unprecedented pace" (p. 16), and in 2008, the National Council of Teachers of English updated its definition

of 21st century *literacies*. Literacy is a complex, multifaceted concept that changes as society changes. Students must not only be able to read and demonstrate understanding but also be able to view and comprehend a wide range of texts and make intertextual connections. Students also must be able to share knowledge through written and oral communication and through visually representing information. According to Williams (2008), the literacy experiences that students bring to the classroom are not the same as they were in the past and will not be the same in the future. Educators must look at the challenges and opportunities presented by the changing view of literacy to prepare students for the future.

To prepare students to be successful with the various discourses they are confronted with on a daily basis, as well as those they will encounter in the future, it is important to move beyond basal reading series and content area textbooks. Students now are expected to understand a much wider variety of texts in multimedia, including texts that inform, persuade, and even those created through technology. These technological texts might include blogs, PowerPoint presentations, WebQuests, and videos. By allowing students to experience a wide range of texts instead of only traditional printed texts, we will assist a large group of students who learn better through other means (Alvermann, 2001b). Research suggests that adolescents most at risk can often be motivated through other forms of text (Alvermann, 2001a; O'Brien, 2001). Often, these students see the relevancy of literacy and their own lives through the use of diverse texts. Therefore, we must use a wide variety of texts in order to meet the needs of all students.

Increased Emphasis on Content Area Learning

This changing view of literacy has had an impact on the view of content literacy development. It is no longer enough for students to perform computational math, list the order of the presidents, and describe the types of clouds they see in the sky. Students are expected to understand more content area knowledge that goes far beyond this, and teachers at all grade levels must strive to ensure that students are able to develop that level of content literacy (Swafford & Kallus, 2002). With globalization, our students are competing with students graduating from schooling systems in other countries. As elementary educators, we are faced with preparing students to succeed in a world that continues to change and grow.

Considering the Role of Standards

No longer can students graduate high school with a minimal level of content area knowledge and succeed in the workforce. While schools must focus on the best way to develop content area knowledge, students must also be able to communicate their understanding in an articulate manner. There is an ever-increasing emphasis on standards that articulate what students are expected to learn during their formal schooling. It is rare to read educational material or watch the news without seeing a reference to educational standards. This educational concern has resulted in professional associations and state departments of education continually revisiting and revising standards as they clarify what they believe students should know and be able to do in the content areas.

At present, there are national standards created for each of the different subject areas (e.g., math, science, social studies) for all grade levels. However, there are also state standards for each subject area, which are based on the national standards created by professional organizations. The continual emphasis on standards articulating the content area knowledge that students must grasp shows that content area knowledge is demanding more and more of an educational focus.

The national standards for social studies, science, and mathematics are developed to ensure a certain level of content area understanding, and yet it is clear that the standards committees recognize the necessity of strong literacy skills in developing that knowledge. The National Council of Teachers of Mathematics (NCTM) standards created in 2000 expect students from prekindergarten through twelfth grade to be able to reflect on mathematical problem solving and display relevant data to answer self-formulated questions. The NCTM standards even have an entire process standard entitled "Communication," which stresses the importance of students from prekindergarten through twelfth grade being able to organize their mathematical thoughts and use the language of mathematics to communicate with those around them. Likewise, the National Curriculum Standards for Social Studies (National Council for the Social Studies [NCSS], 2010) encourages students to reflect on concepts learned through all language modalities. Finally, the National Science Education Standards (National Research Council [NRC], 1996) also seek to develop those who can "engage intelligently in public discourse and debate about important issues that involve science and technology" (p. 1). Possible assessments listed in the standards include portfolios, interviews, investigative reports,

or written essays. To be successful on such assessments, students will need strong literacy skills.

All three content areas involve students working together as part of a collaborative process and encourage the use of technology. While our goal is to develop strong content area knowledge, we can best achieve that by strengthening the literacy skills necessary for such knowledge. When state standards are created, it is evident that literacy skills are necessary to meet the grade-level expectations. Students are expected to be able to interpret, describe, and explain science, math, and social studies information to meet Florida and California standards and Texas Essential Knowledge and Skills (TEKS). Those expectations demand that students use their literacy skills throughout content area material. According to Moss (2005), this standards-based focus, standardized testing, and technology have placed an emphasis on informative texts and, therefore, have shifted interest in content literacy to the elementary grades.

TRY IT OUT

Examine your state standards for math, science, and social studies at the grade level you teach. Determine specific ways that literacy skills are tied to the standards. Look for skills related to reading, writing, oral language, and visual representation. Take notes on what you find and use the information to guide you as you plan meaningful classroom activities that focus on disciplinary literacy skills.

Concerns Regarding Content Area Instruction

Although many people argue that math has always been a priority because of testing, we are now seeing widespread calls from the National Governors Association urging schools to place an even higher level of emphasis on integrating science, technology, engineering, and math (STEM) in the classroom ("The Push," 2008). Statewide STEM initiatives have become a topic of discussion for those involved in education in many states, as government and business leaders urge us to focus on those areas of the curriculum. These initiatives are often directed at high school students and other stakeholders in their education. The importance of creating rigorous high school classes, encouraging early postsecondary and career planning, and helping students compete in the global market are often mentioned.

However, to meet the higher expectations at the secondary level, we have to begin preparing students for the demands of the mathematical field in the elementary grades.

Similarly, the National Assessment of Educational Progress (NAEP) requires that test takers be able to understand not only the narrative text often used in the elementary grades but also the informative text students often experience later in schooling. In fact, 50% of the passages are informative at the fourth-grade level, and that amount increases to 70% in high school. By focusing on content area literacy as early as possible, students are more prepared for assessments such as the NAEP. Yet scores announced in March 2009 show that the nation's fourth graders show no sign of reading improvement from the previous year's test data (see nationsreportcard.gov).

Comments are often made in the media regarding the fact that students in the United States cannot perform up to the ability level seen in other countries. There are international tests that support these claims. The Program for International Student Assessment (PISA) conducts a standardized test that assesses the reading literacy, mathematics literacy, and scientific literacy of 15-year-olds from both public and private schools around the world. Students are expected to apply their knowledge of reading, mathematics, and science to issues that might actually be encountered in real life. According to *Reading Today* ("PISA," 2008), every three years when the assessment is given, it focuses on one of the three literacies. For instance, the 2006 PISA exam focused on scientific literacy. In one sample question, students are presented with a photo and information on the Grand Canyon and then asked which of two questions regarding the Grand Canyon could be answered through scientific investigation. Another question discusses two children creating an experiment related to sunscreen and then asks students which of four questions the two children were trying to answer with their experiment and why they completed certain steps in the experiment. These questions require much more than rote memorization of facts. When one looks at the scores from the U.S. students, it is evident that compared with 29 other countries in the PISA jurisdiction, U.S. students scored lower than 20 of the countries on the combined science literacy scale (Baldi, Jin, Skemer, Green, & Herget, 2007). Although not all students completed the mathematics literacy portion in 2006, again the results are not positive. U.S. students, when compared with students of the 29 other countries,

scored higher than students of only five other countries. Therefore, in order for students to be able to compete globally, they must develop stronger content area knowledge and be able to apply that information in authentic ways.

The most recent Progress in International Reading Literacy Study (PIRLS), completed by fourth graders in 2006, revealed similar findings. Although students in the United States did not show a significant drop in their test scores, the United States overall was ranked significantly lower than in the past. Hong Kong improved its scores on the test so that instead of being far below the United States in ranking, they are actually very far ahead. Chall's research has focused educational attention on the fact that in approximately the fourth grade, students see a shift in expectations. They no longer are expected to learn to read but rather are expected to read to learn. Chall and colleagues (1990) coined the very popular educational term "the fourth-grade slump" to describe the time when students enter fourth grade and cannot meet the literacy demands required of them, and therefore struggle academically. Unfortunately, Chall et al.'s research shows that students from low socioeconomic homes struggle even more than middle class students. In order for students to be successful, they must be exposed to informative text, and attention must focus on building their content knowledge long before the upper grades.

Many in the field of social studies are alarmed at the lack of classroom time focused on social studies education (Jones & Thomas, 2006; Manzo, 2005; Perkins-Gough, 2004). Unfortunately, this is not a new concern. Even when I taught elementary school back in the late 1980s, teachers were required to focus on math and reading. Just as with the current classroom schedule shared at the beginning of the chapter, science and social studies were squeezed in on alternating days of the week if time allowed near the end of the day. Some of the elementary teachers I work with today have voiced similar concerns and stated that they are told they must teach math and reading but that the other subjects need to be "covered" during reading time if they want to teach them.

As conscientious educators, we are concerned about meeting the needs of the students. We need to take innovative measures to ensure that social studies and science content are linked to literacy skills. If this integrated instruction does not occur, we will continue to see students developing less and less knowledge of content area information, and they will be less equipped to deal with out-of-school literacy demands. Also, by using

innovative methods to connect content area knowledge and literacy skills, students are better prepared to develop the disciplinary skills they need to be successful in each of the content areas.

What Makes Content Area Material So Demanding for Elementary Students?

Although many, if not all, of those engaged in the educational community would agree that content area material is much more demanding than other types of text, we need to better understand why that is so. Let's think about some of the differences between an expository or informative text that we might encounter with social studies, math, or science and compare it to the type of fictional reading most students encounter in the elementary grades.

First, there are the vocabulary demands. Vacca and Vacca (2008) refer to three types of vocabulary: general, specialized, and technical. General vocabulary refers to the words we find in everyday speech and text. Therefore, students have extensive opportunities to see, say, hear, and write these words. Overall, everyone understands and agrees on the meaning of these words when the terms are encountered. Specialized words are more difficult. Although they may have general meanings in most situations, they can have specialized meanings within certain content area contexts. These are also called *multimeaning words*. Words such as *yard*, *plot*, and *gross* can have very different meanings depending on whether they are used in reference to everyday objects or within a mathematical context. A term such as *branch* refers to a section of the government in social studies but within everyday context typically refers to a tree. Then, there are homophones, such as *weigh* and *way*, which are confusing to students and especially English learners. Even more difficult than specialized terms, we have technical vocabulary. These terms are only seen and heard in specific content areas. *Circumference*, *legislation*, and *hypothesis* are just a few polysyllabic technical terms that students are expected to learn and be able to use. The complex vocabulary demands in content area material can create a great deal of issues for students.

Second, let's think about the comprehension skills required for content area material. Many of us can sit down and read a novel by our favorite author and understand it rather easily without much guidance. However, if we are presented with a detailed article on health care reform or directions for building an experimental airplane, many of us would struggle. In fact, I

doubt too many of us would want to ride in the airplane we built. Likewise, content area text requires a very different type of reading. It assumes that the reader has a certain level of prior knowledge and specific background experiences. The way the text is read will also vary. The reader will want to make note of important points. This might be accomplished through highlighting, two-column note-taking, or another method of reminding ourselves of key points. Very few of us would even consider using these strategies with narrative text read for enjoyment. Finally, the material must be read critically. It is important to examine the author's view on the topic and determine whether the text contains accurate information or whether the material is propaganda designed to persuade the reader to adopt a specific viewpoint. This means that intertextual connections are even more important with content area texts.

Through Shanahan and Shanahan's (2008) work, it is evident that mathematicians, scientists, and historians must read material very differently. Shanahan and Shanahan found that mathematicians must read material closely and pay attention to every word because even the smallest of words, such as *is* and *of*, which may be insignificant words in many texts, may be important when determining a mathematical answer. Those in scientific fields must often focus on visualizing the material they read and comparing visual aids. In addition, historians must not look at text as if it is factual and must instead be able to compare multiple texts to verify information. They must also be able to read a text to determine the author's point of view and realize that the reader's opinions will also influence the reading of text. Historians must be able to examine and read multiple documents that include multimodal sources to complete their work (Leinhardt & Young, 1996; Wineburg, 1991). All of this is important to consider as students try to understand texts.

Intertextuality (Kristeva, 1984) refers to the ability to take material within a text and relate it to other texts previously read. Many teachers encourage students to make intertextual connections on a daily basis as part of literature circles and other activities conducted with narrative materials. Making these types of connections with narrative text is valuable in helping students see how ideas relate and can strengthen their understanding of material. However, these connections are essential with expository and informative text, too. Many times, these types of intertextual connections are important to corroborate what various authors may be stating on the same topic; for instance, students need to realize that

there are many different types of texts in social studies, including primary and secondary resources. By making connections, students can analyze second-opinion texts on subjects to better understand what is occurring. Not only must students make connections, but they also must know how to locate sources and evaluate the information they are reading. With all of the content area material available on the Internet, it is becoming even more important that students learn to read text in a critical manner.

Finally, students are expected to remember a great deal of information from content area material. If we were asked to read an adolescent novel and then have a book talk with students, most of would easily be able to do it successfully. However, if we were presented with a text on the ancient Greek Olympics, the phases of the moon, or the three branches of the U.S. government and their responsibilities, and then asked to share the information with students, I bet we would react very differently. What would we want to do? I would want to spend time familiarizing myself with the material and studying it. Elementary students would, too. Content area material demands that students develop study skills to learn the material. These skills are not going to occur naturally. Without guidance, students will want to write down everything they read verbatim. That is definitely not going to work, and students need to know how to weed out unimportant information and focus on the facts that need to be learned. Students must also be taught that informative texts have a unique structure (Moss, 2004). By helping students realize the importance of linguistic features, such as diverse fonts, diagrams, and headings, they will be able to navigate through informative text and learn the content within it.

DISCUSSION POINT

Think about the math, science, and social studies texts used at your grade level. What specific difficulties do students have with each of the content areas? Are there certain issues that you have noticed with students regarding the specific linguistic features, vocabulary demands, or content-specific demands? Discuss how it might be possible to prepare students for the content area demands that they might encounter.

Content area texts present many unique demands. Students must be able to deal with complex vocabulary, approach the material differently to comprehend it, realize the potential of multiple sources, and know how

to determine the most important information in the text. They can only gain the abilities to be successful with such material by experiencing it on a consistent basis. Through teacher-guided activities and experience, students can build their background knowledge with math, science, and social studies texts and achieve success.

Content Area Demands Related to Other Aspects of Literacy

When we think about oral communication within diverse content areas, we must consider the vocabulary demands discussed earlier in the chapter. All three content areas require that students have the technical vocabulary as part of their speaking vocabulary, which does not come automatically. During conversations and other types of talk, students may not automatically use mathematical and scientific terms or the metaphors and antiquated words they read in their social studies text. However, there are ways to get students to expand their speaking vocabulary and incorporate the terms. Try reading a word or phrase that is not in your speaking vocabulary. It is extremely difficult, and comprehension is nearly impossible. Furthermore, listening is just as important as speaking, and listening to informative material is very different from listening to a story. In Chapter 4, we expand on these ideas as we seek to develop oral communication in the content areas.

Writing demands also vary. Mathematicians must be able to translate symbols into words and vice versa. Likewise, scientists must understand how various types of writing are effective. Notes written about an experiment will look very different from an article written to persuade people to avoid certain types of food or to "go green." While adolescents who write for various purposes have been shown to improve their scientific writing (Hand & Prain, 2002), we can start this at a much lower grade level through some of the activities shared in Chapter 5. Our budding scientists at the elementary level need to be aware of the various purposes for writing and how that relates to the science they are learning. As previously discussed, those in the field of social studies must be able to critique a variety of materials, understand differing points of view, and gather important facts from texts. They must also be able to develop a deeper understanding of the importance of both primary and secondary sources.

Finally, visual representation and viewing are playing a very important role in all areas of our lives these days. We can help students build these skills by incorporating the Internet throughout the content areas, asking students to tell stories about their content information, allowing them opportunities to create comic strips and newsletters to share knowledge, and asking students to create biographies that show how views of famous people changed through time or differed according to diverse opinions. As we seek to foster young students' ability to visually represent information and critically view text, these are some of the ideas that will be explored in more depth in Chapter 6. At the same time, the activities shared will strengthen students' mathematical, scientific, and social studies knowledge.

Although there are similarities among important skills needed for each of the three content areas, there are also differences. The second part of this book will help students navigate content area texts and articulate their understanding. Through reading, writing, orally communicating, and viewing and visual representation, students will be able to focus on specific content area demands. Although all students will not grow up to be experts in the field of social studies, science, or mathematics, it is still necessary to develop the disciplinary skills in each area so that students can be successful in the older grades and in life.

What Does This Mean for Elementary Educators?

With the widespread emphasis on content area knowledge, the focus on math, science, and social studies learning cannot wait until students are in the secondary classroom. Teachers must focus greater effort in the elementary grades to help students understand and communicate content area knowledge.

Link Literacy Development and Content Instruction

Students are now expected to have deeper and more extensive content area knowledge and be able to not only read and write about information but also communicate their knowledge through other means. Therefore, instead of teaching literacy skills in isolation, these skills must help students successfully interact with diverse materials pertaining to science, social studies, and math. In a study conducted with third graders, students who participated in a program that integrated literacy and science instruction not only improved significantly in their language arts competencies, but

they also showed science gains (Morrow, Pressley, Smith, & Smith, 1997). In addition, third graders who were taught through concept-oriented reading instruction, which integrates science and reading, not only were more intrinsically motivated to read but also had a better self-efficacy for reading (Wigfield, Guthrie, Tonks, & Perencevich, 2004). Likewise, students' situational interest, which is developed in such learning, may be used to increase long-term reading comprehension (Guthrie et al., 2006). Finally, fifth-grade students improved their scores in reading, science, mathematics, and writing on a statewide assessment in Maryland when they were involved with integrated instruction and exposed to a wide variety of resources (Guthrie, Schafer, Von Secker, & Alban, 2000). Research clearly supports that integrating literacy tools across the content areas will increase content-level knowledge and also build and strengthen literacy skills.

Use a Variety of Materials

We must also rethink the texts we use for content area learning and ensure that diverse materials are available for students. Even though there have been many researchers who have criticized the writing in textbooks (Armbruster & Anderson, 1988), many elementary teachers continue to rely on them for content area instruction (Harlen, 1997). Even when trade books are used, research reveals that there is an overreliance in the elementary grades on narrative text. In fact, Kamberelis (1999) has found that students in kindergarten, first grade, and second grade are much more familiar with narrative texts than other genres. Although many elementary classrooms emphasize narrative text, it is not what we encounter as adults (Venezky, 2000). In Chapter 2, we take a closer look at the wide variety of materials that can be incorporated into the classroom in addition to traditional textbooks. As we help students understand diverse math, science, and social studies texts, we are providing them with opportunities to understand the unique demands of each content area.

Encourage Disciplinary Knowledge Skill Development

Shanahan and Shanahan (2008) have created a three-tier pyramid of literacy progression that specifies the types of literacy skills that our students must develop to thrive in society and be contributing members in an ever-changing world. The lowest level of literacy development is basic literacy skills. Skills at that level are often learned during the primary

grades, and by the time most students are in high school, they fully possess these skills. Students at this level understand concepts of print and begin developing automaticity with basic words. When it comes to reading stories, students are familiar with the basic elements and realize the familiar sequence of events often found in a plot. These are literacy skills that are essential to reading, but they represent only the basic level. Students need to possess a much higher level of literacy skills to fully participate in the world around them.

The next level is intermediate literacy. At this level, students not only learn to read polysyllabic words but also expand the number of sight words they possess, develop metacognitive awareness, increase their vocabulary, and read a wider range of texts. Shanahan and Shanahan (2008) point out that although most students develop these skills by the end of middle school, the skills are often not applicable to diverse texts and situations, nor are the skills linked to particular subjects.

Finally, the top level of literacy development is disciplinary literacy, which means developing skills that are specific to the content areas. According to Shanahan and Shanahan (2008), "Progressing higher in the pyramid means learning more sophisticated but less generalizable skills and routines" (p. 45). Although these researchers believe these content area skills are seldom taught at the secondary level, they also note that many middle and high schools have barriers in place that make it difficult to develop effective reading skills.

According to Shanahan and Shanahan (2008), there is often compartmentalization of subjects at the older grades, teachers have less literacy coursework in their educational backgrounds, and parents are traditionally less involved in their children's education. Therefore, it only makes sense to begin efforts in the earlier grades to help students develop disciplinary literacy. As we begin to build their oral, visual, and written skills at the elementary level, we can and must focus on helping them achieve disciplinary literacy skills and ensuring that they will be successful with the diverse and more complicated texts they are exposed to in the older grades.

Many elementary teachers are familiar with K–W–L plus (Carr & Ogle, 1987) and Venn diagrams and use those strategies across various texts that students encounter. Although those are valuable strategies, research suggests that students additionally need even more specialized strategies to fully understand math, science, and social studies texts. In Part II, specific

strategies and activities will be shared that can be used at the elementary grades to begin developing disciplinary knowledge.

Making the Most of Instructional Time With a Content Literacy Focus

Those in the educational community are becoming concerned with the lack of instructional time provided to individual content areas and are strongly advocating for the importance of their specific areas. This continually expanding body of knowledge becomes a concern when looking at the already full schedule of an elementary teacher and accounting for the time spent on noninstructional tasks. When a study was conducted with seventh- and eighth-grade science classrooms (Laine, Bullock, & Ford, 1998), teachers were alarmed when they realized that 20% of the class time was spent with noninstructional tasks. However, many elementary teachers would not be surprised by that finding. Many elementary teachers are all too aware that a great deal of classroom time is spent taking students to assemblies, organizing lunch count and attendance records, lining up and returning to the classroom from various activities, taking bathroom breaks, listening to interruptions on the intercom, dealing with visitors coming to the classroom, handling students' misbehaviors, responding to fire drills, and many more items that have an impact on daily schedules. Thus, we must make every effort possible to take advantage of every instructional moment we have with students.

Focusing on content literacy will actually help us make optimal use of the limited instructional time we have with our students in the classroom because students will be enhancing their literacy skills as they think, read, write, and orally share content information. We must look at various literacies as working not in "competition but cooperation" (Plummer & Kuhlman, 2008, p. 96) with each other. As we incorporate more informational texts into the classroom, it is possible to develop content-knowledgeable students with strong literacy skills (Reutzel, Smith, & Fawson, 2005; Williams, Stafford, Lauer, Hall, & Pollini, 2009). Students will be able to read, write, and articulate their thoughts in a variety of ways across content areas. Literacy skills will literally be woven through the curriculum.

This integration can help make the most of the instructional time available (Rogers & Abell, 2007). Instead of carving out numerous chunks of time for reading, writing, sharing read-alouds, and each of the

content areas, literacy skills can be strengthened by providing students the opportunity to tie in content area concepts throughout the literacy coursework. This ensures that there is time for teaching the content area skills and helps remove the stress of adhering to the schedule so that there is still time by the end of the day to teach all content areas. Along with easing the burden on the teacher, this type of teaching also makes the literacy skill development more meaningful. A great deal of the reading, writing, speaking, and viewing that adults do on a daily basis is tied to the content areas. In the world outside the classroom, there is no barrier between those areas.

Removing the Barriers

It is expected that elementary teachers will have a solid understanding of the developmental stages through which children progress and how to best meet their literacy needs. Many teachers graduated or will graduate with a large number of courses devoted to doing just that. Also, most elementary teacher preparation programs require method courses for each of the content areas. However, the gap comes when trying to determine how best to address the content area needs and develop literate students who can communicate their content area knowledge.

Many elementary teachers are drawn to education because of a love for children and a desire to make a difference in their lives. There is a sense of satisfaction to be gained from watching students grasp the understanding of a concept for the first time. Rarely do educators become elementary teachers because they have an exceptionally high level of knowledge and interest in a specific content area. Research by Harlen (1997) suggests that our self-doubts about our content-level knowledge have had an impact on our teaching of subjects and at times have had an impact on our reliance on the textbook to cover content area material. In addition, research by Gernon and Grisham (2002) found that elementary teachers in California rarely took a content area literacy course during their preservice education. Many teachers completing a teacher preparation program in other states no doubt can attest to a similar undergraduate experience.

Conversely, secondary teachers often become teachers because they love a specific content area, and more often than not that is the only content area they teach. Elementary teachers have many more expectations. They must not only possess a solid understanding in all

content areas but also must be able to help students learn diverse material. Therefore, it is essential that elementary teachers see themselves as content area experts. It is necessary to develop the skills and dispositions needed to strengthen students' math, science, and social studies knowledge and provide them with opportunities to communicate their understanding. By fostering disciplinary literacy at younger grades, students will be better prepared for the advanced content-level expectations of secondary school and can ultimately be contributing members of society.

The educational system often creates artificial barriers between the content areas through the use of space and resources. However, students do not see these barriers (Altieri, 2010). In the world beyond the classroom, literacy is a tool through which students develop and communicate an understanding of science, social studies, and math. By removing the barriers that exist, we help students develop their literacy skills and apply their learning beyond the classroom walls. We also provide rich experiences that will help them develop disciplinary literacy skills necessary for their lives now and in the future.

Considerations for Effective Content Literacy Instruction

There are several areas that must be considered when addressing content area teaching. First, students need the opportunity to feel successful. To achieve that goal, elementary teachers must consider the individual needs of their students. English learners and those with learning disabilities require extra support in developing math, science, and social studies knowledge. To develop content area knowledge, the home–community connection must be strengthened, and students must expand their technological awareness. Each of these areas is pivotal for consideration in effective content area instruction.

Learning Disabilities

Although many students struggle with content area texts, those with learning disabilities need extra guidance to face the challenges presented by the text (Dimino, 2007). Many teachers of young students realize that social studies and science can be very difficult for them because of the vocabulary demands, the unfamiliar expository discourse, and their lack of background knowledge. However, it is often an assumption that math, because it is

based on numbers, is an easier content area for all students to understand. Research suggests differently. According to Templeton, Neel, and Blood (2008), students with emotional and behavioral disorders often have difficulty understanding mathematical concepts. Students must not only learn technical terms specific to the field, but they also will often encounter words they see in everyday life that have very different meanings within the mathematics field. Furthermore, students must be able to understand how numerals, words, and visuals can work together in text and problems. All content areas require additional support when working with students with learning disabilities.

To help all students be successful with subject area content, additional support must be provided for those with special needs, which may include additional hands-on experiences, the opportunity to respond through a variety of modalities, and the modification of assignments and expectations. Through scaffolding, teachers can provide the supports necessary to build content area knowledge so that students can feel confident and be better able to deal with the more complex subject matter that will present itself in later grades.

English Learners

Although oral language proficiency for English learners has been shown to take three to five years or more to develop, it can take much longer for these students to develop proficiency with academic language (Hakuta, Butler, & Witt, 2000). Oral language proficiency involves words used in everyday settings to converse with others. However, many of the concepts and terms in math, science, and social studies are rarely part of oral language. Therefore, special attention must be given to English learners' content area needs to move them beyond basic conversational English to being able to tackle the much more complex content area texts. Students must understand the technical vocabulary, discourse patterns, and the way the text is organized in content areas (Silva, Weinburgh, Smith, Barreto, & Gabel, 2008).

Similar to beliefs regarding students with learning disabilities, it is expected that English learners will have difficulty with social studies and science due to the technical vocabulary, density of concepts, and a less familiar genre. However, research shows that English learners also struggle with mathematical learning. According to Janzen (2008), math is often assumed to be easier than some content areas because it is based on

numbers, but research has shown that math is challenging because it uses a variety of semiotic systems and technical vocabulary (Schleppegrell, 2007). Students must be able to comprehend charts, symbols, and other types of language to understand the content.

Without ignoring the academic demands of math, science, and social studies, teachers must take into account that some students' cultural beliefs may also limit their academic success. Gutstein, Lipman, Hernandez, and de los Reyes (1997) share that sometimes beliefs and cultural values regarding gender roles can influence learning. In a study by Daisey and José-Kampfner (2002), teachers had to show students from Puerto Rico and Mexico that there are Latinas who succeed as engineers and mathematicians to have an impact on students' views. Prior to the study, students had stereotypical beliefs about females and the fields of mathematics and engineering. Although this study dealt with one specific ethnicity, it stresses the importance of considering the impact of students' beliefs and values on their understanding of content learning. If students possess beliefs that may serve as barriers to content area learning, those beliefs must be addressed.

TRY IT OUT

Think about the English learners and students with special needs in your classroom. What activities or modifications do you make related to content area information so that they are able to achieve success? Share your ideas with colleagues. See if you can help each other gain additional ideas that might make math, science, and social studies content easier for these students and, therefore, remove some of the content area barriers.

Home–Community Connection

We must use the literacy experiences and skills students bring to the classroom to foster the specific skills they need to be successful with content texts inside and outside the classroom. Regardless of socioeconomic background or culture, all students have valuable literacy experiences outside the classroom context. However, the educational system values certain types of experiences, and the literacy practices

tend to be associated with middle class values (Walker & Bean, 2005). The deficit view continues to be a barrier in making the home–school connection (McCarthey, 2000).

For instance, consider Taylor and Dorsey-Gaines's (1988) *Growing Up Literate: Learning From Inner-City Families*, which portrays children's literacy development in urban settings; the text was monumental in showing the educational world that all families have literacy experiences at home. Likewise, Heath's (1983) groundbreaking book *Ways With Words: Language, Life, and Work in Communities and Classrooms* demonstrates how two very different communities have both oral and written literacy traditions. Although sometimes it may feel that students who arrive at school predominantly from lower income families have limited literacy experiences, it is not true. Their experiences may simply be different. The educational system often draws parameters around acceptable literacy experiences. For example, students are expected to have knowledge of familiar fairy tales, yet some students may not have that knowledge but instead may have many other literacy skills. We need to strengthen and sustain the home and community connection to cultivate students' content literacy development.

Padak and Rasinski (2007) stress several ways to help encourage independent reading at home, and it is evident that several of their suggestions can easily be applied to the content areas. First, we must keep activities simple so that they are easy to implement, provide texts, and help parents see print wherever it may be found. Parents want to help their children succeed in school but often have limited time and materials. Also, as Padak and Rasinski point out, a trip to the library should not be required in order for parents to be involved in their children's literacy development. Chall and colleagues (1982) conducted longitudinal research with second, fourth, and sixth graders, and the results revealed the powerful influence of the home environment. In fact, word recognition and vocabulary were related to the time the students spent interacting with adults. This type of interaction does not require extensive preparation, a high level of education, specific texts, or any money. Helping parents or other adults realize the significance of their role in facilitating children's literacy skills through activities as simple as oral conversations is vital.

In Chapter 2, we talk about the importance of using a variety of materials to develop content area literacy, and by using a wide range

of materials, parents will see that they can be actively involved in their children's education. As Shockley (1994) states, "Schools often unintentionally deny families access to school literacy by their rigid adherence to packaged programs such as basals" (p. 500). That is also true with the overreliance on content area textbooks. This overreliance perpetuates the myth that the books hold a hidden key in helping students become skilled content literacy learners. Upper elementary content textbooks can be intimidating to many parents. Most educators have to review social studies, science, and math content before they teach it to students, so it is easy to imagine how flipping open a sixth-grade social studies textbook could intimidate many parents. Research shows that parents who believe that it is important to be involved in their children's education and that they are capable of making a difference are much more likely to be involved (Hoover-Dempsey & Sandler, 1997). As educators, we must help parents see the important role they can play in their children's content literacy development. Parents can learn more about the material with their children through the Internet and other texts and can ask their children questions about the topics and assist them with understanding the material.

Furthermore, we realize that it is important for students to be able to understand a large variety of texts, including informational texts, to be successful in today's world. However, exposure to diverse texts varies beyond the classroom walls. We must focus attention on informative texts because research shows that text usage varies according to one's socioeconomic status. Results of Duke's (2000) research with first graders reveals that students from "traditionally disenfranchised social groups" (p. 202) have even less interaction with such texts. Adults are constantly bombarded by a variety of texts and required to make intertextual connections to understand information. Stories encountered in the news often link to prior newspaper stories, and articles often make reference to studies published elsewhere. All students must be able to understand the diverse texts that exist in order to be considered literate. Therefore, we must take into consideration students' home and community connections and the diversity of texts they have been exposed to.

Students have a wealth of experiences related to social studies, math, and science outside of the classroom context. These experiences in their homes and communities can be woven into classroom lessons, and formal

lessons can be taken outside the classroom and applied in home and community situations. By understanding that students are part of cultural contexts and recognizing the community as a resource, we can strengthen their content literacy skills.

Integrating Technology

Students cannot be considered literate today unless they are prepared to use technology in diverse settings and for varied purposes. Technology is playing a larger and larger role in students' literacy development. The STEM initiatives clearly stress that technological skills are essential to be successful in the workforce. Inadequately preparing students to work with technology can affect their ability to obtain jobs and become successful in the world (Finn, 1999). When we examine all of the technologies that students have access to on a daily basis (e.g., e-mail, Internet, Skype, videos), we see the type of knowledge and capabilities that students will need to compete in the workplace (Leu, 2000; Schmar-Dobler, 2003).

In day-to-day living, we are bombarded with technology. Digital cameras, cell phones and smartphones, iPods, and other electronic items play important roles in our lives. With computers, we can watch television, enjoy YouTube videos, communicate with others, read articles, conduct research, surf the Internet, go shopping, and complete banking transactions. Technology is playing an increasingly larger role in our lives. In a similar manner, students are bombarded with technology every day, yet rarely have they been taught to be effective consumers of it. Just as it is our duty to show them that information in books must be analyzed and not taken at surface value, we must encourage students to scrutinize the information they view, read, and listen to from technological sources.

With one click of a key, students can have access to a wide body of knowledge on any topic. Technology makes the world seem like a much smaller place, but it is not enough for students to be able to communicate, view, or read information. The Internet provides almost unlimited access to sources, so we must help students become wise consumers of the information. One Google search on a content area topic can provide hundreds or thousands of possible texts within seconds. Students must understand how to navigate the volumes of files they will encounter online. According to McPherson (2007), we have a responsibility to help our students develop the critical literacy skills necessary or "we risk leaving our children at the mercy of less scrupulous players (e.g., advertisers,

corporations) using the Internet to communicate their own agenda" (p. 69). We must teach students how to learn from technology.

In educational settings, many of us also have much greater access to technology today than even in recent years past. Teachers are able to use smartboards, digital cameras, laptops, and other materials to help students develop content area understanding. According to the National Center for Education Statistics (Kleiner & Farris, 2002), 99% of U.S. schools have Internet access. However, research shows that information on the Internet is not read in the same manner that students read written texts. Viewers click on links and get more in-depth information on some areas and less comprehensive understanding of other topics. Also, students often look to visuals to explain the text (Liu, 2005). Of course, teaching students to use the technology available today is not enough. They must be able to understand technology so that they can adapt to the ever-changing technological landscape.

The world of technology can also help students articulate their ideas with a wider audience beyond the classroom. They can not only access information but also present knowledge through various methods (Ikpeze & Boyd, 2007). Blogs are only one example of an activity students may enjoy outside of the classroom that can easily be adapted to the content areas. Students can work in groups to develop WebQuests for social studies topics, create videos of their science experiments, and analyze mathematical statistics presented by advertisers. It is imperative that we take technology and weave it throughout the content areas to help students learn to use it for real and relevant purposes outside the classroom. We must build on any technological skills they already possess, and take advantage of their interest in technology.

In many of the activities presented in Part II of this book, it is easy to see how some teachers have used technology within the classroom. However, there are many other ways that teachers can incorporate technology into their lessons. Elementary teachers and their students can create the connections based on their own access to technological sources and students' interests and experiences. We must provide students with experiences to analyze various forms of media and be intelligent, knowledgeable consumers of technology so that they are prepared to be truly literate in the content areas. Students must learn to comprehend, synthesize, make intertextual connections, and analyze information and communication technologies.

REFLECTING BACK AND LOOKING FORWARD

As elementary educators, we must continue to reflect on our vision of literacy. We continually find that more and more is expected from students when they leave our classrooms. The content knowledge demands and the literacy skills students are expected to possess are increasing at a tremendous pace. Whereas the expectations are constantly changing, we know that the amount of time students spend with us is not increasing. Therefore, we must help students expand their content literacy skills and their communication skills in an efficient manner.

Although fourth grade and beyond is often thought of as the time when students read to learn, this way of thinking must change. Students must have exposure to informative texts beginning in the earliest years, and they must begin to develop the skills necessary to understand new content area materials to which they might be exposed. Reading and writing are not areas to be mastered but rather skills to be used to help students develop the knowledge necessary to succeed in the world. As the world changes, students will be expected to find answers to increasingly complex issues. Without the literacy skills to deal with the ever-growing and almost unlimited amount of information, students will not be successful. Incorporating students' literacy tools across math, social studies, and science at all levels ensures that they have the level of content area knowledge necessary to actively participate in an ever-changing world. To do this, we must see ourselves as content area teachers.

In the next chapter, a variety of materials are introduced that can help us achieve our goal. According to an article in *Reading Today* ("PISA," 2008), the PIRLS study reveals that the content area textbook serves as the basis for students' reading instruction, but it also shows that students in general are still exposed to more narrative than informational texts. Now is the time to rethink literacy instruction at the younger grades and take a closer look at the materials used in the content areas.

Selecting Materials for Content Area Connections

....

Mr. D.'s second-grade students are studying community helpers. Although the social studies textbook he often uses in class has a short chapter on the topic, he wants to make the topic more relevant to his students and incorporate a variety of texts. He also knows that his students have a range of ability levels. Realizing that the textbook is too difficult for many of his students at this time in the year, he is incorporating many other types of text. Today, we see students in his room working in a variety of small groups to learn more about the topic.

One small group of students is busy skimming and sorting a large stack of mail, which might be delivered by a mailperson. They are categorizing the mail according to its purpose, and planning to make a chart showing the types of mail delivered. Another group is listening to a parent explain her job as an architect. She is showing the students online photos of buildings she helped create. The students are interested in the photos, but they are also eager to learn more about the drawing plans she brought with her. A third group of students is reading Joyce Slayton Mitchell's *Crashed, Smashed, and Mashed: A Trip to Junkyard Heaven* (2001) and *Tractor-Trailer Trucker: A Powerful Truck Book* (2000); both contain amazing photographs. As students flip through the pages, they are looking for jobs related to a junkyard or truck driving and to see what literacy skills are required by these jobs. Two students excitedly show the others in the group the trucker's full-page daily log found in the one book, while another pair of students discusses a photo in the other book of the computer screen listing details about car parts available in the junkyard. The fourth group is viewing a video on veterinarians and using the information in the video to help them prepare questions for a field trip they have planned for later in the week to a local veterinarian's office.

....

In this classroom vignette, Mr. D.'s students are engaged in the topics because he moved beyond the classroom textbook and incorporated a variety of texts into his lesson. Unfortunately, as many teachers are aware, textbooks continue to be the predominant text used for content area teaching (Haury & Rillero, 1994; Henke, Chen, & Goldman, 1999a; Weiss, 1987). In fact, a survey conducted by the U.S. Department of Education examined the instructional practices in elementary and secondary schools from 1994 to 1995 and found that grades 4 through 6 saw the most extensive use of textbooks (Henke, Chen, & Goldman, 1999b). Although using a textbook may be the least time-intensive way to teach and reinforce content, it may also be the least conducive to true learning.

Research shows that textbooks are often not at an appropriate level for students' understanding (Cho & Kahle, 1984), and many researchers and educators argue that there are much better ways to teach and reinforce information. Textbooks are mass produced for districts and often may not focus on state expectations and state assessments (Conley, 2008). In fact, according to the American Association for the Advancement of Science (2002), a review of science textbooks reveals that they do not adequately address standards-based learning goals. Furthermore, others have stressed that textbooks are often confusing for students and are not at a readability level that best meets their needs (Vacca & Vacca, 2008; Wallace, 2005). "Inconsiderate texts" (Armbruster, 1984), or texts that are poorly written, have been a concern of educators for many years. While these texts are confusing for many students, those with exceptionalities may need even more extensive guidance to understand concepts presented in textbooks (Dimino, 2007).

DISCUSSION POINT

What are concerns you have with the textbooks you use for math, science, and social studies? Can you think of ways other types of text might address each of these issues or better meet students' needs?

Many experts have begun to encourage teachers to see the textbook as merely one more resource to draw from (e.g., Dunn, 2000; Walpole, 1998). Textbook writers typically assume that all readers have the same reading ability and the same level of prior knowledge on the topic. A classroom

contains students with a wide range of reading levels, and using one text can create additional burdens for those students who are English learners or are struggling readers. The textbook can also be quite intimidating with its size, print, and method of presentation. For years, educators have argued that the textbook should no longer be the primary text used to gain content area knowledge (Stewart, 1994). However, although we have seen a gradual shift to the use of multiple texts for adolescent social studies teaching (Stahl & Shanahan, 2004), we still have a long way to go.

There are many other texts that teachers might use to more effectively share content knowledge with their students. Conducted at 33 elementary schools, Guthrie and colleagues' (2000) research reveals that in the upper grades, performance on a statewide assessment is related to "integration of curriculum and an abundance of books and resources" (p. 222). Teachers can provide that abundance of resources and books and tailor to students' needs through the use of trade books, imported and local texts, and technological resources.

This chapter begins by illustrating how using multiple texts addresses national and state standards and then discusses the benefits of using trade books, examines the types available, and gives suggestions for selecting quality texts. Because the need for incorporating informational texts into the content areas has been the focus of much recent research, specific guidelines for locating and selecting such texts will be shared. Next, we look at how imported and local texts can also be effective means for developing math, science, and social studies concepts. Both personal and public local texts are discussed so that teachers may find ways to more effectively use the ones they currently have available and gain ideas to enrich their classroom environments through the creation of other texts. Then, we look at other possible texts, including nonprint media. Finally, the most important part of the equation is shared: the teacher's role in making the student–text connection.

Addressing Content Area Standards Through Text Variety

Various national groups support the use of various materials. According to the National Curriculum Standards for Social Studies (NCSS, 2010), students must be encouraged to critically read and view a variety of texts, including media, print, audio, and video content. Likewise, the National

Science Education Standards (NRC, 1996) state that everyone should be able to intelligently participate in discussions and debate regarding important issues related to science and technology. Reading or viewing materials representing diverse views is integral for this to occur, and through a wide variety of materials, we can ensure this happens.

The degree to which individual states encourage the use of diverse texts varies. With the TEKS for social studies, students are expected to be able to examine both primary and secondary sources as well as use the school's media center, technology, and other informational sources. The TEKS specifically encourages a variety of materials, including biographies, folk tales, myths, legends, poetry, songs, and artwork, with the primary grades and expands the suggestions to include novels, speeches, and letters at the older grade levels. The History–Social Science Content Standards for California Public Schools (California Department of Education, 2000) recommend similar materials. Whereas the California science standards mention that supplementary books and materials are available to help students demonstrate mastery of content, Florida's science standards (www.floridastandards.org/Standards/FLStandardSearch.aspx) take that one step further and encourage students to use appropriate reference materials to support their scientific understanding (SC.5.N.1.1; SC.6.N.1.1).

Although using a variety of materials will prepare students for the world in which they live and motivate them to develop content area knowledge, it is clear that using diverse materials is also encouraged and at times required in order for students to demonstrate mastery of content area standards. In the next section, we take a closer look at various texts.

Using Trade Books to Create Content Area Connections

Unlike local texts, which according to Maloch, Hoffman, and Patterson (2004) are "the written texts created or constructed by classroom participants" (p. 130), imported texts are created by others and brought into the classroom context. Trade books are one type of imported text that might help foster content area understanding.

Trade books have been defined by Morrison and Young (2008) as "books which are published for a retail market and are available at bookstores and libraries" (p. 205). These are often the type of books—not textbooks—that students read late at night with a flashlight, beg to hear

orally read to them, and take along to read on vacations. When students want to know more about what it is like to be an astronaut, how to plant a flower garden, or what type of animals live in the desert, they do not look for a textbook to satisfy their curiosity. They find another type of text, and often that type of book is a trade book.

Benefits of Using Trade Books in the Classroom

In-Depth Coverage of Specific Topics. Many articles have been written about the benefits of using trade books to help students develop content area knowledge. According to Lamme and Ledbetter (1990), trade books are better able to provide depth to a concept than textbooks. Obviously, a textbook that is designed to cover science, math, or social studies material for an entire grade level cannot possibly go into detail on individual concepts. Although one chapter in a textbook might be dedicated to simple machines or the U.S. Civil War, teachers can easily find hundreds of children's books written about various aspects of each topic.

Accessibility and Timeliness. These books are readily available and can be tied throughout the content areas. According to Lynch-Brown and Tomlinson (1999), over 120,000 books are in print today, and Huck, Hepler, Hickman, and Kiefer (2001) estimate that 5,000–6,000 new books are published each year. Not only does that allow us to have a wide variety from which to choose, but it also enables us to use recently published texts. Some content area information, such as science and social studies concepts, can become outdated in textbooks. However, because of cost and other factors, many districts adopt new versions approximately every six years. Therefore, textbooks cannot be the sole text presented to students.

Engaging Presentation by Children's Book Authors. Science, mathematics, and social studies textbooks are not traditionally written by children's book authors, and students normally find that trade books are much more interesting and engaging (Hilke, 1999; Ross, 1994). Although a topic such as storms might not seem that exciting, it is amazing how students react when presented with Seymour Simon's (1989) picture book *Storms*. Authors of trade books have an ability to bring to life material that might normally appear dull (Young & Vardell, 1993).

Lois Ehlert and Eric Carle have brought many concepts to life for the youngest of readers, and Julius Lester and Russell Freedman have

enhanced the learning of older students. Research by Guthrie, Schafer, and Huang (2001), conducted with Maryland fourth graders, shows that students who read extensively score higher on the NAEP. This research also reveals that the amount of engaged reading is so powerful that it can mitigate the influence of parents' educational backgrounds on the assessment.

Active Learning. While trade books cannot replace hands-on instruction, they can enhance active learning. Moyer (2000) encourages the use of trade books to create mathematical connections for students. Also, Morrow and Pressley's research (1997) suggests that using trade books along with hands-on science experiments can foster a greater interest and enjoyment in science content. Their research suggests that students in third-grade classrooms that integrate literature and science choose to read more science texts on their own. This is exactly what we need to prepare students for their futures. We must improve students' understanding of science, technology, and engineering content, and by motivating students to read more texts on the topics related to those fields during their free time, we can do that.

Higher Readability for Diverse Needs. Finally, trade books can more easily meet the needs of diverse students. Within a classroom, there is a wide range of reading levels and interests. Yet, a textbook does not take the reader into consideration. Although the same textbook is typically used with all students in a district at a specific grade level, it is easy to find a range of trade books on any topic from the simplest of concept books to more difficult and higher readability material. Thus, it is not surprising that trade books have been shown to benefit students who are struggling with social studies content (Heubach, 1995). In fact, nonfiction texts (Brassell, 2006) and the topics often found within them (Worthy, Moorman, & Turner, 1999) are especially appealing to boys and those students who might normally be reluctant to read text (Collard, 2003). Fuhler (1992) also shows that nonfiction texts can be valuable for students having difficulties with learning to read.

Although students may look at picture books or shorter books with visual aids as "baby books" and those deserving the attention of struggling readers, we know that the majority of reading experiences we encounter in the world are often with short texts. By incorporating these types of texts

during the day through reading aloud, content area connections, and such, we give credibility to them. We show that we value the information the books contain and that they are appropriate for all audiences. As reading role models, students will value what we value.

As we continue to try to meet the needs of a wider range of students, and as our classrooms become more diverse, we need materials that can be tailored to individual students. Trade books offer that possibility. Teachers can take into consideration readability, interests, and prior knowledge of students when selecting trade books to share. In the next section, we look at the different types of trade books that contain content area information.

Types of Trade Books

Research shows that students are exposed to far more fiction than informational text (e.g., Duke 2004; Pressley, Rankin, & Yokoi, 1996). In a study conducted by Yopp and Yopp (2006), only 5% of the texts read aloud to preschool students were informational. Likewise, Duke (2000) reveals that first graders in her study were exposed to only 3.6 minutes of informative texts per day. When I ask elementary teachers to share trade books they might incorporate into content areas, the overwhelming majority of texts they bring to share are fictional. We then discuss Duke's research, and many teachers are not surprised at the findings. Elementary teachers often seek out storybooks to help develop content area knowledge, even though research (Smith, 2000) shows that as adults, we read far more informational texts. Very recent research (Pentimonti, Zucker, Justice, & Kaderavek, 2010) conducted with early childhood classrooms reveals that this is not changing.

TRY IT OUT

Keep a journal over the next 48 hours documenting the types of connected text you read and view for purposes other than teaching. Next to each type of writing, state the purpose of your reading. Was it for gaining information? Did you read for enjoyment? It might be easiest to select key times during the day to write down what you have read so far (e.g., breakfast, lunch, dinner, bedtime) while the memories are fresh. Share your list with a friend and see if you had similar reading experiences and purposes. What does this tell you about the types of reading and viewing students should be doing?

When balancing students' exposure to text, let's first consider content area trade books that might help introduce and reinforce concepts. These trade books do not need to be shared during specific times of the day. They can be tied through lessons, shared by visitors, and read orally during storytime. There are three types of books that can be used to teach and reinforce content area knowledge: poetry, nonfiction, and faction.

Poetry. This genre is often not thought of when one thinks of content area material, but more and more poetry books are being written that can encourage the development of content area knowledge. Along with the benefits associated with other types of trade books, poetry often takes a minimal amount of time to share because it is short in length and easy to integrate throughout the curriculum. It also enables students to learn about poetic elements and see how authors use a less familiar type of text to convey information.

Teachers will find that there are many books of poetry for children that contain numerous poems related to content material, such as J. Patrick Lewis's *Arithme-Tickle: An Even Number of Odd Riddle-Rhymes* (2007a) and *Scien-Trickery: Riddles in Science* (2007b). Often, as is the case with works by Lee Bennett Hopkins, the books serve as compilations of poetry related to a particular subject or topic. Jane Yolen's *A Mirror to Nature: Poems About Reflection* (2009) contains beautiful photographs and poems about alligators, cockles, and redfish, as well as other living creatures found in nature. Along with the poems, facts are shared about each animal. However, there are also books in which an author takes one specific poem, creates illustrations to go along with the text, and makes it into an entire picture book. Rebecca Kai Dotlich's *What Is Science?* (2006) is an example of this type of text.

Nonfiction. It is extremely important that this category be well defined because many educators have very different definitions of *nonfiction books*, and many people use the terms *informational* and *nonfiction* simultaneously (Saul & Dieckman, 2005). I use the term *nonfiction* for the broad category because when teachers go in search of books to connect to content areas, the terms most often used to distinguish between the types are *fiction* and *nonfiction*. As Saul and Dieckman point out, *nonfiction* is also the term used with the Dewey decimal system and the Library of

Congress. Therefore, when media assistants or others help search for materials, this is often the term used.

Moss (1991) believes that nonfiction texts help teachers individualize instruction, are more appealing to students, provide a more in-depth level of knowledge for the reader, are written in an easier to understand format, and provide more current information than textbooks. A large number of nonfiction books recently published in picture book format will appeal to both students and teachers (Gill, 2009). This category includes autobiographies, biographies, and other books that contain factual material.

One important type of nonfiction is informational text, which contain many important features not found in all nonfiction texts. According to Duke and Bennett-Armistead (2003), an informational text not only seeks to provide information about the world but also has "particular linguistic features such as headings and technical vocabulary to help accomplish that purpose" (p. 16). Because many of these books will use headings, a table of contents, a glossary, bold print, illustrations, diagrams, and other features often not found in other types of trade books, incorporating this type of text into the classroom is an opportunity to expand students' schema of trade books. It will also prepare students for the reality of standardized testing, since a great deal of text on standardized tests is informational (Calkins, Montgomery, & Santman, 1998). Because a plot is not present, this type of text often captivates students through the use of visuals, such as maps, photographs, diagrams, and other illustrations, that complement the written words. These books can appeal to a wide range of grade levels.

Although many believe that students prefer storybooks, research suggests differently (Donovan, Smolkin, & Lomax, 2000; Fresch, 1995; Hapgood & Palincsar, 2006; Pappas, 1993). In fact, younger students especially will enjoy concept books that help reinforce specific concepts they may be learning in math or other content areas. Students also love trivia, and many reference books contain content area trivia that will help engage the students further. *Go Figure! A Totally Cool Book About Numbers* by Johnny Ball (2005) is just one example of a nonfiction content area trade book that many students will find interesting. It includes mathematical puzzles and interesting facts about math and demonstrates math's practical application to everyday life. Books with science trivia and experiments belong in this category, as well as books that contain maps of geographic areas or games that children play in other parts of the world.

As a class, brainstorm a list of linguistic features commonly seen in content area trade books. Then, share a book, such as Nic Bishop's (2007) *Spiders*, with students. Determine if the author used any of the text features the class brainstormed or any others they might not have thought about when creating the list. As the class skims through the book, discuss the features that students notice. What makes this book different from narrative texts they have read? For instance, on each full-page spread, there is a small paragraph at the bottom about one specific type of spider. Additionally, one sentence on each page appears in a bright, large font. Students can discuss why an author might do that. A book such as this one provides an excellent opportunity to also introduce students to an index if it is a new feature for them. Show the index and ask why someone might want to use it. What is its value to the reader? How are the words or topics arranged? Finally, *Spiders* also includes a glossary, and its purpose can be explored with students. Sharing books such as this one and drawing students' attention to the textual features can help them learn more from informational texts and also prepare them for much more difficult material they will encounter in the future.

Now, divide the class into small groups. Give each group an assortment of informational books to examine. Ask the students to go on a text hunt and list what linguistic features are used in the books. Are there any features used in some of the informational books but not others? Why does each author use certain text features? Then, each group can share with the rest of the class a few key points about the linguistic features they noticed.

Another favorite is *Actual Size* by Steve Jenkins (2004). Students can relate to each illustration because everything is shown in its actual size. Illustrations include the foot of an African elephant and a great white shark's teeth. Along with allowing students to better grasp exactly how big things are, each page contains additional facts related to concepts such as length, height, and weight in small print.

As teachers get to know their students better and learn more about their students' interests, they may want to recommend other nonfiction texts that pertain to those interests. Whether students' interests include

traveling, animals, or machines, it is easy to locate many nonfiction trade books that will help students develop their reading skills while gaining knowledge about content areas. The importance of student interest cannot be emphasized enough.

For example, Joy Hulme's (2005) *Wild Fibonacci: Nature's Secret Code Revealed* will appeal to students interested in animals and nature. This book introduces the fact that "Fibonacci" creatures all contain a specific shape: a winding coil. Whereas more advanced students can develop a deeper understanding of the information presented in the text, the idea of Fibonacci numbers can be introduced to younger students using this picture book. Also, many teachers may glance at a book title, such as Sarah Campbell's (2010) *Growing Patterns: Fibonacci Numbers in Nature*, and automatically expect the book to be targeting much older students. However, elementary teachers working with students as young as fifth grade have stated that they had students who would absolutely love the text. Although the concept is complex, figuring out the patterns shown in nature would be enough to get some students interested in reading the book.

Faction. According to Avery (2003), this category of content area trade books blends together both fiction and facts. It is a very popular type of children's literature, and many books of this type have been selected for inclusion on the International Reading Association Teachers' Choices reading lists or won *Learning Magazine*'s Teachers' Choice Award or other prestigious awards. These books are written primarily to teach information, but they contain narrative elements. There may be fictionalized characters or settings that do not exist in reality. Although more and more articles in professional journals are discussing and debating the merits of faction and informational picture books, it is important to realize that these books are not new. In fact, more than 50 years ago, people believed that the fictional components present in the texts could help engage students with scientific content (Giblin, 2000).

One example of this type of text is Janet Halfmann's (2007) *Little Skink's Tail*. The story is told through the eyes of a lizard named Little Skink. As she is enjoying life in the forest, a crow swoops down to prey upon her, but she has a trick. She can shed her tail and save her life. Little Skink does just that and then spends the rest of the story thinking about different animals and what it would be like to have their tails. Finally, the daydreaming stops when Little Skink sees in her shadow her own tail,

which has grown back. According to the publishers, this book has been verified for factual information by the director of education for school and family programs at Zoo Atlanta. There are additional activities in the back of the book that encourage students to plot out on a map where Little Skink saw each animal. Students are given the actual footprint of the animals shown in the story and then asked to match the footprint to the one on the map and name the coordinates. Finally, there is a page detailing why a variety of animals have tails and the purpose they serve the animals.

Clearly, *Little Skink's Tail* contains some facts, but it also contains a great deal of fiction. According to Donovan and Smolkin (2002), these texts are hybrids that contain elements of fact and fiction. Many people (Bamford, Kristo, & Lyon, 2002; Smith, 2001) have expressed concern about such texts, arguing that students should be exposed to nonfiction so that they are not confused between what is real or factual and what is fictional. In fact, many educators believe that anthropomorphism, or giving human traits to inanimate objects or animals, should be a quality taken into consideration when selecting texts (Connor et al., 2010). However, many teachers enjoy using texts such as these with young students and believe that the stories capture student attention while teaching and reinforcing information. This book has been categorized as fiction, which makes sense. However, it also blurs the division between fact and fiction. We need to be careful how we use terms such as *nonfiction* and *narrative* when we refer to books with students. The dividing line between narrative and nonfiction is not always clear, and narrative is not always make-believe or untrue.

If we use faction books in our classrooms, we must, as Bamford and Kristo (2000) state, be aware that these books can confuse students. A book such as *Little Skink's Tail* requires discussion with very young students regarding what is factual about the book. Draw students' attention to the story and ask them what elements of the story are true or factual, such as, Can lizards really lose their tail? Do crows eat lizards? Perhaps make a list during a rereading of all of the informational elements. For instance, the acknowledgments page lists the names of the people who verified the accuracy of the information, and when the students look at the back of the text, they see additional facts about other types of tails. Then, examine the text to determine what makes the book similar to narrative stories the students have read. Do lizards talk in voices like this one did? Can a lizard daydream as shown on one page of the text with one hand

under her chin and the other under her elbow with her thoughts shown above? On a large piece of chart paper, write *faction* and *fiction*. Draw a line down the middle to divide the paper into halves. Have students list the facts in the text in the faction column and the narrative part in the fiction column. Another suggestion for a story such as this is to give students sticky notes and have them stick the notes wherever they find a fact in the book. Then, all of the students can share the facts they found.

Similarly, Betsy Franco's (2009) *Pond Circle* is a faction book, written for ages 4–8, that explains the food chain to the rhythm and tune of "This Is the House That Jack Built." Although the little girl in the book, Anna, does not exist in real life, many teachers may choose to use the book to introduce the concept of a food chain. The vocabulary is quite complex, with words such as *mayfly nymph* and *algae*, but the book also includes animals that are familiar to even very young students, such as a raccoon and skunk. The story reads much more like a narrative text than an expository text.

Another recently published text, *The Rainforest Grew All Around* by Susan Mitchell (2007), is a tale of the rainforest that is read or sung to the familiar tune "The Green Grass Grew All Around." There are very few facts, if any, presented within the main part of each page. Each page uses repetition and the familiar lyrical tune so that even the youngest of students will want to follow along. However, there is a lot of detailed factual information in the sidenotes of each page. Students learn that "The Amazon River is over 4,000 miles long," and "kapok trees can grow between 150 and 200 feet" (n.p.). However, similar to books such as those in the Magic School Bus series, the students must read the sidenotes to gain a lot of the information on the text's topic. According to teachers with whom I shared *The Rainforest Grew All Around*, the sidebars are not conducive to reading aloud with students because of the lyrical nature of the text, so the teachers would probably read the main part of the pages and not share what was in the sidebars. The concern then becomes the value of the book for students. Whereas young students will enjoy the tune of the book, much older students would be ready to learn information from the sidebars, such as "Pineapples are bromeliads" (n.p.). This book has won numerous awards, including NAPPA Gold and *Learning Magazine*'s Teachers' Choice Award, was selected for IRA's Teachers' Choices reading list, and was a Mom's Choice Awards finalist.

There are those who will argue for or against the use of such texts. Although informational texts can convey a lot more content information

and should be used as much as possible with students, faction can still have a place in the curriculum. The important thing is to think about how we can help students gain the greatest benefit from the use of these texts. Keep in mind that even if we only integrate informational books into math, science, and social studies, students will still read faction on their own or have these types of books read to them. Students need to have the tools necessary to help them distinguish what is real from what is make-believe to gain the most from such texts. By providing students with the proper tools, we can help them develop metacognitive awareness when they are reading faction and be aware that while there may be facts, there will also be fiction.

Locating the Texts

The first step in using quality trade books with students is locating texts that can be used to reinforce content area information. Publishers of textbooks often include a recommended list of specific trade books that relate to units of study discussed within their texts. However, research has shown (Hunsader, 2004) that not all of the books recommended by textbook publishers are quality texts. Therefore, teachers do not want to automatically assume that the trade books recommended will be useful in the classroom. Fortunately, there are many other resources where teachers can locate quality content area trade books.

One idea is to review award winners. Many teachers are familiar with both the Caldecott and Newbery medals. The Caldecott is awarded each year for the illustrations in a text, and the Newbery is given for literary quality. Often, award winners do not relate to a specific content area, but with the large number of informational books being published, more and more awards are given to texts that integrate math, science, and social studies, and they can be used to teach content area knowledge. For instance, *Song of the Water Boatman: And Other Pond Poems* by Joyce Sidman (2005) was named as a Caldecott Honor Book and received a Blue Ribbon for Nonfiction from *The Bulletin of the Center for Children's Books*, and Sarah Campbell's (2008) *Wolfsnail: A Backyard Predator* was chosen as a Theodor Seuss Geisel Honor Book.

Educators can also examine the October issue of *The Reading Teacher* for the Children's Choices reading list and the November issue for the Teachers' Choices. Every year, teachers, reading specialists, and librarians

from across the country create the Teachers' Choices booklist. Additionally, the International Reading Association and the Children's Book Council sponsor the Children's Choices booklist, which is created each year from the books chosen by 10,000 students in grades K–6. Although it is not unusual to locate content area trade books on these lists, many other types of books are also included. Similarly, teachers can examine winners of the Teachers' Choice Awards given by *Learning Magazine*. To win the award, educational products, not just books, are reviewed to determine their quality, instructional value, ease of use, and innovation, then the materials and books that score the best in those areas are honored. It is important to note that teachers are the ones who are determining the educational materials or books worthy of this award.

Fortunately, many content areas have committees that also select award winners. Teachers should examine texts that receive the G. Woodson Book Award, which is given to social science texts, and the Children's Science Book Awards. Various content area committees publish lists of recommended books. Since 1972, the NCSS and the Children's Book Council have reviewed and recommended trade books with social studies themes in *Social Education*. In a similar manner, the National Science Teachers Association (NSTA) and the Children's Book Council compile a list of recommended science trade books for K–12 students. This information is available in the NSTA's journals *Science and Children*, *The Science Teacher*, and *Science Scope*. Teachers can also look at NSTA Recommends online (newsite.nsta.org/recommends) to find reviews of a number of different resources. Duke and Tower (2004, p. 114) also list the following publications that regularly print reviews of nonfiction texts:

- *Appraisal: Science Books for Young People*
- *Book Links*
- *Booklist*
- *Horn Book Magazine*
- *School Library Journal*
- *Science and Children*
- *Science Books and Films*

Additionally, the Database of Award-Winning Children's Literature website (www.dawcl.com) makes it much easier to find specific types of

books for students. On this website, it is possible to narrow down a search by specifying awards won, publication year, ethnicity of main character, age and gender of protagonist, historical time period, and many other variables. Created by a librarian in 1997, this website is very easy to use when searching for recently published content area award winners, and a detailed description of each award is provided through links.

TRY IT OUT

Working with a group of preservice or inservice teachers, think about the topics students will be learning in science and social studies. Divide up the topics among the teachers. Then, individually go to the Database of Award-Winning Children's Literature website (www.dawcl.com). Use the options on the website to narrow search options and see if each person in the group can locate recently published, award-winning informational trade books that might be used to introduce, teach, or reinforce content. At the next meeting, share what everyone found. Between the school and public libraries, it may be possible for group members to work together to find the texts. Working together to get the books will take much less time and provide a wider variety of books for the students.

Evaluating the Texts

Although many great resources are listed in this chapter, it is still important to be able to evaluate trade books. All trade books used with students should be quality literature (Norton & Norton, 2003). With all of the books available, it is possible to find ones that are quality literature and effectively reinforce content area information. Since new trade books are continuously being introduced on the market, there are many excellent ones that might not make the lists. Also, although the panels reviewing books for published lists often are composed of persons in the educational field, individual teachers know their students and the goals they wish to achieve.

With time being limited and such a large number of trade books available, what qualities do teachers look for when selecting texts? Donovan and Smolkin (2001) examined teachers' selections of science texts and found that teachers consider the content presented, visual features,

readability of the text, developmental level necessary to benefit from the material, and books they believed students would enjoy. Those are all important considerations when determining texts that might be used to develop content area knowledge. However, it is important to be able to compare texts as easily as possible within time constraints.

Because evaluating potential texts for use in a classroom is so important, many educators have sought to create instruments that can be used to assess trade books. Many of these instruments are specific to a content area. Originally, Schiro (1997) created an instrument to evaluate both the literary criteria and the mathematical content of trade books. A few years later, Hunsader (2004) revised the assessment to be more manageable for teachers. Likewise, Donovan and Smolkin (2002) created an assessment for science trade books and stressed three key features: genre, content, and visuals. Recently, Atkinson, Matusevich, and Huber (2009) created a rubric specific to the selection of science texts.

Table 1 contains a set of content area trade book evaluation guidelines based on criteria and suggestions from a variety of sources (Atkinson et al., 2009; Cullinan, 1989; Donovan & Smolkin, 2002; Harvey & Goudvis, 2007; Saul & Dieckman, 2005; Sudol & King, 1996). You can use the reproducible Content Area Trade Book Evaluation sheet provided on page 208 in the Appendix to list and rate each book you would like to evaluate, using 1 for *does not meet expectations*, 3 for *meets expectations*, and 5 for *exceeds expectations*. There is also room to list outstanding features about each text. This tool provides a relatively quick way to assess trade books. By formally analyzing texts, it ensures that we move beyond using texts that are easily accessible, visually attractive, or appealing but may lack the qualities we seek in quality content area trade books. Now, let's take a look at the criteria in more detail.

Accuracy of Content

Accuracy is obviously one of the most important aspects to consider when selecting trade books to share. According to Rice (2002), teachers must assess books not only for inaccurate information but also for omissions. However, having inaccurate information or an omission does not mean the book cannot be used with students. It might be possible to choose to use only part of the text. Also, the text may provide the opportunity to teach students that everything in print is not necessarily accurate, and students need to ask questions, seek out information, and critically read all print.

Table 1. Content Area Trade Book Selection Guidelines

Criterion	What to Look For
Accuracy of content	• Author's experience and background are provided. • Photo credits are included. • References are cited. • Information is current.
Cohesion of ideas	• Words and phrases (e.g., *because, therefore, as a result*) signal within-paragraph connections explicitly. • All ideas belong together as arranged. • Abstract concepts are introduced appropriately (e.g., one at a time, concrete and relevant examples).
Organization and layout	• Text layout according to the table of contents is logical. • Text features (e.g., chapter titles, subheadings, glossary, index, visual aids) serve a purpose. • Text pattern is the one most appropriate.
Specialized vocabulary	• Vocabulary is adequately explained through the text, visuals, or glossary.
Student considerations	• Students have the appropriate background knowledge necessary to digest the text. • Format is appropriate (i.e., page and print size). • Positive gender and racial/ethnic role models are provided. • Will interest students
Teacher goals	• Is useful according to teacher goals (e.g., use, standards)

This can be especially critical with social studies texts. Guidance is vital when using books containing inaccurate information or omissions.

Determine if the author's experience and background are adequate to write the text. Many in the educational field refer to this as the integrity of the author. Some publishers list the author's background on the book cover or in the back of the book. It is important that the author has the necessary knowledge to write on a specific topic. This criterion is closely related to the accuracy of content. One small publisher of numerous science and math trade books, Sylvan Dell Publishing, often informs the reader on the book cover that either the author has the necessary knowledge or that the text was reviewed by someone with appropriate background prior to publishing. Likewise, other trade books written by children's authors will often cite consultants or others who reviewed the book for accuracy.

Some experts (e.g., Kiefer, 2007) are concerned that some teachers may lack the specified knowledge to know whether content is accurate. If you find yourself questioning your level of knowledge of a specific content area or topic, this is a great time to use other resources. After closely examining any background information provided on the author, work in groups so that teachers with stronger backgrounds in different content areas can assist with examining the texts. Content area teachers at the middle and high school levels can also work with elementary teachers and share their science, social studies, and math knowledge. Elementary teachers can use their expertise and experiences to narrow down the trade books they are interested in using with their students, and educators who have a stronger background in a specific area can examine the selected texts to ensure that the information is accurate. All of us have the same goals for our students and want to see them expand their content area literacy skills, and we can achieve that goal by working together.

Other things to consider when examining accuracy of content include determining whether photo credits are included within the book's pages and references are cited. Finally, examine if the information is current. As discussed previously, there are many books continually being published, so we can easily find ones that contain up-to-date information.

Cohesion of Ideas

This criterion will vary depending on the type of book being examined. If teachers are looking at informational types of text, they will still want to examine the cohesion of ideas, but the writing will look very different from narrative texts. With expository writing, the types of words and phrases that help connect ideas is important. Are words and phrases such as *because*, *therefore*, and *as a result* used? Does the text flow logically? Are concepts that might be abstract appropriately introduced? We cannot have a conceptual load that is too difficult for the students. Concepts need to be introduced in a concrete manner, with appropriate examples that students can relate to and understand.

If teachers are looking at faction storybooks, in addition to analyzing the content area information, teachers will also want to ensure that it is a well-written text with which students will engage. To assess the literary quality of storybooks, it is important that the plot, characters, and style be analyzed. The plot should be well developed through the text's pages. Also, students enjoy imaginative and creative story lines that capture their

attention and engage them with the material. The characters, if there are any in the story, are ideally not flat, but rather well-developed characters that express their feelings, views, and values to the reader through their actions and words. Finally, it is important to consider the author's writing style, such as word choices and the way words and sentences are combined to create the text.

Organization and Layout

When examining trade books, it is important to examine the illustrations, photographs, graphics (e.g., diagrams, tables), and words. The visuals should be appealing to the students, relevant to the text, and ones to which the students can relate. Books that encourage engagement with the text because of their visual presentation are valuable. Students need to be able to relate to the visuals in the text, and they should be shown from a child's perspective. One of my favorite books is *What in the Wild? Mysteries of Nature Concealed...and Revealed* by David Schwartz and Yael Schy (2010). Each photograph contains a mystery in nature and is accompanied by a short poem containing clues about the mystery. When students lift the flap on each page, they find more amazing photos, the answer to the mystery, and scientific details about the topic. Students will want to learn more about the earthworm castings, star-nosed mole, the meadow vole, and other interesting topics found in the book.

Also, it is important to analyze the placement of text. The words should not only complement the visuals but also be arranged on the pages so that they are appealing to the eye and easy to follow. The font likewise must be taken into consideration. Although font and page layout may seem trivial, think about how students react to the format found on standardized tests. We want students to be engaged and confident when they interact with a book. At a later date, take text from one that the students enjoy and show how it can be made to look intimidating through the use of font and layout; then, students will realize they can handle material found in other sources such as tests. While choosing books for classroom use, remember that they should draw the reader into the pages.

Text features such as chapter headings, subheadings, glossary, and table of contents should serve a purpose. Do they help the students understand the material, or do they create confusion? Teachers must help students use such text features to understand text. Therefore, we must ensure that they actually serve a purpose in helping the reader gain meaning from the text.

Specialized Vocabulary

We must examine how vocabulary terms are introduced to the reader. Are they explained through the context, visuals, or glossary? Are the vocabulary words explained adequately so that students understand the meaning of the terms? Are specialized vocabulary terms introduced within the context so that they do not overwhelm the reader? Students need to develop their vocabulary by being introduced to new terms within text, but the vocabulary should not create frustration for the reader.

Student Considerations

Although it is important to determine if a specific trade book is appropriate for the audience, it is vital that teachers realize that expectations can constantly change. This category is much more static than other criteria previously discussed. We must ensure that the book is at an appropriate readability level, which will be determined by how the book will be used. If the book is read to students, then it may be written at a higher readability level because the teacher will be present to scaffold learning and facilitate a discussion about the contents. If the book is being sent home for the student to read, then it needs to be at the independent level so that he or she can successfully read the text without assistance.

Also, determine if the format is appropriate for the intended students. Are the number of pages and the print size realistic for the age of the students? Will the book appeal to students? Although specific content area topics need to be taught, there are many different ways they can be presented to students. It is important to determine if the text presents the material so as to encourage student interest in the topic.

It is also important to determine whether the degree of detail is developmentally appropriate for the class. Although students need to learn about geometric shapes, the level of depth they need in second grade is very different from the depth needed by sixth-grade students. Not only is it important to take into consideration the current level of the students, but also it is important to realize that a book that may not be appropriate now may be appropriate later. As students improve their reading skills and develop background knowledge, some books may be appropriate to use even though the texts would not have been selected earlier in the year.

Finally, it is essential to determine if positive gender and racial/ethnic role models are provided. Examine the illustrations and the text.

Are males, females, and various ethnic groups represented? As discussed previously in this chapter, it is important to examine literature for its portrayal of people. According to Daisey (1994), minorities and women have been absent or poorly represented in science textbooks. We need to ensure that that is not the case in any of the trade books we select to share with students.

Teacher Goals

For this aspect of the assessment, think about the content of the text and your goals for the lesson. Think about the specific math, science, or social studies standards or topics that need to be addressed. Can the book be used to adequately foster an understanding of them?

Although there are many great assessments available to evaluate trade books related to specific content areas, the purpose of the assessment guidelines in Table 1 is to be able to quickly assess whether a book is appropriate for developing content area knowledge. Try to work in grade-level groups to examine texts and complete the evaluation sheet. Using a short period of time during grade-level meetings might be ideal for this task. If that is not possible, complete the sheet individually and then meet to discuss findings. I believe there is value in discussion, and it is important that more than one person review the same book.

The evaluation sheet makes it more difficult to select a book based on emotional appeal. We have all seen trade books that grab us from the moment we open the cover, and we cannot wait to use them with students. However, by analyzing trade books, we will ensure that our selections have the characteristics we seek in quality content area trade books. After reviewing a number of books, the assessment guidelines will be internalized, so the process will become much faster.

TRY IT OUT

Meeting in a small group, try out the Content Area Trade Book Evaluation Sheet reproducible in the Appendix with several trade books you enjoy using in the content areas. How do the books compare according to the assessment guidelines? Do the results confirm that the books are worthwhile texts to use with students, or do the results perhaps encourage the selection of alternative texts?

Determining Whether the Text Is a Good Fit for the Students

After locating books we want to use on various topics and evaluating their content, we have one final but very important consideration: We must also determine if the books are appropriate to use with students. It is often a struggle to determine if a book is a good fit. Decisions have to be made regarding whether the book is appropriate for the students to read independently or perhaps more suited to reading in class where students have access to more guidance. However, there are a lot of time constraints, so activities need to be quick to administer and meet the purpose. Although the Raygor (1977) and Fry (1977) readability formulas are often used to determine an approximate grade range for a text, they do not take into consideration the reader who will be interacting with the text or the way it will be used in the classroom. The formulas only consider word difficulty—determined by length of word or number of syllables, depending on the formula chosen—and sentence length. Vacca and Vacca (2008) refer to these formulas as "rubber rulers" (p. 129) because they are meant to give estimates rather than specific levels.

This section highlights four ideas that might be used to determine the appropriateness of a text for a specific reader. Although the first method, fluency snapshots, relies heavily on teacher judgment, the other three—FLIP; easy, just-right, and challenging books; and using a compass to navigate texts—allow the students to play a key role in determining whether a text is suitable for their reading purpose. All four ideas look at very different things, so review each one and decide which ones best meet your needs. Also, keep in mind that even though these four ideas were designed to be used with trade books, they are easily applied to other forms of text. Internet resources, documentaries, and other media can also be analyzed to see if the texts are at an appropriate level for students.

Fluency Snapshots

Fluency plays an important role in comprehension of text. Students who read word for word or those who must spend a great deal of effort to decode each word have difficulty understanding or comprehending the text. Therefore, one way to determine if the text is appropriate for students is to capture a fluency snapshot (Blachowicz, Sullivan, & Cieply, 2001). When we think of a snapshot, we think of something quick that represents

Table 2. Rate of Oral Reading Fluency

Grade Level	Oral Reading Rate
1	30–70
2	60–90
3	80–120
4	100–130
5	120–150

Note. Adapted by Morris, Gilmore, & McCracken, as cited in *Reading Diagnosis for Teachers: An Instructional Approach* (3rd ed.), by R. Barr, C.L.Z. Blachowicz, & M. Wogman-Sadow, 1995, White Plains, NY: Longman; and "Curriculum-Based Oral Reading Fluency Norms for Students in Grades 2 Through 5," by J.E. Hasbrouck & G. Tindal, 1992, *Teaching Exceptional Children, 24*(3), pp. 41–44.

one moment in time. The fluency snapshot is a quick tool that gauges a student's fluency level with a text. The chart in Table 2 shows the rate of oral reading fluency one would expect for various grade levels in the elementary school.

To capture a fluency snapshot, have each student individually read a passage from the content text orally for one minute. Then, determine the total words read minus the miscues, or deviations from text, to arrive at the student's oral reading rate. Taking into consideration the student's grade, it may be determined that the text is too difficult to read independently, or perhaps more additional guidance will be necessary for the child to comprehend the text. The fluency snapshot is especially valuable because a variety of content area texts will be used with students. The assessment takes minimal time to administer, so when questions arise as to whether a series of books may be appropriate, it is possible to determine within 60 seconds whether the texts are appropriate or whether it might be better to select ones that are easier or more challenging for the students.

FLIP

FLIP, which stands for *friendliness*, *language*, *interest*, and *prior knowledge* (Schumm & Mangrum, 1991), is a strategy often used with middle and high school students for content area material, but it can be modified so that even younger students can use it to determine if a text is right for them. Each of the four elements is rated on a scale of 1–10. A 10 would be an excellent rating for a text, whereas a 1 would mean the text did not score well on the element.

When students rate a text on friendliness, they are looking at linguistic features. Are there highlighted words, headings, a table of contents, or other elements that help explain the text? Language refers to the difficulty of the reading assignment in regard to the number of new words. Students are directed to read three random paragraphs to determine if the vocabulary or long sentences are confusing. To assess interest, students are directed to read the headings, the beginning and end of the passage, and any visual features included. Finally, the FLIP method asks students to determine their level of prior knowledge. Again, students think about what they read to determine interest and rate their prior knowledge level from 1, meaning they know very little of the content, to 10, which means the text is very familiar. There is also a follow-up aspect of the strategy that asks students to determine their purpose and reading rate and budget the amount of time it will take them to read and study the material.

To begin, write the letters *F*, *L*, *I*, and *P* spread out across the smartboard or chart paper. Then, as a class, look through an informative book that students might choose to read on their own and ask them to rate each of the areas. Start with the letter *F* (friendliness). Ask students to think about the types of features they often see in informative books. Brainstorm with them a list of features (e.g., italics, bold type, headings, fact boxes, glossary, table of contents, charts, sidebars, diagrams, pictures) that they might see in text and write them under the *F*. Then, have the class rate the friendliness level of this text. Is it really friendly, a little friendly, or not at all? After students rate the friendliness, ask them to think about the words and sentence meanings. Again, direct their attention to the headings, the bold print, and perhaps the introductory and summary paragraphs. Determine if there are a lot of really difficult words and sentences, whether the students can read most of the words and sentences, or whether they know all of the words and can easily read the sentences. Again, students should rate the level of language difficulty. Next, ask them to think about their interest. After all that they have read, how interested are they in reading the text? Are they very interested, not really interested (i.e., they do not really care whether they read the book), or definitely do not want to read the book. Finally, ask them to think about their prior knowledge. They should again think about what they have read so far. Do they know a lot about the topic, something about it, or almost nothing? After rating each area, ask students how they might use their

findings to determine whether a book is appropriate for them, offering guidance as needed.

Students can then be given the FLIP Assessment Sheet reproducible found on page 209 in the Appendix and be allowed to rate another book in pairs or independently. They can draw a face, with a smile, frown, or straight line for indifference, or write a number (1–10) for each area. An alternative is to give the youngest students the Lift-the-Flap FLIP Assessment Sheet reproducible, which can be found on page 210 in the Appendix. After folding the paper and cutting the flaps, students can write the numeral or draw a face underneath each of the four letters.

With the original FLIP strategy, Schumm and Mangrum (1991) added a caution against students trying to quantify something that is very difficult to quantify. Therefore, it is unnecessary to average numbers and focus on the result. Also, the purpose is for students to internalize the process. They do not have to complete a sheet every time they want to read an informative text. However, after using the sheets for a while, students will know the qualities they might consider in a book so that they can tell if it is an appropriate text for them.

The FLIP strategy gets students thinking about books. Instead of selecting a text based on a cursory glance at the back cover or a few pictures, students realize that many other features can have an impact on whether a book is a good fit for them. Sometimes, students are required to use a specific text. In that case, the results of the FLIP assessment can help determine what additional support may be necessary for the students who will be involved with the book. Perhaps more prior knowledge is needed on the topic. If it is readily apparent that students do not have a strong interest in the text, then extra discussion may be necessary to tie the book into the students' lives. By better understanding whether a text is appropriate for students, it is easier to create lessons and activities that meet our students' needs.

Easy, Just-Right, and Challenging Books

Harvey and Goudvis (2007) encourage students to think about books as belonging in one of three categories: easy, just-right, or challenging. As Harvey and Goudvis suggest, many students are unaware that adults cannot read everything. Therefore, as we talk about each of the three levels with our students, we need to provide our own examples of texts that might belong in each category. I prefer to share the three

categories in the following order to provide a logical, linear continuum for students:

- **Easy books**—Students can read all of the text and understand everything that is presented.
- **Just-right books**—Some words or ideas may not be understood, but most of the text can be read.
- **Challenging books**—Many of the words and ideas are not understood.

Students need to know that it is acceptable to read books from all three levels, but the majority should be just-right books. If presented with challenging books on a regular basis, the students will get frustrated. Those books might best be read at a later time, or perhaps someone can read them aloud. The text is too complex, and little learning can occur when reading them independently. Likewise, easy books are just that, too easy. Although it is fine to read these books for enjoyment and relaxation, we want to grow as readers. Therefore, the majority of books we read will belong in the just-right category. For most literate adults, easy books might be series narratives or books read as children, just-right books are probably those related to career fields or written about hobbies, and challenging books might be books related to entirely new, complex fields in which there is minimal background knowledge.

These three categories continually change. Books that might be challenging at one point can become just-right books as time passes, other texts are read, experiences occur, and the reading skills and background necessary to read them are built. Likewise, books that are just right may find themselves in the easy category after repeated readings. When students have an interest in a content area topic, or teachers want to recommend books on a specific topic, encourage students to skim the book, read a page or two, and determine which category the book falls into. If it is a challenging book, a student might still take the book home to read with parents or perhaps be paired with a student with stronger reading skills to read together. Although these categories were written to describe books, it is evident that the categories can be applied to a lot of other texts that students encounter.

Using a Compass to Navigate Texts

When traveling in unfamiliar territories, it is often important to use a compass to help guide us in the right direction. Students can use the

Compass for Navigating Words in Text reproducible, located in the Appendix on page 211, to determine if a text is at an appropriate level for them. The reproducible is based on the idea of knowledge ratings (Blachowicz, 1986), in which readers are asked to rate their knowledge of a text's vocabulary on a continuum. Readers determine and rate words according to word difficulty level. Instead of providing students with specific words from the text, as is done with the knowledge ratings strategy, the compass asks students to examine the text and determine the level of knowledge they may have of the text based on an overview of words.

First, model with a think-aloud the use of the compass sheet. Ask students to skim a selection or passage of material. The amount of material will depend on the grade level of the students. If it is a longer selection or an informational trade book, students might read a couple of pages and also skim the headlines and words in bold print. Then, have students look at their compass sheet. In the northwest (NW) quadrant, students can list content words they "know well," using the *n* and *w* as a mnemonic. In the northeast (NE) quadrant, students can list content words they "know but don't *ever* use." These are words that the students have seen or heard, can say, and may even know a basic definition for; however, the students do not believe they could use the words easily, have a really in-depth knowledge of the definitions with the connotative meanings, or can share ways the words might be used. The southwest (SW) quadrant contains words that are "somewhat familiar." Students have seen or heard these words but have no idea what they mean. Finally, there is the southeast (SE) quadrant for words labeled "strange encounters."

If the majority of student-written words are listed on the compass in the NE and NW quadrants, then travel will be smooth sailing. The text is pretty much on target, and students can probably read it independently. If the majority of words are in the NE and SW sections, students will need a moderate amount of word strategy to tackle the text. With support, this text can be read and is probably at their instructional level. However, if the majority of words are in the SW and SE quadrants, then perhaps the students should reconsider their current travel plan and navigate through other texts on the topic. If using these texts as part of the classroom instruction, be aware of the difficulty level for those students and provide extensive support. If a peer reading program is established, books in the last category might be good ones for the older partners to share when they visit the classroom.

Beyond Trade Books: Including Other Types of Imported Texts

When we talk about content area material, attention must also be given to imported texts that are not in book format but can help students develop literacy skills and content area knowledge. Imported texts are brought into the educational setting, not created within the classroom. These texts are present throughout communities and homes (e.g., maps, travel brochures, directions, recipe books, newspapers, comic strips) and can easily be tied to content area learning. Students often enjoy these texts because they have seen them used for authentic purposes outside of formal settings, such as schools and libraries. Imported texts provide yet another type of print that will help expand students' content literacy knowledge.

Through the incorporation of these texts, teachers can help students see that literacy extends beyond the classroom and connects with the community. One such example is when parents or others bring in published recipes to share with the class. Students not only understand the value of literacy skills beyond the educational context but also can also develop reading fluency and mathematical skills as they share and talk about the recipes.

Although recipes have similar traits to other types of writing with which students are familiar (e.g., words are read top to bottom and left to right), recipes are often an unfamiliar type of text for young students. First, all of the ingredients are listed at the top. Then, in the narrative part that follows, directions are given for completing the recipe. Sentences often contain few extraneous details and only the words needed. Finally, the amount produced by the recipe is noted. I have used recipes with third graders to compare quantities produced, amounts of ingredients needed, and even differences in temperature settings. It is clear that when a new format of text is used with students, they often try to read it as they would a more familiar format such as storybooks. Students must realize that different types of text require different types of reading. Recipes require a specific type of reading and have their own specialized vocabulary. There are also visual features such as headings (e.g., "Ingredients") as well as abbreviations that must be learned. Recipes are one more way to show students how texts vary. Just as students can be successful and easily learn to read that type of text, they can also learn to read and comprehend science, social studies, and math texts, which are also written differently than narrative texts.

Likewise, directions to create or build items or conduct a science experiment are often difficult for students to follow. However, these are important types of text with which students should be familiar. They must learn that steps should be followed in a specific manner so that the proper results are attained. Often, there are diagrams or illustrations that accompany the text, and if analyzed correctly, those visuals can help the reader comprehend the directions. Students must also develop metacognitive awareness so that they know what to do if it appears they are not understanding and following the steps correctly and can retrace their steps to see where they made a mistake. Through the incorporation of diverse types of imported text, we further expand students' knowledge of text and prepare them for the vast types of text they need to comprehend to be literate in today's world.

English learners can often talk with friends and demonstrate conversational English skills much faster than they can actively participate in content area discussions. Although students generally find content area materials more difficult to comprehend than narrative stories, think about the demands of math, science, and social studies texts for English learners. The vocabulary demands and density of concepts in each of those content areas can create additional issues for at-risk readers. By incorporating a wide variety of imported texts, students can expand their understanding of text and textual demands as they develop content area competence. These texts can not only help by providing visuals to reinforce science, social studies, and math learning, but they also serve to encourage academic language growth as concepts are explained and discussed.

Local Texts: Empowering Students as Creators and Authors

According to Maloch and colleagues (2004), local texts are created within the classroom and designed for use with students. Similar to imported texts, local texts are often easily attainable and cost little to nothing to produce. The texts also help contribute to a print-rich environment. With very little work and time, this type of text can be a valuable part of any science, social studies, or math lesson.

The benefits of local text are many. Students often have an added sense of pride and interest when they are involved in the creation of text.

They learn that what they write is valuable and that their writing conveys meaning. Likewise, teachers often play an important role in local text because they help facilitate and lead the creation of the material. Also, the texts are often created through collaboration, so students are developing social skills as well as academic skills as they work with peers. The following are a few examples of local text that might be created to convey or connect content area knowledge:

- Student-created informative books
- Journal entries written from the perspective of a specific historical time period
- Directions for building models of volcanoes
- Wall charts with poems and stories containing mathematical concepts
- Posters and diagrams encouraging students to protect the environment
- Word walls containing math, science, and social studies terms
- Timelines of historic events
- A science notebook documenting the steps of an experiment
- Graphic organizers that help students solve story problems
- Student-created websites for sharing content area projects

Guidelines for Selection and Usage

Although the availability of local texts is important, it is even more important to look at their use. Maloch and colleagues (2004) suggest the following seven guidelines for the use of local texts:

1. Read your room.
2. Read other rooms.
3. Think locally.
4. Think relationally.
5. Think across the curriculum.
6. Think dynamically.
7. Create space and design.

These guidelines, which are expanded on in this section, ask the teacher to reflect on how local texts are used in the classroom and throughout the school, the relationship of local texts to other texts, and the static nature of local text.

What Does This Mean for the Content Areas?

Each of the seven guidelines (Maloch et al., 2004) can be applied to the analysis of local text, which might be tied to content area learning. While reading a classroom, look for text created within the classroom. The first area to examine may be the classroom library. Are there student-created texts that help develop mathematical, science, and social studies skills? Are these texts displayed and organized to encourage student involvement? Also, look at other areas of the room. Are student-created texts that share content area information displayed on the walls and in centers? Students must learn to understand timelines, diagrams, and other visuals found in many content area books and can often begin by relating the visuals to their own lives and experiences. For example, timelines can be created to show specific key events in their own lives, and students can be encouraged to connect those examples to visuals they see in books and other texts. This connection of texts to other texts (i.e., intertextuality) is vital for people to make sense of what they learn (Lemke, 1989). As adults, we connect everything we learn to other experiences and knowledge that we have in order for meaning to occur. Likewise, students need to see how various types of text connect to what they see in other situations.

When reading the room, it is important to see that local text is integrated throughout the classroom. Also, can you tell whether all of the students were involved in the texts' creation? Students need to feel a sense of ownership and know that they can contribute content area–related local text to their classroom. It is also important to look more closely at the local texts. While quantity is important, quality is even more important. To gain additional ideas, visit other classrooms and talk to colleagues. Then, brainstorm ideas to facilitate the use of local texts.

TRY IT OUT

Get together with a colleague and read each other's rooms. Reading your own classroom may be more difficult than reading someone else's because you know what you are hoping to communicate. It is similar to reading something you wrote versus reading what someone else wrote. Help each other see what others see inside your classrooms. What do you notice about the local text? Is it tied to the different content areas? Does it represent a variety of students? Does it enhance the learning environment? What changes would you suggest to improve the use of local text?

Relationships between texts are important. Maloch and colleagues (2004) talk about public and personal texts. Think about the public texts that are displayed in the classroom. Are there ways to tie personal texts, or texts that only the authors see, to the public texts? For instance, if students write a class poem about slavery, they can create personal stories, poems, videos, or podcasts that tie to the information.

Local texts can be tied to hands-on lessons and imported texts, or texts created elsewhere and brought into the classroom. If a science trade book related to gardening in spring is shared with the class, students can plant seeds similar to the ones discussed in the text. The class can also develop a weekly chart, or a public text, so that the class can monitor their plants' growth. After reading and discussing the book and seeds, students retrieve their science logs and write down the steps they followed. Through these activities, the students are linking their private texts to the imported text and the public text that was created.

Thinking dynamically refers to the fact that classrooms must be engaging and interesting to students. Classrooms that are exciting centers for learning are constantly changing. Therefore, determine if the local texts have been used recently. If not, is there a way that they can be worked into the curriculum again to reinforce content area knowledge? Once students no longer notice the text, it may have outlived its purpose and no longer be valuable. Local text is inexpensive and easy to create. Therefore, it can easily be replaced with other local text when it no longer serves a purpose.

Finally, think about the space and design of the classroom. Displayed print needs to serve a purpose. Does the print help create an environment that is conducive to learning? Can students benefit from the print displayed, or is it so cluttered that it creates more confusion than clarification? Quality must be considered as well as quantity.

Local text is valuable. It helps establish a sense of community in the classroom, as students feel that they are important and contributing members. It also increases student exposure to text and adds to the print-rich environment. Finally, it serves as one more important type of text that can be used to help improve reading skills and the depth of content area learning.

Nonprint Media

Technology is playing an increasingly important role in our lives. In fact, Ikpeze and Boyd (2007) refer to the overwhelming amount of information

available as a "knowledge explosion" (p. 644). McPherson (2007) believes that if we do not help students learn to navigate nonprint media, then we are hindering them. In order for students to be successful and able to compete in the constantly changing world, they must be prepared to use "powerful literacy" (Finn, 1999, p. xi). While suggestions for incorporating technology into the content areas are shared in various chapters of this book, it is important to include nonprint media as an additional form of text that should be incorporated into the classroom.

Nonprint media might include videos, DVDs, websites, databases, commercials, and audiobooks. Although many of those types of media require the use of the Internet, schools are changing to help teachers meet the need. Years ago, it would not have been easy to have access to the Internet in schools. However, 99% of schools are now listed as having Internet access (Kleiner & Farris, 2002). While schools in some areas still have very limited access, other forms of nonprint media can and should be incorporated into the classroom.

It is obvious that the various professional groups responsible for writing the content area standards are aware of the increasing importance of technology. The NCTM (2000) includes technology as one of six overarching principles that guide the teaching of mathematics. The National Science Education Standards (NRC, 1996) focus on the importance of developing a "scientifically literate populace," which requires exposing students to a "rich array of learning materials" (p. 2). These materials need to include technology. Finally, the National Curriculum Standards for Social Studies (NCSS, 2010) state that students should be able to use a variety of media including films and PowerPoint presentations, and the NCSS include "science, technology, and society" (p. 218) as one of the 10 themes that are important at all levels in schools.

Liu (2005) states that material in a digital environment is read differently than traditional printed text. Students often look for visuals that help them understand the text, are less apt to reread material, and tend to read much more selectively online. Instead of reading digital material in a linear manner as a chunk of text, viewers choose bits that catch their interest and read those. While we must help students maximize learning from nonprint media, these forms of text are often some of the most familiar to students. Digital texts serve to connect students' lives outside of school with their experiences within the classroom, and many students already have a familiarity with and an interest in the use of online tools.

Also, it is essential that nonprint materials be included so that students develop technological competency.

DISCUSSION POINT

Discuss with your students how they use technology on a daily basis. What types of technological items do your students use each day? What types of technologically related activities do they participate in, and what type of literacy demands do they encounter? How are these literacy demands similar to or different from the literacy demands encountered in the classroom math, science, and social studies lessons?

Kamil, Kim, and Lane (2004) provide guidelines for selecting multimedia documents and recommend that they contain appropriate visual representation. The visuals can help students comprehend what they are reading in the same manner that they use graphics in a printed book. Also, the authors believe that verbal and visual information should be presented together so that one type of information reinforces the other. It is also recommended that students' prior knowledge and developmental levels be taken into consideration when selecting the documents. As with any text, students who have limited background experiences with the topic will experience difficulty understanding the content. Likewise, research conducted with fifth, seventh, and ninth graders who were reading science texts containing multimedia aspects (Moore & Scevak, 1997) has shown that younger students may have difficulty integrating the components of multimedia documents. Students may have more difficulty linking text and visual aids present in the material. Educators need to be aware of the demands placed on students by such texts and work to help them gain the most from technological resources.

The Important Link Between Texts and Students

While the purpose of this chapter is to explain the value of incorporating various forms of text into the classroom, the most important link between students and the text they use is the teacher. The texts discussed in this chapter should not be relegated to a classroom library, sent home for independent reading, or available only during free time. Although those

may be additional ways of providing access to the materials, we can do so much more. Trade books can be valuable, but they must be accompanied by meaningful activities to help students learn (Macken, 2003), which is also true for local text and nonprint media. Educators used to lament that children's literature could become basalized and used more like the old basal readers with their lockstep approach. Now, research (e.g., Palmer & Stewart, 1997) shows that sometimes trade books are used in the same manner as textbooks. Unfortunately, as electronic text becomes more prevalent in school settings, I believe it could also be used similar to textbook material. However, that would not be making the best use of the materials. All texts are not meant to be used in the same manner, and by taking into consideration the needs of our students, and the unique qualities of the wide diversity of texts available, we can best address our students' needs.

Teachers know their students and know which texts might interest students and which might frustrate them. Through a teacher's decision making, students are able to appreciate texts that are appropriate for them. Teachers not only help students select texts but also help them make sense of the texts. Through their valuable interaction, teachers are able to help students better understand concepts discussed and elaborate on topics presented (Varelas, Pappas, Barry, & O'Neill, 2001). Meaningful activities for using the texts are shared in the remaining chapters of this book. Through the teacher's facilitation, students can not only enhance their literacy skills but also develop a stronger knowledge of math, science, and social studies through the use of texts discussed in this chapter.

REFLECTING BACK AND LOOKING FORWARD

This chapter outlined a variety of texts that can cultivate content literacy skills. Whether students are kindergartners or sixth graders, it is important to expose them to a wide variety of quality texts. Some texts are "inconsiderate" (Armbruster, 1984), and these poorly written texts are confusing and extremely difficult for students to understand. These texts lack structure and coherence of ideas and are unsuitable for the audience. However, with the wealth of texts available, students can easily have access to "considerate" texts that present information in a reader-friendly manner. Just as Atkinson and colleagues (2009) recommend that teachers engage

in "collegial conversations about trade book evaluation among themselves and content area experts" so that decisions are no longer "based simply on availability, whim, or the blanket recommendations offered by publishers or experts" (p. 496), I believe this is true for any type of text we bring into the classroom.

Through the use of a variety of trade books, imported and local texts, and nonprint media, we can enhance students' educational experiences. According to Palmer and Stewart (1997), it is crucial that educators use multiple texts in the classroom so that "independent learning, rich discussion, and critical thinking" (p. 631) can take place. As we help students work with a range of texts and make intertextual connections, our classrooms will become places where content learning is relevant to the outside world. As our classrooms and the world continue to change, we must prepare our students to participate actively in the world in which they live. We can do this by creating classrooms that reflect the type of reading that will be demanded in the world outside of school. Although we will never be able to expose students to every text imaginable or use every type of nonprint media they may encounter, we can prepare them to be effective and flexible thinkers with the ability to gain information from new texts that they may encounter. However, this is not possible when we limit students' experiences to one text: the textbook.

Trying It Out:
Activities for Fostering
Disciplinary Literacy Skills
in Math, Science,
and Social Studies

Meeting the Reading Comprehension Demands of Each Content Area

Let's begin by thinking about what we mean by *reading* and more specifically what it means to read in math, science, and social studies. Reading is a complex skill that many of us spend a great deal of time focusing on in our elementary classrooms. Think about all of the reading skills that our students must learn. Very young students must develop concepts of print. Students need to learn that we read from top to bottom and left to right, and that we read words not illustrations. Additionally, we teach Dolch and other sight vocabulary words that students must recognize. As part of our early literacy instruction, we foster decoding skills through phonemic analysis so that students can figure out unfamiliar words that they encounter. Finally, we encourage students to use picture cues, skipping and rereading, and metacognitive monitoring to help them with unfamiliar words in the text.

As students master these basic skills and move beyond the primary grades, we move on to what Shanahan and Shanahan (2008) call "intermediate literacy" (p. 45). We help students at this level comprehend by encouraging a wide variety of literacy strategies. K–W–L plus, directed reading thinking activity, Venn diagrams, and other strategies expand students' background knowledge, strengthen their vocabulary, and encourage metacognition.

Our goal in developing these reading skills is to enable our students to understand that print has meaning and to ensure that they have a wealth of strategies in their toolbox when they encounter words they cannot read. Research suggests that we are very successful at developing these levels of literacy. Our students are reading markedly better than they did years ago, and our standardized scores demonstrate that (Perie, Grigg, & Donahue, 2005). However, as students progress in their schooling and move beyond

elementary school, they are unprepared for the textual demands they encounter.

Shanahan and Barr (1995) have a wonderful analogy for this trend in literacy thinking, which they refer to as the "vaccination approach." It is often believed that if early literacy issues are funded and strengthened—if students are "vaccinated" early on—students will continue to read without problems for years to come. Unfortunately, that does not appear to be the case. The great improvements we are seeing with younger students are not lasting after they leave our elementary classrooms and proceed on in life. Keeping with the vaccination analogy, this type of approach in actuality is similar to the flu shot. The vaccination approach, with a strong emphasis on basic and intermediate literacy skills, helps students at the lower literacy levels. However, the approach leaves students unprotected for all strains, or types, of literacy demands they encounter later. When our older students are faced with the demands of specific content area reading, they are unprepared to be successful readers. In fact, Greenwood (2004) stresses that middle school students actually encounter a wall with content area reading. This wall can be removed by presenting students with the skills and knowledge they need to be prepared for math, science, and social studies reading.

As elementary teachers, we want our students to be successful throughout life in their reading. Even though we must focus on the basic and intermediate literacy skills, we must also begin at even the youngest of ages to focus on the reading demands found in disciplinary literacy. Although it sounds like one more task to add to an ever-lengthening list of material to cover and items to teach, it just means that we need to rethink how we present material and strategies. We need to draw students' attention to the unique reading demands of the field of mathematics and help them realize that they must consider content areas when reading. When we read a math word problem, a document on the U.S. Civil War, or a section of text explaining how we digest food, we read the text very differently.

DISCUSSION POINT

Think about the important role that comprehension plays in reading. How does the way students read in math vary from the way they read in social studies and science? How can we draw their attention to the fact that reading requires different skills and strategies in different content areas?

What Does This Mean for the Content Areas?

If I asked you to review a letter, a book, or an online article on a significant historical event, you would not be surprised if I told you to read it and then invited you to talk about it without looking back at the text. What would happen? You would summarize what you learned and discuss the gist of your reading, which would probably work. However, if I asked you to read a math word problem and then turn over the sheet and tell me the gist of what you read, you would probably be shocked, to say the least. With math, we must teach close reading and rereading of text. Students must realize what the problem is asking them to do and be able to sift out erroneous information, which is just one example of how reading in science, social studies, and math differs. Therefore, let's now look at each of the three content areas to determine the types of reading skills we need to develop in our students, the goals we have for them in those areas, and the types of activities they may participate in to be successful with the reading demands of these subjects.

Mathematical reading requires a very unique type of reading. Let's think about what we expect students to know and be able to do when it comes to reading related to mathematics. Throughout their schooling experience, students are presented with word problems and expected to be able to determine the best way to solve the problem. Even when students are presented with problems within trade books, they must often approach the text as they would a word problem in a textbook. They must determine what information is important and what is not important to solve the math problem. Students must therefore understand the value in close reading and rereading as two extremely important strategies to use with text.

With scientific reading, students are often required to look at text and then diagrams and charts that extend the information present in the printed words. As they read, students must be able to visualize what they are reading. Moving from reading printed words to visuals on a page and back to printed words is a sophisticated process. It means students are not using the skills of beginning at the top of the page and reading until the end of the text as they may have traditionally done with narrative text. Students stop, start, and stop again as they seek to understand the relationship of the visuals and the text and gain meaning from the print. They need to read a great deal of factual information and be able to understand it.

Social studies text requires an entirely different type of reading. As we all know, this type of text is quite dense, with a great deal of information discussed in very few words. Let's think about some of the textual demands that students might encounter while reading through a social studies text. Shanahan and Shanahan (2008) point out that although there may be fewer technical terms in social studies, the general difficulty of words is high. When I reviewed two elementary-level books pertaining to the Civil War, I found words such as *advisor, resigned, stroke, honored,* and *majority.* Although those words may not be familiar to many students, they are not words that readers would anticipate seeing in Civil War texts. Learning and reading about famous people is valuable, but how were events and people a part of the bigger scheme of things back then? How did it all fit within trends we see in history? We must assist students so that they can continue to successfully read social studies text and understand the textual demands. Students must also understand how to compare multiple sources through careful analysis and understand how others impose their opinions on text. According to VanSledright (2002), this is difficult to learn because students from a very young age are taught to see texts as factual and true accounts of what really occurred. With all of the information bombarding students now in the informational age, it is especially important to help them critically evaluate texts.

The following activities are not all inclusive. There are many ways that we can prepare students to read text related to specific disciplines. However, these activities are meant to provide concrete ideas for drawing students' attention and interest to thinking about how they read in math, science, and social studies. When we ask a young student about reading, chances are they will talk about words and books. Students will not intuitively think about reading within various content areas as requiring different skills unless we help them with this important process, which must begin in the elementary grades.

Math

Word problems may be the greatest mystery of all time. When teachers tell me that students struggle with word problems, it is clear that some things never change. Has there ever been a time when word problems were easy for students? I remember struggling with them as a child. If I said to an adult, "The train leaves the station at…," I am sure many eyes will

roll. It is so much easier to solve math when it is involves symbols, such as $2 + 2 = \underline{}$, because we know what we must add to determine an answer. In word problems, the mathematical operations required to determine the answer are never explicit. We must take words and translate them into symbols and vice versa. All three of the strategies shared in this section show students that math is similar to a puzzle. The first strategy is designed to help them translate words into symbols. The second strategy draws students' attention to mathematics and requires them to use color to help "read" the words in a problem. Finally, the third activity is designed to help students think about everything they read in math and determine what is and is not important in the problem.

Word Problem Code Breaker

This strategy helps students translate words into math symbols and vice versa (Altieri, 2010). It is a way to help students learn what keywords in math word problems mean. Students will come to associate specific mathematical symbols with various words they might see in word problems.

Students must realize that when they read mathematical text, they must read every word. Although polysyllabic technical words might be the ones that create difficulty in other content areas, many math teachers have shared the difficulty in getting students to realize that small words such as *is* and *of* must be noticed because they can have an impact on the answer to a problem. With social studies text, it may be enough to get the gist of the material, but mathematics is different. Students must not only pay attention to specific words but also be able to understand their meanings specific to the field of mathematics.

The Word Problem Code Breaker is a great strategy regardless of the age level (see page 212 in the Appendix for the reproducible). Young students can complete the sheet as a whole-class activity and will only be able to complete sections for the operations they have learned. Older students may work in groups to complete individual sheets that they can keep and use to help them solve future word problems they encounter. Students can continue to add words to their sheet as they deal with progressively more difficult problems.

The purpose of this strategy is not to stop using concrete objects to complete math problems but to enhance the use of such methods. The purpose of the reproducible is to introduce the idea that reading in

mathematics is done very differently from other types of reading with which students may be more familiar.

How It Works

1. Provide students with a copy of the Word Problem Code Breaker reproducible. First, explain that the sheet has the equal sign in the middle of the page and areas to brainstorm all of the words that students might see for each operation (i.e., addition, subtraction, multiplication, division). It is often less confusing for students to complete the page counterclockwise to align with the order in which they learned the mathematical operations, denoted by the large *C* on the sheet. The *C* is a reminder for students to proceed counterclockwise, in the same direction that they typically write a C. Therefore, students will begin by brainstorming words that might mean *addition* in the top right section of the paper.

2. Divide the class into small groups and ask them to brainstorm words they see or have seen in word problems that are used to mean each of the operations on the sheet. To do this, they may want to look at their math books or children's books that contain word problems.

3. Begin with addition. Ask one group to share all of the words they brainstormed. After the first group of students shares what they wrote in the addition section of their sheets, the other groups can give additional ideas. Everyone in the class can add terms to their own papers as ideas are shared. Continue on with each group sharing until the last group shares what they put in the oval in the middle of the page, and others have shared additional ideas for the term *equal*.

Very young students may be presented with the following problem:

> There are six cats sitting on a fence. Four of those cats get off the fence. How many cats are left?

The students may draw and write out their answer to the problem. Many times students at this age are also expected to write the number model. For this example, the answer expected might be $6 - 4 = 2$. Students may draw six cats and put an X over four of the cats. Even a simple problem such as this has words that have mathematical meaning.

How do the students know that they are not adding the number of cats but instead are subtracting? Many very young students will respond that it makes sense. They draw their illustration, and since some cats are no

longer there, they illustrate "take the cats away" by drawing an X through four of the individual cat pictures. Take that moment to point out that the words "are left" often means that the reader is being asked to subtract and not add. Similarly, problems geared to the youngest of ages that ask "for the total" in a math problem often require adding. The students can reread or listen as the recently solved problem is reread and compare other problems they have completed to see if those problems had a similar wording and if they subtracted in those problems.

This strategy can also be easily used with word problems written for much older students. Older students may read the following:

The sum of three times a number plus 10 is 25. Find the number.

Students could read through the word problem and determine which words are code words for mathematical operations. *Sum* refers to addition, *times* refers to multiplication, and *is* means equals. This strategy is a very versatile one for math because it can be modified and used at a variety of grade levels.

Additional Ways to Try It Out

Although very young students will not be ready for the Word Problem Code Breaker sheet, they may be introduced to a modified version. You can create a chart or even a section of a wall with only the plus and minus signs on it. As students read and notice similar words in the problems they solve, these words can be added near the correct symbol. For example, they might list words such as *more*, *adds*, *in all*, and *plus* in the + section. Under the − sign, they may also list words such as *take away*, *minus*, *leaves*, *removes*, and *are left* that gave them cues to use subtraction.

The Color Connection

The Color Connection is a strategy primarily geared for upper elementary students and uses color as a way to help them develop mathematical literacy. This strategy requires students to read words and translate them into symbols. Therefore, students can translate a word problem into its symbolic form. This strategy also emphasizes a close reading of equations. The Word Problem Code Breaker sheet (see previous activity) can be tied into this activity.

How It Works

1. Provide students with a written equation such as the following:

 A rectangle's perimeter is equal to two times the length plus two times the width.

2. Ask students to underline or highlight the words that mean "equal to" in a specific color.

 A rectangle's perimeter <u>is equal to</u> two times the length plus two times the width.

3. Then, ask students to change the underlined words to their symbolic equivalent, the equal sign, and highlight that symbol with the same color. This separates the sentence into two distinct parts, to the left and right of the equal sign, and shows that there are two sides to the equation.

 A rectangle's perimeter = two times the length plus two times the width.

4. Have the class highlight the first part of the sentence in a new color and the second part in yet another color (denoted by **bold** and *italics* here).

 A rectangle's perimeter = *two times the length plus two times the width.*

5. Students should look at their Word Problem Code Breaker sheet and circle the operation words they found in the word problem.

6. The circled words should be replaced by their mathematical symbols. For "times," the students can use an × or a multiplication dot (·). In addition, the plus sign represents "plus" in the equation. Students insert the symbols for those words.

 A rectangle's perimeter = two × the length + two × the width.

7. Talk about how the numbers in the sentence must be changed into their symbolic representation so that there are fewer words at the final steps. There are only two numbers in this problem, so when they are changed into their symbolic representations, students have the following:

 A rectangle's perimeter = 2 × the length + 2 × the width.

8. Discuss how the variables must represent exactly what they measure. If the reader does not know how much he or she has of something, then that is the unknown, or variable, quantity. Perimeter could be represented by P, length could be represented by L, and width could be represented by W. Insert those letters into the equation to represent those words.

(Now that we are working with an entirely symbolic problem, the period is deleted, which is how students will most often see these types of problems.)

$$P = 2 \times L + 2 \times W$$

9. Students have just translated words into symbols. They have gone from the English language to the algebra language. Older students may understand that $2 \times L$ is equal to $2L$ and that $2 \times W$ is equal to $2W$. If so, both $\times$ symbols can be removed.

$$P = 2L + 2W$$

10. Reread the answer and compare it to the original written equation.

Many students are visual learners and respond to color. This activity initially uses color to focus students' attention on translating a written problem into its symbolic equation. Using color makes each step clearer to the students as they go through the mathematical process.

Stoplight Strategy

Even the youngest students understand the meaning of the colors on a stoplight. Often in the early grades, teachers use a stoplight system for behavioral management. Green means that students should keep doing what they are doing, yellow means that they must use caution and think about how they should change their behavior, and red means to stop and change behavior. Whether it is a stoplight on which students have individual clothespins signifying their current behavior or some other method of denoting behavior with colors, the very youngest of students understand those three important colors.

That is why I like to use those colors to help students know what to do when they are reading the text in a word problem. They first get the green light to read through the word problem and then they must stop. When stopping, they have to ask themselves some very important questions. What is the word problem asking them to do? The students can either determine the problem orally as a group or individually write the problem, depending on their age and experience with the strategy. Then, they proceed with caution as they decide what is important or unimportant textual information to answer the question. Understanding what is

important in a word problem and what is not important is a very difficult concept for young students, but with teacher assistance, even those at the younger grade levels realize that they must read mathematical problems and stories differently. They must also monitor their understanding as they complete the steps.

How It Works

1. Begin by talking about the colors on a traffic light and let students explain what those colors mean to drivers. Why must we have traffic lights? Then, tell the students that they will be using those same three colors to help read word problems.

2. Read through and discuss the following steps with students:

Green = Go
Carefully read the word problem.

Red = Stop
Think about what you read. Before going on, state the problem that you must solve.

Yellow = Proceed with caution.

Look at the text and list all of the information as either important or unimportant.

Red = Stop
Can we take the important information in the problem and write out the steps we need to complete?

Yellow = Proceed with caution
Let's look at the steps to see if we can determine the answer.

Red = Stop
Does the answer make sense? How do we know that it is reasonable?

3. As a class, work through one word problem together using the Stoplight Strategy for Solving Word Problems reproducible, found on page 213 in the Appendix, which may be used with students to help them through the process.

4. Next, students should work in groups or individually to see if they can apply the strategy to other math problems they encounter. The

reproducible should not have to be photocopied every time students try to answer word problems. Instead, keep the steps on a chart posted in the classroom for students to reference. As time passes, they will internalize the types of thinking they must do to solve word problems.

Students in the early grades often work with very simple word problems. When students get to step 4, they may only have one step to complete their problem. However, those at older levels may have several steps required to determine the answer.

A Look Inside One Classroom
The following word problem is very similar to ones that might be completed in second grade. The following shows how the Stoplight Strategy might look in action:

Green = Go

Teacher: Let's read through the word problem.

Second graders had a field day. There were 3 teams of second graders created for the races. Those teams competed in wheelbarrow races, sack races, and an obstacle course. There were 4 children on each team. How many children were in the races altogether?

Red = Stop

Teacher: After reading through this word problem, what problem are they asking us to solve?

Student: We have to figure out how many second-grade kids were in a relay race.

Yellow = Proceed with caution

Teacher: Let's see if we can figure out what is important information and what is not important information from the text and create lists. If we aren't sure, we'll let the information stay in the important information part of our chart.

Student: I don't think we really have to know the types of races they had that day.

Teacher: That's right. Which sentence contains that information?

Student: The third one.

Teacher: Can we just remove that sentence? Let's read it out loud and make sure there isn't anything we need to know to help us figure out the problem. If we agree, then we'll draw a line through the unimportant information.

Some second graders had a field day. There were 3 teams of second graders created for the races. ~~Those teams competed in wheelbarrow races, sack races, and an obstacle course.~~ There were 4 children on each team. How many children were in the races altogether?

Teacher: Is there anything else that we can remove?
Student: The first sentence doesn't really tell us anything important either.
Teacher: What does it tell us?
Student: It just tells us the grade and that they were having a field day.
Teacher: Does everyone agree? Let's go ahead and draw a line through that sentence, too. That was a good point because it doesn't really matter what grade the children are in in the story. Let's also remove part of the second sentence.

~~Some second graders had a field day.~~ There were 3 teams ~~of second graders~~ created for the races. ~~Those teams competed in wheelbarrow races, sack races, and an obstacle course.~~ There were 4 children on each team. How many children were in the races altogether?

Red = Stop

Teacher: Let's look at the problem we have left and write down the important information we know.

There are three teams for the races.
Four children are on each team.
We need to determine how many children there are altogether.

Teacher: Let's rewrite this information as a math problem with numbers and symbols.

$3 \times 4 = ?$

Yellow = Proceed with caution

Teacher: Let's try to solve our problem.

$3 \times 4 = 12$

Red = Stop

Teacher:	Does 12 make sense for an answer?
Class:	Yes.
Teacher:	How do we know it is reasonable?
Student:	The answer has to be larger than the number of teams, and it has to be bigger than the number of kids on each team.

The Stoplight Strategy encourages students to closely read and reread word problems. By getting students to use their metacognitive skills and think about each step, we help them realize that math word problems must be read differently than many of the texts they encounter on a daily basis.

Science

As we think about the demands of scientific reading, we realize that we often must read factual information and develop a complete understanding of the material. Similarly to math, readers must know what is important and what is not important. They also encounter technical vocabulary that may not be familiar. Often as readers, we get caught up in the narrative and forget to focus on the facts provided within the text. Furthermore, scientific writing often contains an assortment of graphic aids. Charts, diagrams, and graphs are often found within the pages, and students are expected to be able to shift between reading words to looking at visuals and vice versa. If they are not taught the importance of such visuals, many students will merely skip the visual aids and read the actual text.

The activities that follow help students determine important textual information, encourage the expansion of technical vocabulary, and focus their attention on the importance of visuals related to science texts. The first activity, Talking Drawings is a great way to introduce the importance of visuals to students by engaging them in creating pictures. Next, the Text Roles activity is designed to focus students' attention on the skills they need to navigate science text. Each role develops specific disciplinary literacy skills related to science.

Talking Drawings

Originally developed by McConnell (1993), this strategy is a great way to help students focus on the importance of visuals. Because visuals play a

key role in many science texts, it is important that students see drawings as a source of information when reading science content. Through student-generated drawings, students are able to share their knowledge and technical information (Fello, Paquette, & Jalongo, 2006). Not only will this activity help them visualize what they hear or read about in texts, but it also can provide them with additional opportunities to increase their understanding of specialized words. While some strategies must be modified to work with a range of ages, Talking Drawings is one that can be successfully used for various grades with only minor modifications to better suit the needs of the teacher and students.

Although students may read the science text to themselves to complete the activity, this strategy is an excellent way to tie in teacher read-alouds with informative texts and content area material. Tying comprehension strategies with science content is an excellent way to support student learning (Connor et al., 2010), and this strategy is an excellent way to do just that. Research strongly supports the importance of orally reading aloud informative texts to students (Smolkin & Donovan, 2001). Although teachers have read stories aloud to students for years, the text of choice was often a narrative book. However, as the focus on the use of informative texts in the classrooms increases, it is important that these texts be seen as viable for read-aloud time with students. Through the oral reading, students can build background knowledge, develop a better understanding of the technical vocabulary and content information in the text (Webster, 2009), and focus on the linguistic features present in such texts (Jalongo, 2006). Furthermore, according to Pappas (2006), the discussion that ensues allows teachers to model scientific language.

How It Works

1. Choose a science topic that students are preparing to study or just beginning to study.

2. Select a quality informative text pertaining to the topic. Chapter 2 contains many ideas for locating such texts. Since the text is to be read aloud, be sure to read it aloud on your own or to a peer several times before sharing it with students. Often, informative texts are more difficult to read aloud than the narrative ones, which is often due to a lack of experience with reading such texts aloud and the linguistic features that mark such texts. Locate several discussion points in the book where you

might want to stop and have a discussion with the class. Decide how you will draw the students' attention to linguistic features that the author uses in the book. Just as with a narrative text, and even more so with an informative text, engage the students throughout the read-aloud. Asking questions at the end will not keep them engaged with the text, and there is no way to know what they are and are not learning as the text progresses.

3. Introduce the science topic and text to the students. Explain that before the book is read to the class, they should draw an illustration of the topic. Discuss what they may gain from drawings and other types of visuals they create or view. It is often easier to draw a picture than to write about a topic because students may lack the language skills or knowledge of content-specific terms. While drawing, students are able to think about any prior knowledge they may have on a topic and may remember other information as the drawing progresses. Finally, ask them to think about how authors use such visuals to help readers gain a better understanding of text. Have they ever seen information presented in pictures and found it easier to understand than the written words? Rebus stories are often used when students start reading. These books contain pictures in lieu of some words. Likewise, pictures are equally important as students progress through the grades. Instead of replacing words, visual aids are often used to add important information to the text. Talk about maps, graphs, and other types of illustrations they have seen.

4. Allow time for students to create an illustration on the topic. Ask them to draw a picture to share what they know about the topic. They may label items, write phrases, or just draw.

5. Have students share their drawings with the rest of the class.

6. Orally read and discuss the selected text with the students.

7. Ask students to then modify their drawings, or if it is easier, they can create entirely new ones for the topic based on the text they just heard. Have them add information they learned. Encourage them to label parts of their illustrations and use any new technical terms they heard in the story.

8. Talk about the strategy. Have students share their illustrations with the rest of the class. They can talk about what they changed after the story was read or share their two drawings if they made a new one after hearing the text. By listening to others share their drawings, students are having technical vocabulary reinforced and perhaps hearing information they missed when

the text was read. Encourage them to refer back to the book read when discussing why they added certain information to their pictures.

For example, if young students are learning about birds, they may draw a picture of a tree, some birds, and grass prior to listening to a text such as *What Bluebirds Do* by Pamela Kirby (2009). After reading and discussing the text, students may choose to add details and labels to their drawings. Based on information gained from the text, students may choose to draw a knothole on the tree and label it "cavity," or they may add a nest box to the tree. They may also show a group of nesting boxes and label it "bluebird trail." Smaller birds may be labeled "chicks," or a group of chicks may be labeled "brood." Since the first flight is referred to as a fledging, a student may draw a chick in the air and label it "fledgling" (the name of the chick after its first flight). Even parts of the chick might be labeled, such as the down (the hair on a recently born chick) or the beak.

After the second drawing is created or the first one is modified, let students work in groups or pairs to share their drawings with each other. Students will reinforce the technical science vocabulary they are developing and expand their vocabulary and content knowledge by talking with others. Listening skills and cooperative learning will also be strengthened. While they are reinforcing the skills and background information they need to read science texts, it is evident that they are also learning to visually represent and view visuals that they did not create.

A Look Inside One Classroom

A first-grade teacher was teaching a two-day unit on turtles. She began by letting students know that they would be learning about turtles. Before they began, she encouraged them to show her what they knew by drawing a picture. They could label parts of the picture or write a sentence on it if they wanted to do so.

The teacher then had the students orally share their pictures. Many of the pictures did not have labels. Most students just drew pictures of turtles, and some included sand, water, and eggs. After sharing the pictures, the teacher orally read the informative text *Sea Turtles* by Gail Gibbons (1999). The book talks about eight different types of sea turtles and goes into detail about each type's characteristics. The pictures in this book for young learners are clearly labeled. After reading the book, the teacher had the students give her facts about sea turtles, and she listed those on the smartboard.

Finally, they drew a second picture showing what they knew after listening to and discussing the book. The students, even at this young age, did a great job. Some of their new pictures looked entirely different from their first ones. One student's original picture depicted a turtle and eggs on the sand with water nearby. This student's postreading picture showed only a turtle, but six parts of its body were labeled: "tal," "shell," "bacfliprs," "fliprs," "yis," and "mouth." Another student chose to keep his before and after drawings almost the same with an illustration of a turtle, sand, and water. However, on his after picture, he labeled "weeds," "water," "baby trtl," and "sand." When the teacher asked why, he said he was showing what he had learned from the read-aloud.

One of the more interesting examples is Shannon's drawings. Her before and after pictures are shown in Figure 1. Many books for young readers use anthropomorphism, giving inanimate objects and animals human characteristics. This practice is often criticized in informative trade books because children have trouble differentiating between real and make-believe. In Shannon's before picture (Figure 1A), the four turtles look almost human. Two of the turtles have long eyelashes and big, pink lips. I would venture to guess that she was showing boy turtles and girl turtles in this drawing. After hearing the informative text by Gibbons, this first grader made a much more scientific drawing (see Figure 1B). She clearly labeled with arrows the sea, eggs, fin, and shell. Also, she showed the turtle leaving the sand after laying the eggs to return to the sea. This correct sequence of events shows that Shannon has an understanding of how sea turtles lay their eggs.

All of the students' drawings demonstrated a gain in knowledge after hearing the book. Not only did Shannon's second picture show a better understanding about sea turtles, but it appears that her initial picture may have been influenced by fictional books or movies that she may have seen previously. Although she may not know how to distinguish male and female turtles, real females do not have big, pink lips and eyelashes. Shannon's second drawing appears to focus more on scientific aspects of turtles. The results demonstrate the importance of providing informative books for students on various scientific concepts.

Additional Ways to Try It Out

If desired, this activity can also become progressive talking pictures. Teachers may select several trade books to read aloud that are based on

Figure 1. A First-Grade Student's Talking Drawings

Note. These drawings were made before and after the teacher read a book on sea turtles to the students.

the same topic. Each day, the students can add to their drawings after the trade book is read or create new ones. The discussion with a partner is still a critical element, because students learn a lot through collaboration. This discussion can clarify misunderstandings that students may have about the content. When the trade books are all read, students can look at their drawings and see how much information they gained through the successive texts. Students may also use a different color to label items after each text is read to them, so they can see how exponentially their content knowledge is increasing.

Visuals play a key role in science content. As students progress through the grades, that role can become more and more important. Through talking drawings, students explore the importance of visuals and the knowledge that can be gained from them. The collaborative nature of the strategy adds further learning potential, and the small-group sharing is essential. Through this strategy, students gain new technical vocabulary and background knowledge that will help them when they are presented with future science material on the topic.

Text Roles

Teachers over the years have enjoyed using roles in literature circles with a variety of grades (Daniels, 2002). Literature circle roles provide students with a purpose for their reading and a task to complete prior to a class discussion of a text. The teacher divides the class into small groups, or literature circles, and then individual students within each group are assigned a role. Daniels is quick to point out that although teachers will want to provide printed copies of the tasks to use with students when first introducing them to literature roles, eventually the students will internalize the roles and not need the printed copies. Many teachers designate tasks for each student, such as seeking out vocabulary words, illustrating an aspect of the story, leading the discussion, making connections to other material, or providing a summary. Teachers may take these roles a step further and use roles that are specific to a content area, which can foster the type of reading skills necessary to develop disciplinary literacy knowledge.

Let's look at the skills necessary to understand scientific text. As previously discussed, students must learn how to shift their focus from visuals

to text and vice versa, summarize the material and eliminate unimportant information, develop technical vocabulary, relate the information to the world around them, and read critically. Each of the roles in this activity focuses on some of those goals. Therefore, it is critical that students alternate roles, so they have an opportunity to develop a variety of disciplinary literacy skills.

How It Works

1. Begin by determining a scientific topic for students to explore. This topic may be broad (e.g., habitats) or may be more specific (e.g., changes that occur in nature during winter).

2. Find a variety of texts related specifically to the topic. Look through suggestions shared in Chapter 2 for finding recently published, quality texts. The suggestions can also be used to determine if texts are at a suitable level for the students. Students can play a part in this decision process by also sharing ideas for texts. If students are currently learning about habitats, the teacher may share book talks on texts such as *What Bluebirds Do*, *Wolfsnail*, Tannis Bill's (2010) *Pika: Life in the Rocks*, or *The New York Times* bestseller *Turtle Summer: A Journal for My Daughter* by Mary Alice Monroe (2007). Then, the teacher might let the students determine which books they want to read. By having them participate in the decision process, they have choice, which is a powerful motivator in the classroom.

3. Determine how you want to use the content area text with the text roles. There are two ways these roles might be used: Teachers can have each group read the same text or read an informative text based on a specific topic. Both of these methods can be used with the same role sheets. For example, if the class is learning about nature, each group may choose to read texts specific to one aspect of nature. One group may select texts related to winter or, more specifically, what happens to nature in winter. *Wings of Light: The Migration of the Yellow Butterfly* by Stephen Swinburne (2006), *Bugs and Bugsicles: Insects in the Winter* by Amy Hansen (2010), and *Under the Snow* by Melissa Stewart (2009), which describes what happens under snow in a variety of habitats, all pertain to the topic, yet they are representative of a range of difficulty levels. It is important to ensure that the text options meet the needs of the struggling readers as well as the most proficient and skilled readers.

4. Discuss with the entire class each of the possible roles that students may be assigned. As Daniels (2002) states, the role sheets he shares in

Literature Circles: Voice and Choice in Book Clubs and Reading Groups
are meant as "book club training wheels" (p. 99), and the same is true with
the reproducible role sheets in the Appendix (see pages 214–218). The
goal is for students to begin to think like scientists and draw attention to
the skills they need to develop. As students experience the roles, they will
think about key points, visuals, vocabulary, and connections outside the
text, and eventually they will not need to have a role assignment to discuss
a text pertaining to a specific topic. The following is an overview of each
of the roles.

Visual Expert. Students must learn to view and create visuals that contain
scientific information. Students have a great deal of experience seeing
visuals but not necessarily viewing them with skill. Visuals are found in the
media, on the Internet, and in books, but to be experts at viewing them,
students must be able to analyze the information presented and understand
the purpose of the author or creator of the visual. Although students may
be tempted to skip over visuals to save time while reading text, because
they do not really understand the importance of the graphs, charts, and
illustrations, this role focuses attention on those visuals. Students must
carefully analyze the visuals in the text and determine whether they serve a
purpose or could have been modified to be more informative or interesting.
Students can also be invited to create visuals that they think might be more
appropriate for the text they are reading. The visual expert's contribution to
the group dialogue will engage the other group members to also examine
and discuss the visuals within the text (see page 214 for the Visual Expert
Role Sheet reproducible).

   As an example, the teacher may take a picture walk through a book
such as *Cicadas! Strange and Wonderful* by Laurence Pringle (2010).
Within the pages, students can identify many types of visuals that are used
to enhance the text. There are labeled pictures, diagrams, charts showing
the life cycle, sequentially numbered pictures, and even maps. As the class
looks through the text, they can discuss the types of visuals they see and
how they enhance the text. Then, students can look at the visuals in other
quality books, such as *Mysteries of the Komodo Dragon: The Biggest,
Deadliest Lizard Gives Up Its Secrets* by Marty Crump (2010) or *Seed,
Soil, Sun: Earth's Recipe for Food* by Cris Peterson (2010). These two
books have amazing photographs that accompany the text but limited
visual aids common to informative texts.

Students can then discuss what types of visual aids might make reading those books easier. Perhaps maps or a timeline would add visual knowledge to Peterson's text. Students might suggest adding a diagram of the Komodo National Park to Crump's text because it is mentioned in the book. They may also suggest a map showing the different locations of zoos mentioned that have Komodo dragons. The text discusses the size of their eggs and the length of the babies when they hatch. A life-size drawing for the text, scaled to size, might make that information even more interesting. Perhaps a timeline could be used to show some of the dates mentioned in the book. Finally, students might consider fact boxes, which could highlight amazing trivia mentioned in the text. Many students will be interested in knowing that Komodo dragons' saliva kills their prey or that they can also sniff out dead animals from seven miles away.

Mad Scientist. With this role, students are encouraged to think about the mad scientists they have seen in various media or read about in texts, and be just as obsessed with science as the mad scientists. Students are encouraged to read the text and then search for outside information on the topic or even the author (see page 215 for the Mad Scientist Role Sheet reproducible). They are encouraged to be creative and keep their eyes open for any type of brochures, websites, experts, and other sources that might add information through text or personal interviews. This role will lead students to make intertextual connections (Kristeva, 1984) as they compare information found in multiple sources. The role sheet has a place for students to list a source, a page number if they are examining a written text so that they can easily locate what they want to share, and a few key pieces of information they gained from the source.

Time Machine Traveler. This role asks students to take a ride in a hypothetical time machine and think about how the scientific information in the book may be important not just now but also in the future. They think about the relationship between the material and their present-day lives and the world in general (see page 216 for the Time Machine Traveler Role Sheet reproducible). Students also consider the reasons behind the scientific information's significance. Then, they are asked to brainstorm how they will use the information they gained in the future. If necessary, students can ask other group members or interview outside sources who might explain the importance of the content. These sources might be

students in older grades, adults in specific careers, or even adults who use the material or information in their daily lives.

Science Newscaster. Newscasters must summarize a great deal of important information on a topic in a very brief amount of time. They have to make sure they are focused on the key points they want to share in their newscasts. The purpose of this role is to focus students' attention on the main points in their text. They then prepare a breaking news alert to share with other group members later (see page 217 for the Science Newscaster Role Sheet reproducible).

Word Magician. Magicians can do amazing things with simple objects. Word magicians can take a single word, weave their magic, and provide so much more information on the word. Students who fulfill this role locate interesting words in the text that they believe others should know (see page 218 for the Word Magician Role Sheet reproducible). This role is a modified version of the visual and verbal word association strategy for building vocabulary (Eeds & Cockrum, 1985; Readence, Bean, & Baldwin, 2004). Students state an interesting word they found in the text, write a sentence using the word, explain the definition of it as it is used in the text, and draw an illustration so that they remember the word. The reproducibile also has a section where students can list other forms of the word, such as morphemes and affixes. By looking for other forms of the word, students are manipulating words. The more students see, think about, and use words, the deeper their understanding will be of the terms.

5. Once teachers and students have selected the texts and reviewed the roles, it is time to establish the text groups. These groups should each have approximately five students.

The teacher may assign the roles to the students or let them select the roles they wish to take for the text. Let the students know that they will have the opportunity to participate in each role during the science circles. The rotation of roles is important because it not only keeps students interested but also ensures that they are thinking like scientists and developing the various disciplinary skills necessary for dealing with more difficult text and concepts in later years. A chart can be used to ensure that each group member participates in each of the scientific roles at some time within the small groups.

Students not only realize the importance of visuals but also realize that they must decode unknown words. Students must also comprehend the main idea, without getting caught up in extraneous details, and apply what they are learning to situations outside the classroom. If there are not five students in each group, the teacher may decide to have a student handle two roles. Another idea is to demonstrate with the entire class how the roles work and model through one of the roles, then allow the students to complete the other role sheets within their groups as usual. If it is not possible to use all of the role sheets at one time, it is still important to try all of them at one time or another so that all of the skill areas are targeted.

6. After each of the students has a role, provide them with adequate time to complete their role descriptions. This will probably require at least two to three days. Let students know when their role sheets must be completed by so that they are ready to share in groups. Some teachers may even choose to use topic roles on a specific day of the week, such as Monday or Friday. Science roles might even be used in lieu of sustained silent reading one day a week. The science roles will not only strengthen content knowledge and encourage the reading of informational books but also strengthen students' disciplinary knowledge, which is necessary for future science reading.

7. On the assigned role sharing day, talk about what makes a good listener. Listening is just as important as talking, and in order for each person to have a chance to share in groups, everyone must be a good listener. After groups discuss the texts using their completed role sheets, the students can discuss as a class what went well with the groups and what they may want to change the next time they use roles with an informative text. Using roles is a process, and it will take time to see what works best with the class.

Additional Ways to Try It Out

While the groups are meeting, act as a facilitator and observe what is occurring in the groups. Also, groups may want to evaluate their experience either orally or in writing. In lieu of oral sharing, students may complete exit slips to share what went well and what was difficult for them. This feedback is essential in order for the teacher to be able to modify the roles for future texts.

If texts are long or students are very young, have students read only a portion of the book for each meeting. In this scenario, students can experience a variety of roles with one text. Another possibility with young students is to work with older students as partners. If the older students are struggling readers at their level, they will benefit from helping younger students by improving attitudes toward reading and building self-confidence. An older student can read aloud a short informative text to a group of younger students. Each of the younger students can then complete their roles and share the information they learned at a later date. If this idea is used, it will be important to also let parents know what book the students are reading, so parents can help their students find the information necessary to complete the assigned roles. The added benefit is that parents also are aware of the reading demands that their children might experience with science texts.

Social Studies

Reading social studies–related material requires unique skills. To begin with, students must be aware that social studies text is dense, as a large period of time may be discussed within very few pages. Therefore, it is often difficult to determine the main idea when there is such a large amount of information in a passage. Also, students must analyze the sources they read and develop an understanding of the difference between primary and secondary documents. Historical documents are influenced by the author of the material, and therefore it is important to compare what several documents or texts might say about the same topic. Finally, point of view is an especially important aspect to consider when reading social studies texts.

Three of the activities in this section—Analyzing Like an ARTIST, Multiple Gists, and I-Charts—require students to examine multiple texts. The ability to compare texts is a higher level skill that is important for those reading social studies texts. Through text comparisons, students can determine if information is consistent within different sources, analyze viewpoints, and learn to succinctly summarize key information. Furthermore, as discussed in Chapter 1, the overall vocabulary found in social studies texts can be difficult. Therefore, the 10 Important Words Plus and Word Puzzles activities focus students' attention on the words found in texts and provide a number of ideas for strengthening their understanding of the words.

Analyzing Like an ARTIST

Famous Movie Star Admits to Prior Life as a Grapefruit! Trained Dog Saved From the Pound Cleans Owner's House as a Father's Day Gesture! Have you ever seen headlines similar to these in tabloids as you stood in line at the grocery store? Even more important, have you ever had someone actually repeat information they read in such texts as factual information? Unfortunately, there are a lot of people who read a text and then repeat the information as if it were factual without taking into consideration the author, the author's intent, or even the type of document. The ability to read information and make educated decisions is a skill that must be taught to students. This is especially true with documents related to social studies content.

With this document analysis strategy, students are required to examine a number of details about a text. Artists are known for having a very keen eye for analyzing the world around them, and students are encouraged to think as artists. They must not read the material as factual, but rather they must critically examine the text. Students must understand that there are both primary and secondary sources and that the type of document can have an impact on what they read about an event, place, or person. Also, social studies text can be affected by the author's bias about the person, place, or event. Students must take all of this into consideration as they seek to understand and develop social studies disciplinary knowledge.

Students can use the ARTIST Document Analysis reproducible to examine text (see page 219 in the Appendix). This form encourages the reader to consider the audience, the type of document, the reason why it was created, important details contained in the text, the source for the information provided, and the time period during which the text was created. On the sheet they complete, students provide any information related to each of these six aspects.

How It Works

1. Begin the discussion by asking students if they have ever seen something in writing that they did not believe was true. As they discuss this, ask them what made them rethink what they were reading. Perhaps they knew that the source was a tabloid website known for rumors about famous stars. Maybe they questioned the text because they could tell the author had a strong opinion and was writing to sway the opinion of the reader,

or perhaps they knew the author was someone who had a stake in the information the reader took away from the text. An article written on the important role animals have played historically in medical research would be very different if written by a scientist versus a member of People for the Ethical Treatment of Animals.

2. Prior to beginning the lesson, locate several texts related to a topic of study in social studies. These texts might be from the Internet, a newspaper, or other books specifically about the topic. Then, present students with one of the sample texts.

3. Explain to the students that there are several things they must take into consideration when reviewing texts. As a class, talk about each of the sections of the ARTIST Document Analysis sheet. Why is it important to think about each area? What types of information might we find?

4. As a class, use the sheet to record a text analysis. If there is no information known for a section, the section can be left blank. Discuss the results.

5. Groups of students can then use the sheet to analyze another document on the same subject.

6. After students have completed their analysis, discuss what they found. Were there any interesting findings that they may not have noticed had they not considered each aspect on the sheet? Each group can share an overview of the results of their text critiques.

7. Explain that it is extremely important to analyze social studies material. With older students, take this opportunity to talk about primary and secondary sources. Reading primary sources is similar to hearing information firsthand, and reading secondary sources is similar to being told something secondhand from a friend.

8. As a class, look at other documents related to the topic being studied. Compare several documents authored or created by different people, so students can understand that information can be presented differently by different people. Be sure to include a variety of texts, including those in the media, printed texts, and perhaps even interviews. Discuss how each of the sources might affect the information shared.

A Look Inside One Classroom
A sixth-grade class was studying the Crusades and looked at a variety of texts as part of the classroom instruction. The students began by

analyzing a copy of a painting from the Crusades Era and writing their observations directly on their photocopies. Students also looked at maps showing Christian-dominated areas, Muslim-dominated areas, and those that were a mix of the two religions. Students made inferences based on their observations from both the photographs and the map. Then, the teacher modeled the use of the ARTIST Document Analysis sheet with the photograph. Students were asked if they could tell who the painting was created for, which religion's side was favored in the painting, and during what time period the painting was created. During class discussion, they had to explain how they determined the information shared. The teacher wanted to encourage students to analyze documents carefully and not just look at them superficially.

Then, the teacher passed out two separate persuasive paragraphs. One was written from the perspective of a Christian nobleman during the Crusades, and the other was written from the perspective of a Muslim leader. Students used the reproducible independently to analyze these short texts. The teacher found that the strategy encouraged students to focus closely on document details. Locating emotionally loaded words and determining the time when the document was created was an easy task for all of the students. However, some students needed additional help with other aspects of the analysis. Identifying the document's intended audience, the type of document, and the reason or purpose for the author creating the document seemed to be especially difficult for these students. Through additional discussion, they soon achieved success.

Additional Ways to Try It Out

After students have completed the activity, consider completing a scavenger hunt activity with a narrow aspect of the next topic discussed in social studies. The class can brainstorm the various types of text that might be located on the topic. Students can then work in groups to find a wide variety of materials or texts on the topic. Each group can have a copy of the brainstormed list so that they can work together to make sure the texts they locate come from a variety of sources. For example, if students are studying the government, they may be instructed to find texts related to the vice president. Students might find newspaper articles, magazine and television interviews, political cartoons, press releases, letters, and even charts and tables showing results of polls.

On a designated day, the students can work in their groups to analyze the documents they found, then present their findings to the class. Even the youngest of students can begin to develop the understanding that readers must read critically and compare texts. Young students can understand that two texts on the same topic may share very different information for a variety of reasons. Wineburg (1991) discusses how historians must corroborate information across multiple texts and closely examine the authors' backgrounds and perspectives. This strategy can help young students start developing those skills.

Multiple Gists

As the saying goes, brevity is a virtue. Unfortunately, brevity is something that does not come easy for most people. When we are asked to retell an event that occurred or a book we read, we often go into great detail about not only the main idea but also aspects and details that interested us. As adults, we might notice eyes glazing when we realize that our audience truly stopped listening after the first few minutes. Brevity is why many of us will never be able to tweet or text well without running out of space or developing carpal tunnel syndrome. However, we expect students to be able to succinctly tell us the main idea of a passage. The ability to summarize briefly is an important skill, but it is difficult with social studies because of the amount of content contained within very few pages.

Cunningham (1982) originally developed gist as a strategy to get students thinking about the main idea of a social studies passage. Then, Manderino (2007) adapted the strategy so that students can use it to compare multiple texts. Students read one document and create a 20-word gist. After reading the second document, they take their first gist and the information in the second document to create a new 20-word gist. This continues as students read more documents. Students can use up to 30 words in their final gist. This strategy is a great way for students to make intertextual connections and learn to succinctly comprehend the main idea of diverse informative texts. Multiple Gists can easily be modified for a range of ages.

How It Works

1. Select a passage for students to read. The length of the passage will depend on the age of the students. For young students, share a very brief

informative book on a specific topic. Older elementary students may read a chapter, a section of a trade book, or an online article.

2. Place students in groups and have them retell the passage in complete sentences totaling 20 words. This limits the facts the students can retell, but they also have the opportunity to go into enough detail to explain the main idea. Many teachers who use this strategy with younger students give them a sheet with 20 short lines, so the students can write one word per line to keep track of how many words they have written. Then, students go back to their writing and modify it as necessary. This step in the process is easier if the students turn over the passage after reading it and before trying to write the gist. Otherwise, they may have a great deal of difficulty with limiting their information to the main idea.

3. Ask groups to share their completed gists with the rest of the class. This is a good time for students to share why they did or did not include specific information. They can talk about the difficulty level of the activity and perhaps brainstorm ideas that might make the task easier in the future. Discuss how linguistic features, such as bold terms, italicized print, and headings, might cue them in on the main ideas of their passages.

4. After creating the first 20-word gist, students read another text, then try to synthesize the information in their first gist with information from the second passage and create a new 20-word gist of all of the material they have read.

5. Discuss with students the importance of removing details from text when locating the main idea. Main idea is a difficult concept for many students to understand. However, this activity limits the words they can use. As students continue to synthesize across various texts, they may use additional words for their multiple gists. Allow students to have between 20 and 30 words in their gists as the number of texts they read increases.

If students encounter difficulty with this strategy, have them complete a gist on one text. Then, progressively increase the number of texts students use with Multiple Gist in the future. This strategy can easily be modified in this way to meet the needs and ability levels of diverse students.

I-Charts

As students are expected to read more and more advanced material in social studies, they must be able to compare various sources, corroborate

information they read in texts, and pay attention to the source of the information. Although inquiry charts, commonly known as I-charts (Hoffman, 1992), are often suggested as a way to prepare older students for that type of reading, a modified version can be used with younger students. This strategy is a great way for them to organize the information they read in different sources, and it encourages the use of various types of text. An additional benefit of this strategy is that students organize their thoughts for writing. For primary grades, complete the I-chart as a whole-class activity. However, students in the upper elementary grades may be able to complete the I-charts in small groups after a sample is completed as a model with the entire class.

How It Works

1. Think about a topic related to social studies that is currently being studied. Then, brainstorm with the students to determine three or more questions that they want to answer about the historical subject.

2. Introduce the I-chart (see page 220 in the Appendix for a reproducible). Tell students that, similar to K–W–L, the chart has a place to write what they think they know in relation to each of the questions they brainstormed. Ask the students for any information they know in relation to each question and list that information in the corresponding columns in the first row. If there is other important information they learned in regard to the topic, list that information in the appropriate columns also.

3. Now it is time to consult other sources. Explain that different information can be found in various texts, and sometimes similar information is read. Brainstorm with students other texts that they might read to find out more about the topic. Depending on the topic, they may consult informative texts, the Internet, newspapers, magazines, or even the course textbook.

4. Explain to students that whenever they consult a printed book, they will want to note the title, author, and copyright year of the text in the left column of their I-charts. In addition to that information, they can list the page numbers and edition when the source is a magazine or newspaper. Finally, they can list the website where they found information on their topic when they use the Internet as a source. If they cannot find information on the topic in a source related to one of their questions, they can leave that row blank except for the first column. Encourage students to make sure this column is completed each time they fill in a row to avoid forgetting where they found the information.

5. Using one source at a time, students complete each row.

6. Then, students take the information they learned in relation to the first question and write a brief summary in the final row under question 1. This is repeated for each of the other questions.

7. When charts are complete, students can talk about what they read as a class. Did they find similar information in more than one text? Did they find any information that differed between texts? These charts can also help students organize information from various sources so that they can use their summaries to write four paragraphs on the topic.

I-Charts are an excellent way to visually represent information gained from a variety of texts. As part of the activity, students are also involved in many higher level thinking skills as they compare and synthesize information gained from a number of sources. Similar to Multiple Gists, the number of texts used for this activity can easily vary according to the ability level of students present in the class and the experiences that students have had with comparing diverse texts.

10 Important Words Plus

Have you ever been intrigued by a word you saw in print for the first time? Did hearing it roll off your tongue make you enjoy using it every once in a while just for fun in conversation? Well, students are the same way. They can jump into the wonderful, wacky world of words quite easily by seeking out new and interesting words they want to learn. Rather than providing specific words and definitions to the students to learn, the teacher is in the role of facilitating vocabulary development. Students sense this and want to learn the new words and use them to complete word puzzles later.

This strategy is an excellent way to create word consciousness, which is a curiosity and interest in words, and it is essential for developing vocabulary. Memorizing definitions of assigned words does not help students remember the words after the vocabulary test, and it more than likely will not lead to students applying the words to other contexts. Although many vocabulary strategies require students to be told which words are important to learn, this strategy is unique because it allows students to select the words they want to learn. By allowing students to play a part in the process, they are more easily engaged and curious about the words. While students select

the words for 10 Important Words Plus, it is still very easy to ensure that any words the teacher wants to bring to the attention of the students will be focused on in the lesson.

According to Shanahan and Shanahan (2008), many scholars believe that the general vocabulary found in social studies texts can be very difficult. However, using this strategy in social studies is an excellent opportunity to let students select the words that are important to them from the text. Although many believe there may be less technical vocabulary in social studies than other content areas, even everyday words, or general vocabulary, can be unfamiliar to students. Through teacher guidance, the teacher still has a role in the words ultimately selected for further exploration. Yopp and Yopp (2003) have outlined the steps, as described in the section that follows.

How It Works

1. Ask students to read through a piece of text. The amount of text will depend on the age and ability levels of the students.

2. After students finish reading the text, have each of the students determine 10 words they think are important. Each word can be written on its own sticky note.

3. Then, have students create a class bar graph based on the words selected. By creating a graph with the sticky notes, students can determine which words others also felt were important.

4. Lead a class discussion so that students not only discuss the 10 words they individually selected but also talk about other words students listed on the graph. There is nothing magical about 10 words, and teachers can modify the strategy for younger students and shorter text by having the students locate fewer words.

5. This strategy can then be extended with small-group activities. The teacher provides each student with a task written on a color-coded card. Each card color represents a different task. These tasks can include listing synonyms or antonyms, telling where a word might be encountered, listing other forms of the word, drawing pictures to depict its meaning, creating a graphic aid to show the relationship between the word and other words, acting out the word, or finding sentences in which it was used (Yopp & Yopp, 2007).

6. After the color-coded cards are handed out, all of the students with the same color work together to complete the activity stated on the card with a

teacher-selected word from the class graph. This is where the teacher can focus students' attention on words he or she might feel are valuable for this text and future texts.

7. Once the task is accomplished, each group takes a turn sharing the results. Then, the task is repeated several times, with the teacher assigning another important word from the graph to each group. After students are adept at their task, the groups switch colors to complete a different task with a new word.

A Look Inside One Classroom

One first-grade teacher used this strategy with two pages of text on the topic of natural resources. Because of the younger grade level, the class was divided into five groups of three students each. Also, the teacher instructed each group to find five important words in the text rather than 10. After they completed that task, the teacher listed the five words brainstormed by each group:

Group 1	Group 2	Group 3	Group 4	Group 5
land	water	food	resource	trees
resource	air	people	natural	water
earth	land	water	water	land
trees	fruits	air	land	resource
water	trees	land	needs	natural

Then, the students had a chance to talk about the words. During this discussion, the students noticed which words were on more than one list. One student pointed out that the word *air* was listed under two different groups. Another student stated that the word *needs* was only on one list. The teacher then asked the students to see if there were any words that occurred on three or more of the lists. There were five such words: *land, trees, water, resource,* and *earth.* The class decided that these words were important to most of the class, so the teacher wrote them on the smartboard for future reinforcement.

Additional Ways to Try It Out

Because many classes can have 20 or more students, it would be difficult to handle 200 sticky notes. Therefore, consider dividing large classes

into groups of three or four students. Each group is given copies of the informative text to read, and as a group, the students come to an agreement on the 10 words they want to post on the graph. It is important that every group member has a chance to contribute at least one word to the group list. One sheet is compiled with the 10 words for each group. Older students may not only write the word on the sheet but also note where they saw the word and why they chose it. Although students do not read all of the information on the sheet aloud to the class, it can serve as a prompt for discussions that ensue about the words.

Often, students will go back into the text to locate a word mentioned if they do not remember seeing it, and because words are often used multiple times in a text, students will end up discussing the various places where the word is found. Also, students can list more than one reason for why the word was selected or where it is located in the text. This initial group work adds extra collaboration and encourages even more dialogue. Furthermore, students are gaining experience skimming text and rereading portions of it, which are highly valued skills in the content areas. Students are not only reading new words and expanding their sight vocabulary but also getting the terms into their oral vocabulary.

There is also another way this strategy can be modified. Since research (Heisey & Kucan, 2010) encourages the use of multiple texts even with very young students, because it strengthens students' understanding of content, teachers may choose to select a handful of books on a specific topic instead of having the entire class read the same brief text. Then, a brief book talk can be done on the books before each group is given a short informative text to review. Next, students proceed to select the important words in their text and compile a list of them. Because of the overlap in content/topic, students may have some words that are found in all of the books, yet there will be some unique words also added to the class graph from each text.

Each group takes a turn orally sharing the first five words on their lists with the rest of the class. By having each group begin by sharing only the first five listed, each group will have the opportunity to introduce some new words to the class graph. Then, the groups repeat by sharing the last five words on their lists. Start with the group that shared last and let them share first when sharing the final five words on their lists. As groups share, write the words on the smartboard or a sheet of chart paper to create a class graph. Then, chorally read the words on the graph so that they move into the students' speaking vocabulary.

Lead the discussion by asking what interesting things students notice about the graph. Are there several forms of a word listed? Were there any words that very few or very many students selected? Are there any proper nouns? Are there any words that students think are important that they did not notice when they first read the list, and why do students think so? If time is of the essence, students might complete an exit slip for the teacher. The next day, some of the exit slips might be shared before continuing on with the activity.

For more advanced or older students, they can then work in groups to find other creative ways to share the graph results. They might develop a scatterplot or another visual aid. Also, they may decide to categorize their results. Perhaps students want to develop a graph that categorizes the words according to the part of speech. Maybe they wish to create graphs that show how the words are presented in the text. Those included within headings (e.g., chapter, subsections, visual) might be in one category, those words that are presented in different types of fonts in another, and words that are only part of the chapter text in a third. All of these strategies get students thinking, talking, and writing words. Therefore, they build their vocabulary as they are repeatedly exposed to the words.

Word Puzzles

Students can complete word puzzles (or word tasks, but the term *puzzles* sounds much more motivating) on individual words within a social studies text. Puzzles are a motivating way to focus students' attention on vocabulary words, and students see these tasks merely as fun. The amount of time required to complete the word puzzles will depend on which ones are selected by the teacher. Therefore, the activity can easily be modified to fit within the time constraints of the classroom.

How It Works

1. After students have read through a text, select a different mystery word for each group and write it on a card. The students in each group do not show the other groups their word. Although each group will pass the word card among the students in the group, they will want to only whisper the word in hushed tones to keep the word a mystery. Some of

the word puzzles that teachers might ask students to complete include the following:

- Create a riddle. List up to four clues for your word. Start with a general clue and then give a more specific one. When the time comes, share your riddle with the class to see if the other students can guess your word. As you contemplate clues to share, you might think about part of speech, the definition, or contexts where you might see the word.

- Find another text that uses the word. This may be difficult with print, but it should be fairly easy if students have access to the Internet. If time permits, the students can also look outside of the classroom for examples of the term. When the time comes to share, read the paragraphs or example you found to the class to see if the other students can guess which word was yours. Students will have to be thinking about the original text as they listen to the new text presented.

- Create a visual that incorporates the important word into the visual. When the groups share their visuals, allow other groups to guess the meaning behind the visual before explaining why you created it. What does it represent? Are there any symbols that have meaning to you that are related to the word? As discussed in Chapter 2, these visuals may become part of the local text in the classroom.

- Share the word with another class. Become roving reporters ready to report back to the classroom. Had the other students heard of the word? What did they think it meant? Where had they seen it? What did you learn about the word? If the other students did not know the word, were you able to find a creative way to teach it to the other students?

- See the connection. Groups select two or three words from the class graph and show the similarities and differences using a Venn diagram. Unlike the other word puzzles suggested, this activity allows the students to select the words. While this can be a difficult activity, students might find that two of the three words on the list might sometimes have the same affix added at the beginning or end. Perhaps two of the words have multiple meanings, but the third does not. It is easiest to compare two words with a traditional Venn diagram, but more advanced students may enjoy the challenge of creating one to compare three of the words.

2. At a designated time, have the groups share their completed word puzzles with the rest of the class. Discuss how they completed their tasks, any challenges that were encountered, and any other interesting words that students may have learned in the process. Students might even create word puzzles that the teacher can use with future words.

There are many more options for word puzzles. Since social studies text contains very difficult words, but fewer technically challenging words specific to just those texts, this strategy is a great activity to create word consciousness and build students' vocabulary without directly teaching a specific list of words.

REFLECTING BACK AND LOOKING FORWARD

The strategies discussed in this chapter encourage students to understand the intricacies of reading math, science, and social studies texts. For students, these content areas are often viewed as subjects they must learn in school. Therefore, students often use the decoding strategies they learned in the "learning to read" phase and believe that they can continue to read each of the content area materials in the same manner. However, to be successful in content areas, students must understand the demands of each specific area.

Although disciplinary literacy skills are often discussed in reference to older students in middle and high school, it is possible to start building the foundation in the elementary grades. In the earliest grades, students can begin to understand that all texts are not read in a similar fashion, and older students can develop a more in-depth understanding of specific disciplinary literacy skills. The reading demands shared in this chapter that are unique to each content area can be introduced and discussed with the class.

Instead of reading math, science, and social studies in the same manner, students might choose to read a narrative tale. They must think about the specific content area, the literacy demands of the field, and how they can best approach the text. *Reading* is truly a multimeaning word. While reading always involves comprehension, the skills and strategies necessary to comprehend varies according to the subject matter. This knowledge will help students later in life, as they encounter more difficult content materials, and also prepare them for the literacy demands of the world beyond the classroom.

CHAPTER 4

Orally Communicating Content Area Knowledge

When we think about developing oral communication skills in the elementary grades, we often think about teaching students to listen carefully and articulate their thoughts through speech. We seek to develop these skills so that students become confident in their ability to share ideas and listen and comprehend information they receive. When we look at math, science, and social studies, and at the specific demands of these content areas, we realize that our communication activities must be designed specifically to develop content area knowledge in each subject.

All of the activities discussed within this chapter help with reading, writing, and visual communication, but the focus will be on how elementary teachers can help students improve their oral communication in the content areas. What oral language skills are necessary to develop students' content literacy knowledge and prepare them for future content area material? How might we encourage oral language development in each of the content areas?

DISCUSSION POINT

Think about the oral language classroom activities in which students participate on a daily basis. How are these activities developing students' prior knowledge; enhancing their understanding; and reinforcing their mathematical, science, and social studies knowledge? Are oral language activities specifically tied to each of the three content areas? Are there changes that might be made to the curriculum to strengthen students' oral language in any of the specific content areas?

What Does This Mean for the Content Areas?

As discussed in previous chapters, both math and science texts have very specialized words that students must learn. Some of these words, especially in math, are multimeaning words. They may have a math-specific meaning but also have a general meaning with which students may be more familiar. Words such as *yard*, *mass*, *scale*, and *volume* are some examples. Other terms are homophones (e.g., *wait/weight*); they sound alike but are spelled differently. It is important that when students use these terms, we ensure that they are familiar with the correct term through clearly articulated oral examples. Finally, many mathematical terms sound similar to words students hear every day. When I was teaching first grade, one student insisted that she already knew the definition of *liter* when it was introduced to the class. At her insistence, I asked her to explain the term. She stated that a "liter" is the first person in line to sharpen pencils. At that point, it was obvious that we still had a lot of mathematical learning ahead of us.

For English learners, the large number of technical terms in science and math can be very confusing. We must work to get these terms into students' speaking vocabulary so that they can say the terms and recognize them in printed form. If students cannot orally use a word, it is extremely difficult, if not impossible, to read terms when they are encountered in print. Therefore, it is vital that students be able to orally state specialized words without stumbling over pronunciation. Many math and science words are not encountered in students' day-to-day lives, so we must take extra care to ensure that we create activities designed to facilitate the discussion of the terms.

In social studies, students are confronted with different types of demands. Comprehending social studies material requires students to understand figurative language, which is difficult for many of them. It is not enough to look at the literal meanings of many terms that students may encounter in social studies and need to understand to comprehend the passage. Figurative language, which includes metaphorical references, provides a continuous challenge to students. Through oral language activities, they can better understand what the phrases mean. Students are also expected to be able to articulate cause and effect. Students must not only read and try to remember facts in text but also realize the impact of events on history. When students read about a historical event, they

must think about what happened prior to this occurrence and what might come after it. They need to see and understand the bigger picture of the past. Finally, as discussed in Chapter 3, students must understand varying viewpoints on text. Therefore, the activities in this chapter are designed to develop these skills while reinforcing students' oral language development.

> ### DISCUSSION POINT
>
> Observe some English learners in your classroom. Pay specific attention to difficulties that they may encounter with science, math, and social studies texts. Think about how you can modify currently used classroom activities and those in this chapter to better meet the specific needs of those students.

Math

The activities in this section engage students in using their speaking and listening skills with mathematical terms. As students orally explain their answers during Name the Numeral, other students in the classroom will listen and gain additional ideas that they did not think of prior to the activity. Show Me the Shape gets kids away from their desks and actively moving during the activity. However, they must listen closely as they work with others in order to successfully complete the activity. Classroom Labels is an activity used by many early childhood teachers to build students' vocabulary, and here we see how the activity might be used at any age to expand vocabulary related to mathematics. Finally, "…Is" Poetry is a great way for even the youngest of students to orally discuss their mathematical learning. Through these poems, teachers can tailor the activity so that students review broad concepts such as mathematics or much narrower subjects such as shapes or numbers. All four of the activities in this section take minimal preparation time for the teacher and can be modified to take as little or as much classroom time as is available.

Name the Numeral

In order for students to be able to use and read math terms, it is essential that students be able to also say them. Name the Numeral is designed for

just that. The purpose of the activity is to get kids thinking and talking about numbers. Start off each day with a Name the Numeral activity to get students interested in math and focused on the math to follow. The teacher may even choose a special numeral each day for this activity. After the class lists all of the names they can think of to identify the possible significance of the numeral, the teacher can share why it was selected for the day. Perhaps 100 would be used on the 100th day of school, or 36 might be chosen 36 days prior to Thanksgiving. Students might also enjoy taking turns selecting the numeral for the day. The goal is not to have students correctly guess the reason the numeral was chosen, but rather the idea is to build their interest in numerals while talking about them and listen to classmates' ideas.

How It Works

1. Present students with the numeral of the day. For younger students, it can be basic. For example, tell the students that today's numeral is 13. They can then work with partners or in small groups to brainstorm as many ways as possible to name that numeral without actually using it. The following are some possibilities for the numeral 13:

- The numeral is the same as one foot plus one inch.
- The numeral is the number of days left in the month.
- The numeral is the number of cookies in a baker's dozen.
- The numeral is the number of girls in the class when two are absent.
- The numeral is the same as one 10 block and three 1 blocks.
- If you take a quarter of an hour and subtract two minutes, you get this numeral.

2. Each group can take a turn orally sharing one way to name the numeral of the day. Each suggestion is listed on the smartboard or a large sheet of paper. This step is repeated until none of the groups can think of additional ways to name the numeral. Teachers can encourage students to listen closely to classmates' ideas because those ideas may help others think of even more ways to name the numeral.

With older students the number may be more difficult, and the ways students name it can also be much more detailed.

Additional Ways to Try It Out

Instead of limiting math talk to numerals, teachers may ask students to tell the term, which opens up the dialogue to more descriptions than just numerals. Provide a shape or mathematical concept and ask students to describe it in one sentence. Students can brainstorm various places where they see shapes such as rhombuses, trapezoids, and ovals. They may also describe mathematical operations such as subtraction, addition, and multiplication.

Show Me the Shape

This activity gets students moving around and actively involved with math. It can also be used to encourage them to talk about other mathematical concepts, such as symmetry and patterns.

How It Works

1. Divide the class into groups of four. Give each group a long ribbon, string, or piece of yarn.

2. Write the name of the shape on the smartboard or a large sheet of paper.

3. Ask students to work in their groups to create that shape using the long ribbon.

4. When all of the groups are done, ask each group to tell about its shape. What did the group members make? How did they create their shape? Is it similar to any other shapes they might make?

For example, the term *rectangle* may be written, and students must then decide if all four members in the group will create the shape or only two. What did they have to take into consideration to make it? Students might mention that a rectangle has four angles or four sides, so they knew they needed to either have one student at each corner to make four angles or two students to do it with outstretched arms.

To make it more difficult, the teacher can continue to modify the term on the board. After the groups make the rectangle or another mathematical shape, each group may be given another string, and the teacher may then write the word *symmetry* on the board. The students now have to determine how they can show symmetry with their shape. It may mean that those groups that used four students to create the shape may decide that

two of them can show the four sides while the two other students take the string and divide it symmetrically, or perhaps all four students retain their spots, but the shape is still divided in the middle.

This activity can be modified for different mathematical concepts. Along with getting students away from their desks and actively moving around while learning math concepts, this strategy encourages oral language development. As students work together to determine the best way to create each shape, they must listen to others' ideas and work together to successfully complete the shape. Then, they must explain the steps they took to create it, which helps build their vocabulary and fosters their language skills.

Classroom Labels

When we walk into early childhood classrooms, we often see lots and lots of print in the environment. There may be print in the dramatic play centers for students to play with, such as phone books, postcards, fake prescriptions, and charts in a veterinarian center. Students might also play in a kitchen or store center surrounded by coupons, labeled food containers, and grocery advertisements. Additionally, many educators advocate the importance of surrounding the students with other types of print. We might see directions listed on the wall, the class guinea pig's cage labeled, students' desks tagged, and even signs for the bathroom, door, pencil sharpener, and clock. Although environmental print is often associated with very young students, it is also an excellent way to help older students reinforce math-specific terms.

Using mathematical terms as part of the environmental print in a classroom can be done in any of the grades. By labeling aspects of the classroom with mathematical terms, students are gaining not only from the immediate conversation but also from later dialogue that might occur with the print. Labeling also reinforces that math is all around us, and students can compare different mathematical terms. Then, as teaching occurs and the terms are encountered, students' attention can easily be directed to the terms in their environment. As discussed in Chapter 2, this is an easy way to incorporate local text into the environment. Labeling is also text that can be changed easily and inexpensively.

How It Works

1. As mathematical terms are introduced through hands-on activities during the school year, have the students talk about how the concept is seen in the world around them. While younger students may learn and then discuss basic shapes, for older students the mathematical concepts might include perpendicular and parallel lines, obtuse and acute angles, radius, circumference, area, and perimeter.

2. Ask students to locate places in the classroom where they see examples of various concepts. As they explain the various examples they see around them, students are enhancing their oral language skills. Each item mentioned should be a clear example of the term and easily visible to all of the students. By having math terms readily visible in the classroom, students will have repeated exposure to the terms. Therefore, learning the technical vocabulary will be much easier than if students only encounter the words in textbooks.

3. Throughout the school year, refer back to labels in the classroom to reinforce past mathematical learning. Also, add labels as the year continues and students learn more mathematical concepts. Labels may even need to be modified as knowledge of terms deepens, and students find better examples of places that might be labeled with math terms. For example, if students begin the school year knowing the term *angle*, they may later learn about acute and obtuse angles.

A Look Inside One Classroom

One sixth-grade teacher posted the following mathematical terms in her classroom when the students were learning geometry:

- Right angles (placed in the corner)
- Straight angles (on bricks to model 90 degrees)
- Supplementary angles (drawn on the wall with masking tape)
- Complementary angles (drawn on the wall with masking tape)
- Center of rotation (modeled on the clock and pencil sharpener)

Students can orally compare different terms and explain other places where they might see examples of the concepts outside of the classroom. This is also an excellent way to provide English learners with concrete examples of specific concepts. As students hear the terms used, see the

labels, and make the terms part of their speaking vocabulary, they will develop the technical vocabulary necessary to read mathematical text.

"...Is" Poetry

Students love writing poetry, and poetry is meant to be read aloud. By tying it into math, students can enhance their content knowledge and develop their oral vocabulary. Educators stress the importance of allowing even the youngest of students the opportunity to create poetry (Routman, 2000). Older students can modify and expand its forms to create more elaborate poetry. Although students often associate it with rhyming, it often is unnecessary and usually makes poetry writing more difficult for students. Trying to find words that rhyme for the ends of lines limits the word choice and makes writing poetry much more difficult. Rhyming also does not really enhance the learning that occurs.

"...Is" poetry is easy for even young students to write. To create these poems, teachers may choose to have students define a broad concept such as mathematics. Of course, the topic for an "...is" poem can be much narrower than a content area. In mathematics, a student may choose to write an entire poem about even or odd numbers, a specific type of angle, or even a shape (Altieri, 2005). This type of poetry can easily be connected to any mathematical skill. When the poems are shared with the rest of the class, students foster their oral language development.

How It Works

1. Decide on the topic for the poem. Perhaps it may be a specific number, a geometric concept the class has been learning, or a type of measurement.

2. Introduce "...is" poetry by having the class write one as a group. Encourage students to think about quality instead of quantity when writing the poem. Although many students will want to write as many lines as possible, use the class-created poem as a way to model how lines might be combined to create better ones and a shorter poem. Students should be encouraged to examine word choice and select those lines that have specific details about the topic for the final draft.

Once students realize the importance of word choice, they can be encouraged to elaborate even further. Even many second graders are ready for the challenge. If the class is writing a poem on circles, and a student

states, "A circle is the sun," try to encourage the student to extend that line to perhaps "A circle is the sun on a bright and shiny day," or "A circle is the sun when the clouds do not cover it." Although that is not necessarily increasing their mathematical vocabulary, it is enhancing their literacy skills.

Because "...is" poetry is one of the easier types of poetry to write, many students will strive to write a very long poem. Other educators have also seen students equate length with quality of writing (Walter, 2006). I often find myself asking students to select their favorite five or 10 lines for a final draft. Rereading their creation to narrow down the number of lines encourages students to reflect on the content they are sharing and make judgments while writing. As a class, the students can talk about why certain lines might be chosen instead of others.

3. After the class has created a class poem and read it aloud, it is time for students to create their own mathematical definition poems. They might select the topic of the poem, or there might even be a mystery bag from which students select a card with a mathematical concept written on it.

4. Provide an opportunity for students to orally share their poems. The teacher can have a mathematical poetry day and invite another class to listen to the poems. Another idea is to have students create a booklet and read their poems into a digital media player.

As students explain and listen to other students share their ideas about a math concept, they not only expand their specialized vocabulary but also strengthen their understanding of concepts previously introduced. While the actual written poem has a great deal of value, it is important that the role the oral discussion plays in this activity is not forgotten.

A Look Inside One Classroom

One kindergarten teacher decided to review with her students what they had learned that year in mathematics. She asked them to explain math, and they came up with a lot of ideas. One student said that they learned to count by twos, and another added that they also learned to count by fives. Then, a third student volunteered that they learned to sort. The teacher asked the students what they had learned about sorting. She explained that saying "math is sorting" is true but that the statement could be even more detailed. By explaining the concept of sorting further, they would improve that statement. The students had a number of suggestions, and several mentioned sorting by color, shapes, and even size.

This classroom discussion was important because students had the opportunity to listen to their peers' ideas. This served as a valuable review because students used their oral language skills to articulate what they learned about mathematical concepts and what they remembered about specific hands-on activities in which they participated. Sharing these memories also helped students use their listening skills and then remember other mathematical concepts they had learned. The teacher listed students' ideas on the board as they brainstormed everything they learned about math. Then, she did a think-aloud to explain how they might combine some of the lines to make better lines. In the end, they had written a class "...is" poem. The following is the final draft:

Math is...

when you study numbers
making patterns
counting to 100
learning to tell time
sorting by color, shape and size
counting by 2's, 5's and 10's
being able to count pennies, nickels and dimes
knowing that four quarters equals a dollar
graphing the weather

The class then chorally read their poem several times. By creating and reading it, the students realized that they had learned many mathematical concepts during the year. This reading reinforced literacy concepts, as the teacher could draw the students' attention to sight words such as *the* and specific vowel patterns that the students recognized. The activity also built their vocabulary as they saw and read mathematical terms such as *patterns*, *time*, and *shape*. Finally, the teacher could use this type of poetry to reinforce strategies for reading unfamiliar words. Often, context clues could help determine the meanings of words in some lines. For instance, in the eighth line, the use of context clues could help students figure out the word *quarters*.

Of course, the quality of the poem can be influenced by the experiences that students have with writing, their individual ability, whether they are English learners, and their grade level. Students may choose to keep their poems in a specific portfolio, and as their writing improves during the year, teachers may allow them the opportunity to select some poems in their portfolio to revise. This will allow the students and teacher to see student growth.

Science

Scientific writing is identified as having a high degree of lexical density, that is, a high percentage of content words versus regular words (Shanahan & Shanahan, 2008). This is unsurprising when we look at the scientific words that students encounter in texts and are expected to learn in the primary grades. Each of the four activities discussed in this section focuses on reinforcing those challenging terms in a nonthreatening manner so that the students will enjoy orally building their scientific vocabulary.

Games make learning fun. Any time students feel as if they are playing a game, they are often eager to actively engage with the topic. Beach Ball Vocabulary and Snowball Fight are two games designed for use with an entire class. Both activities are designed to review terms that the students are learning. The games are appropriate for a wide range of grade levels, and the difficulty is dependent on the terms selected. These activities also get students out of their seats and actively involved in learning. Therefore, these two vocabulary strategies provide an additional way to reinforce vocabulary that students have learned in the scientific field.

The last two activities provided, List-Group-Label and Two by Two, might not get students moving around the classroom, but they do involve students working with classmates as they discuss similarities and differences among scientific concepts. List-Group-Label is a brainstorming activity in which there is no one correct answer. The discussion that occurs during List-Group-Label provides a great deal of opportunity for learning to occur and vocabulary to be enhanced. The final activity, Two by Two, will appeal to students because it will remind them of other card games they have played, but the key difference is that this one builds their vocabulary skills.

Beach Ball Vocabulary

Any type of ball can be used for this game, and if the students are outside, it might work to have a large, rubber ball. The ball can even be bounced instead of tossed if you are playing with a basketball or another type of ball that bounces well. However, because students are typically inside the classroom when they review terms, a beach ball is recommended. This is a noncompetitive game in which everyone wins.

How It Works

1. To prepare for the game, students are seated in a circle. Explain to them that today they are going to review terms related to a specific scientific topic.

2. The teacher selects a term, states a question related to it, and then tosses the ball to a student. After catching the ball, the student must repeat the term and try to answer the question. If the student answers it correctly, he or she tosses the ball back to the teacher. If the student cannot answer the question, he or she may call on a classmate for help. However, the student with the ball must ask for help before peers volunteer their advice. The goal of the game is to review the terms, so there is nothing wrong with students helping each other. The students still hear the term and must listen to others to understand the answer, and the original student still has to repeat the correct answer before throwing the ball back.

A Look Inside One Classroom

The following terms are found in a second-grade weather unit:

- anemometer
- barometer
- cirrus
- condensation
- cumulus
- evaporation
- precipitation
- rain gauge
- stratus
- temperature

The following is a vignette showing how these terms might be used with this review activity:

Teacher: *Precipitation*. Name a habitat that gets a lot of precipitation. [tosses the ball to a student]

Student: *Precipitation*. The rainforest gets a lot of precipitation. *Precipitation*. [tosses the ball back to the teacher]

Teacher: *Condensation*. Give me an example of where you have seen condensation. [tosses the ball to another student]

Student: *Condensation*. I saw condensation when it rained, and then it froze on my mom's car window. *Condensation*. [tosses the ball back to the teacher]

Teacher: What is the difference between *anemometer* and *barometer*? [tosses the ball to another student]

As can be seen by this example, the game is not limited to reviewing definitions of terms. Students might give examples of terms or even compare terms that are confusing.

Additional Ways to Try It Out

Older students will enjoy making up some of the review questions. List the terms on the board. After the class reviews the terms, a student can create a question and toss the ball to a classmate. Then, after a student successfully answers the question, the student can make up the next question and then choose another student to whom to throw the ball. If students make up the questions, encourage them to move beyond yes-and-no ones.

The game can also be modified so that the student describes one of the words with a set number of clues without actually using the term and then throws the ball to another student. The receiving student must then listen carefully to determine which technical term is being described and state the term.

Snowball Fight

Anytime students are encouraged by a teacher to ball up a piece of paper and throw it, they are engaged. Therefore, this game is an easy way to reinforce scientific terms and their definitions, while students see the oral review as another game.

How It Works

1. Divide the class into pairs. Each pair is given a sheet of paper to tear or cut in half. On one half of the paper, one student writes a specific, assigned science vocabulary term. On the other half, the other student writes the definition for that term in collaboration with the partner. Each of the students now has either a vocabulary term or a definition.

2. Half of the class stands on one side of the classroom, and half of the class stands on the other side. Everyone wads up their piece of paper to create "snowballs."

3. When the teacher rings a bell, the snowball fight begins. The snowballs are tossed back and forth across the classroom.

4. When the bell rings a second time, the snowball fight stops. Each student selects a snowball, opens it up, and silently reads what it says. Then, they must find the person with the matching sheet as quickly as possible.

5. Next, one of the new pairs reads their word and definition to the class. After the first pair of students reads aloud, they select the next pair of students to use the first shared word in a sentence before the second pair of students reads their word and definition aloud. After the last pair shares, the first pair uses this last shared term in a sentence, which completes the game.

The following is an example of what second graders might say during this step:

Pair 1:   We had *temperature*. It means how hot or cold something is in degrees. [selects next pair]

Pair 2:   They had *temperature*. The temperature outside is hot, so I didn't have to wear a coat today. Our word is *weather*. It means what the sky looks like outside.

Stating the term and definition aloud keeps all of the students listening because they do not know who will be asked next to use the term in a sentence.

Additional Ways to Try It Out

The teacher may choose to have students use the text to write the definitions. Doing so encourages students to go back into the text and reread as they look for the terms. Another idea, if noise is an issue, is to not allow any talking while partners are trying to find each other at the end. The students can only read what is written on other students' sheets to find their partners. Students will still be orally stating the terms, reading the definitions, and sharing sentences that include the terms at the end of the activity.

Both vocabulary games will be enjoyed by students and can play an important role in reinforcing previously learned concepts. By modifying the games as necessary to meet the needs of the students and target the material studied, not only will the activities serve to develop oral language skills, but also students will remain interested in the activities.

List-Group-Label

Enabling students to see similarities and differences among concepts and terms has always been a goal of educators. Many of these activities begin in early childhood programs. Very young students might be encouraged to take a box of objects and attempt to put them into groups according to their similarities and differences. Although Barbara Mariconda's *Sort It Out!* (2008) is a faction book, it is still a popular book to use with younger students as they see similarities and differences between everyday objects sorted by color, shape, material, and texture. Even the youngest of students in school are encouraged to complete word sorts that require them to analyze words for word families.

Developed by Taba (1967), the List-Group-Label activity encourages students at a variety of grade levels to look for similarities and differences among scientific word meanings. Categorization is a valuable disciplinary literacy skill in science. As students participate in the steps of List-Group-Label, they develop a stronger scientific vocabulary as they brainstorm and discuss the words, orally read the terms, view them in texts, and then use them again in oral language while working in groups to discuss and categorize the words.

How It Works

1. As a class, students brainstorm 25 words related to a scientific topic. As they dictate the terms, write them on a large sheet of paper or smartboard.

2. After listing the words in five columns, read through the list while pointing at each term read. Then, have the class chorally read the list so that all of the terms become part of the students' oral language.

3. Small groups of students categorize the terms in groups of approximately three to five. If students create a category of 10 terms, encourage them to think more closely about the words and determine if there is a way to make two smaller categories out of the large category. By limiting the numbers of words that students can place in their categories, students must think more thoroughly about all aspects of the term. Students will need to listen carefully to ideas expressed by other students in the group in order to be able to develop the categories.

4. After a category is developed, a title is given to the group of words. It is important to note that words can be used in more than one group, and

there can be a miscellaneous category for words that do not belong in any groups. However, the miscellaneous category should be very small. Often, by modifying categories, it is easy to use most, if not all, of the terms without needing a miscellaneous category.

5. Ask each group of students to share one category they believe is truly unique.

A Look Inside One Classroom

One first-grade teacher chose to introduce List-Group-Label to her class as part of their ocean unit at the end of the year. The teacher orally shared the informative book *Super Swimmers: Whales, Dolphins, and Other Mammals of the Sea* by Caroline Arnold (2007) with the students. Prior to the oral reading, the teacher informed the students that they would be asked to come up with 25 words about mammals later, and then they would group the terms.

After reading the children's book, the class brainstormed the following list of terms:

- whales
- dolphins
- sea otters
- polar bears
- sea lions
- fast
- flippers
- leopard seal
- acrobat
- lob tailing
- blow hole
- strong
- walrus
- elephant seal
- seal
- short limbs
- swimmers
- spy
- hopping
- graceful
- brave
- breaching
- porpoises
- mothers
- harbor
- tiny ears
- torpedo shaped

Initially, the students were just listing mammals. To broaden the types of words being shared, the teacher directed them to also think about characteristics of mammals. The teacher felt that a benefit of the strategy was that it would limit students to giving one word and summarizing their thoughts into one word because the students often tell stories. The students had to really work hard to state only one word that might be added to the list instead of stating a sentence.

Because the students were first graders, the teacher had the entire class work together to put the terms into categories: marine mammals, land

and water mammals, types of swimming, appearance, and traits. Working together as a class, students were able to group all of the terms into one of those categories. Because it was a new strategy for these young students, the teacher did not have them put terms in more than one group, as she felt it would be too confusing at this age.

Additional Ways to Try It Out

There is a lot of value in encouraging students to look within student-created categories and use words in more than one category because it can help students think more deeply about terms. By doing this, students realize that science terms can have similarities to other terms that they may not have originally considered. However, many primary teachers choose to eliminate that step. If the idea of placing terms in more than one category will create confusion, teachers may wish to initially complete the activity as a whole class in the same manner as the teacher mentioned previously.

Although all of the initial 25 words may be written in black, it will work better to use a different color for each of the individual categories created. In this case, the terms grouped together as marine mammals might be in blue, land and water mammals could be in green, types of swimming in red, appearance in orange, and traits in purple.

After all of the color-coded groups are formed, direct students to take one more look at the groupings. Do they see any words in different categories that could be used to create an extra category? Facilitate the process by suggesting some words and asking the students to name the category. For example, seals could be another category that would contain *elephant seal*, *fast*, *flippers*, *tiny ears*, *acrobat*, and *mothers*. The seals category would include words from the categories land and water mammals, types of swimming, traits, and appearance.

The activity may be connected to writing. Each student can select a favorite group and write a paragraph on the group's topic. In their writing, students can use all of the terms within that category and perhaps even some from the other groups. While completing this activity, students orally use technical vocabulary, read the terms, and use them in their writing.

Two by Two

Concentration, Uno, and Go Fish are familiar card games for many adults and children. Regardless of age, almost anyone can think of card games

that they have played, and people enjoy various types of card games from their preschool years to well into their prime. Card games are inexpensive, relatively easy to learn, require minimal preparation, and can be played within small amounts of time and space. These same traits are what make vocabulary cards a great way for students to have fun and gain repeated exposure to vocabulary terms.

Teachers may select terms that were recently encountered in science texts, ask students to help contribute terms they want to learn related to a topic of study, or use the terms generated from a List-Group-Label activity completed with a class. The more students encounter technical terms, say them, read them, and think about them, the more likely they will be to have the terms become part of their long-term memory. Two by Two is a card game, which is played similar to dominoes, that reinforces technical vocabulary. It is designed to be used with two or three students, but once multiple packets of cards are created, numerous small groups of students can play at the same time with words related to different topics.

How It Works

1. Gather index cards or similarly sized cards and a list of recently introduced vocabulary terms. Write two different vocabulary words on one side of each card, one at the bottom and one at the top, and leave the other side blank. To make the game challenging, approximately 30 words will be used for the activity. If some words are more difficult for students, put those words on more than one card so that the terms are used more often. If possible, clip art for the more difficult terms might be printed, cut out, and glued or taped next to the corresponding terms to scaffold English learners or any students who may need additional assistance to remind them of the terms.

2. A pair of students then divides the cards between themselves. One player begins by selecting one of his or her cards, putting it on the table face up, and reading the two terms.

3. The other student then chooses one of his or her cards and places it next to the card already on the table so that one of the terms on the first card touches one of the terms on the second card. There is no one correct answer, but the student must orally explain how the two terms that touch are related. For example, if the first student places on the table a card that has "lob tailing" written on one half of the card and "graceful" written on

the other half, the second student then has to pick one of his or her cards and attach one of its terms to either "lob tailing" or "graceful." The second student must then state why a term on his or her card was placed next to one of the two terms on the first card and what the two adjoining words have in common. By listening to the other student's explanation, a student can gain ideas for other terms that may be related to the concept. Figure 2 is an example of how cards might look after seven turns and includes some of the terms brainstormed in the previous List-Group-Label activity.

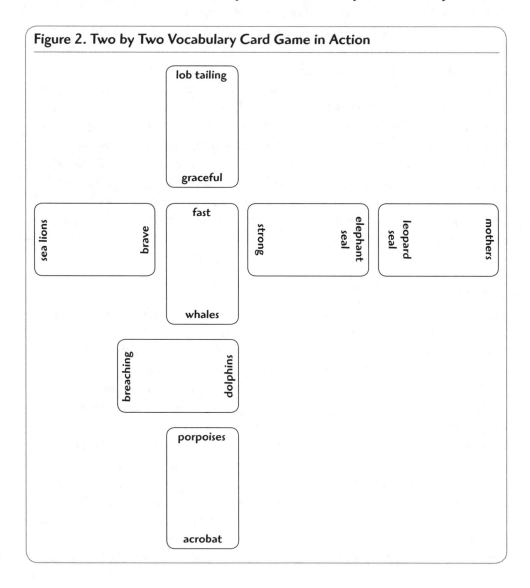

Figure 2. Two by Two Vocabulary Card Game in Action

Additional Ways to Try It Out

Cards are so versatile that it is easy to think of other activities and games that can be played with the same sets of cards. For example, students might lay all the cards out on the table face down. Then, one student selects a card and silently chooses one of the words but does not tell the other students in the group the secret word. The student with the secret then poses a series of yes-and-no questions to the other students until they narrow down the possibilities and determine the secret term. The winner gets to choose the next secret word from a new card.

Students can also create word jars based on a thematic unit that they are learning in science. The words can be written on small card-shaped pieces of paper. *Donovan's Word Jar* by Monalisa DeGross (1998) is about a young boy who loves learning new words. He writes words that he finds interesting and intriguing on individual slips of paper and puts them in a jar. This book can serve as an excellent tie-in to creating word jars or word boxes full of terms related to a scientific topic. As the class learns about a theme, students can seek out new words by discussing the topic with their parents or even looking in other topic-related texts. At the end of each week, the teacher can select a word from the jar and use it as the word of the day. This strategy enlarges students' scientific vocabulary.

Social Studies

Social studies information places special demands on students: They must not only look at details but also understand broad concepts. Additionally, students must understand other viewpoints and the fact that the presentation of information can be affected by an author's point of view.

The three activities in this section develop oral language skills related to the demands of social studies content. In Carousel Brainstorming, small groups of students orally discuss what they learned about a broad concept. As they share the information they find and listen to other classmates' ideas, students determine which ideas might be the most important to share with others. The Looks Can Be Deceiving activity allows students to determine the meaning of figurative phrases often seen in social studies. Students love trivia and learning unique information, so they will view this activity as a game. It will also encourage them to be aware of figurative language in social studies texts so that such phrases will create fewer issues

during future reading. Speed Sharing encourages students to listen closely to other viewpoints on a topic so that they can share their own opinions. By listening to others, students are able to modify and more clearly articulate their own opinions.

Carousel Brainstorming

Which came first, the chicken or the egg? Does thinking about that question make your head hurt? Although there may be no correct answer to that question, determining cause and effect can be extremely difficult for students. Truly understanding a topic and being able to discuss causes and effects takes a lot of practice. However, understanding cause and effect in relation to social studies content plays an important role in the development of disciplinary literacy skills. Carousel Brainstorming is a great way to introduce students to cause and effect.

If you were asked to brainstorm a list of concepts related to a key event in history, chances are that you might be able to come up with a small but succinct list of ideas. However, if you had the opportunity to brainstorm with a small group of peers, the list would probably be much bigger and show a much deeper level of understanding of the event. Although class discussion can help students develop a better understanding of content material, working in small groups to brainstorm information on a topic can result in a much higher level of knowledge on the subject.

With Carousel Brainstorming, students work together in collaborative groups to discuss the importance of concepts related to social studies. While each small group brainstorms a list of ideas related to a key concept, the students have the opportunity to articulate their thoughts so that others understand the importance of their ideas. As the lists are shared and discussed, groups will think of other ideas to share. While students work in small groups, they have the opportunity to hear ideas and viewpoints from all of their classmates as they read what others have written.

Because students are writing brief phrases instead of paragraphs, oral language is developed not only through small-group sharing but also at the end of the class when students discuss their final products. It is important to have students explain why they chose the key phrases they listed for each concept.

How It Works

1. Select five or six key events or concepts related to a social studies topic. Then, take five or six large pieces of chart paper and write one concept or event in a circle in the middle of each paper.

2. Divide the class into groups and give each group one of the large sheets of paper with a concept or event written on it. Give each group a different colored marker, so no two groups have the same color. Since each group has a different color, it is easy to see which groups added ideas to each topic sheet. At the end of the activity, there should be ideas written in a different color from each group.

The group's goal is to take a couple of minutes and orally brainstorm everything they can about the key event or concept listed in the circle. As part of this process, students might look at informational texts on the topic or even notes they may have taken in class. Each group can choose a student as the recorder to write the ideas discussed onto the paper. Because a lot of ideas will be shared, the goal should be to list phrases or words instead of entire sentences. This method will help limit the number of ideas each group writes so that all of the groups will have an opportunity to add to each sheet.

3. After a few minutes, all of the students must stop writing. Then, the sheets are passed so that each group now has a new topic to analyze and discuss. Each group must look at the new sheet and review what the other group wrote on the topic. Another person in each group now has the opportunity to be the recorder and write down the group's ideas for the new topic.

4. This process is repeated until all of the groups have had a chance to write on each of the large sheets of paper containing a key event or concept. The sheets are then returned to their original groups. Before sharing orally, each group will need to review all of the additions to the brainstorming sheet from the other groups. When students first start using this strategy, they may sometimes list very similar ideas with different phrases. This is a good time to point out the importance of looking at the relationship among ideas brainstormed. Students might even categorize some of the phrases and talk in general about what those phrases show. As each group of students shares the ideas listed on their paper, the students in the group will want to look at all of the ideas to determine the key points for the topic. The students may even be instructed to orally share five of

the most important ideas they see listed for their topic and discuss why they believe those ideas are important to the event or concept.

5. Then, each group can share the ideas brainstormed on their concept with the rest of the class. Through discussion of the ideas shared, students can understand key events that might have influenced the concept or the effect that concept may have had on other events that took place.

A Look Inside One Classroom

One third-grade class began this activity with the teacher explaining brainstorming. The teacher then told the students that they would be brainstorming in groups on the U.S. Civil War and focusing on its causes and effects. As a class, they brainstormed on the topic of Abraham Lincoln. Students came up with words such as *war, reconstruction, Emancipation Proclamation, assassinated, blockade,* and *freed slaves.* Afterward, the students orally expanded on the terms they brainstormed. The teacher asked if Lincoln caused slaves to be freed, and the class agreed. Then, the teacher asked how the war was tied to everything. Freeing the slaves caused an effect, the war. Lincoln did not cause assassination, but the class stated that because of what he did for the country, the assassination was an unfortunate effect of his accomplishments. The class continued discussing the rest of the concepts that they had brainstormed on the topic of Abraham Lincoln.

The teacher then divided the class into five heterogeneous groups and gathered five large sheets of paper. In black marker, he wrote a key concept on each sheet in big letters. Each group of students was given one of the sheets. Because the class was spending the final weeks of the year reviewing the Civil War, the five concepts listed were cotton gin, abolitionists, states' rights, slavery, and General William T. Sherman. Although the teacher had used a variety of texts during the unit, he chose to focus students back into their content area text. On the smartboard, the teacher listed the page numbers from their text pertaining to each concept. Therefore, students could go back into the text to review key information. Each group was given a different colored marker so that it would be obvious which contributions were written by which groups at the end of the activity.

Each group was expected to list important causes and effects for each topic. The students were told to list their three best ideas so that students would not try to fill the sheet of paper with as many ideas as

possible. When the groups were ready and had reviewed the material, they were given one to two minutes to brainstorm their ideas on the sheet of paper.

Then, each group of students gave their sheet to the next group. Before students repeated the process, they had to look at what was listed on their new sheet by previous groups before putting down their own ideas. Given their age and experience, there were still times when very similar causes and effects were listed, but overall, the students came up with many ideas.

At the end of the activity, each group was given their original sheet. Using the same color marker they originally used to write down their three ideas, the groups were instructed to read through all of the ideas that they and their classmates had written on the sheet and circle the three they felt were the most important. Figure 3 shows what was written on two of the groups' sheets. This activity required the students to work together. It made them prioritize important concepts related to cause and effect and distinguish details as a group. Also, the students compared concepts listed on the sheet so that they did not circle three terms that were very similar.

Each group of students then shared their sheet with the rest of the class. The teacher took this opportunity to help students see where he may have chosen something different to circle. For example, on the first sheet of paper (shown in Figure 3A), the teacher shared that because "led to war" and "Civil war" are very similar terms, he may have chosen to circle just one of them. The students discussed which other phrase they might have circled.

Additional Ways to Try It Out

Another idea is to place the large sheets of paper at various stations in the room. Then, the students can move from topic to topic instead of passing papers. This will also work better if a variety of informational texts and other sources related to each concept are available for the students at each station.

Depending on the age and ability levels, students can also categorize the ideas shared on their sheet. Then, they may be able to develop a semantic map showing the relationship between some of the key terms listed for their topic.

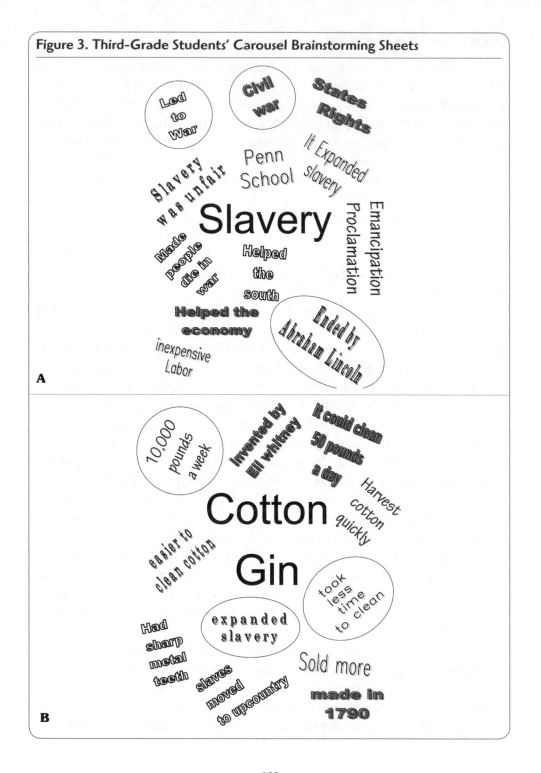

Figure 3. Third-Grade Students' Carousel Brainstorming Sheets

A

Led to War

Civil war

States Rights

Slavery was unfair

Penn School

It Expanded slavery

Slavery

Emancipation Proclamation

Made people die in war

Helped the south

Helped the economy

inexpensive Labor

Ended by Abraham Lincoln

B

10,000 pounds a week

Invented by Eli whitney

it could clean 50 pounds a day

Harvest cotton quickly

Cotton Gin

easier to clean cotton

took less time to clean

Had sharp metal teeth

expanded slavery

slaves moved to upcountry

Sold more

made in 1790

Looks Can Be Deceiving

"If I've told you once, I've told you a thousand times that it drives me up the wall when I can't get all eyes on me." "Kids, you're hearing it straight from the horse's mouth." "I want everyone to do well and reach for the stars!" Excuse me, but what did you just say? If you were talking to a student just learning English, chances are the student would have no idea what you meant by these statements. In fact, although English learners often read words literally, because they are unfamiliar with figures of speech found in everyday language, many other students also have difficulty when encountering idioms, metaphors, and multimeaning words. The English language is peculiar. Social studies texts contain many figures of speech that can trip students up (oops, another idiom) when they are trying to understand content. For English learners, these terms can be even more difficult to learn.

When introducing unique figures of speech, there are many books that might be helpful to share with students. Fred Gwynne's *The King Who Rained* (1988) and *A Chocolate Moose for Dinner* (1976) are both picture books containing homophones and homonyms. Numerous examples in his books, such as "gorilla war" and "coat of arms," pertain to social studies. These examples might be shared with the class, and the accompanying illustrations as well as the figurative meanings can be discussed.

Denise Brennan-Nelson has also written many books that play on words and share idioms. *My Momma Likes to Say* (2003), *My Grandma Likes to Say* (2007), *My Daddy Likes to Say* (2009), and *My Teacher Likes to Say* (2004) are four books that she has written to explain a variety of adages. Within the pages of her rhyming and rhythmic picture books, the students can read about many common idioms that they may have heard their parents or other adults say. The interesting part of the book lies in the historical background given for each idiom and the trivia the author shares. After listening to one of the books, students might ask adults they know for additional idioms, then go in search of the origins of the idioms on the Internet and in other texts.

Jon Agee, a mastermind of wordplay, has authored books containing anagrams, palindromes, oxymorons, and spoonerisms. Oxymorons, which pair two contradictory terms, can be seen in his book *Who Ordered the Jumbo Shrimp? And Other Oxymorons* (2002). Many of the examples shared in that text may also be encountered in social studies texts. When

introducing wordplay to students, Marvin Terban's (1983) *In a Pickle, and Other Funny Idioms* is another book worth considering. Also, Loreen Leedy and Pat Street's (2003) *There's a Frog in My Throat! 440 Animal Sayings a Little Bird Told Me* is a book that students might enjoy.

The following is a list of figurative terms that students might encounter in social studies:

- airplane hangar
- American culture
- arms race
- baby boom
- Black Death
- Black Thursday
- bomb shelter
- branch of government
- calculated risk
- Civil War
- coat of arms

- Cold War
- Communist Party
- cradle of civilization
- Gilded Age
- Great Depression
- Great Divide
- guerrilla war
- in the pen
- Iron Curtain
- king who reigned
- labor union

- Little Bighorn
- live in the present
- living legend
- Middle Ages
- New World
- old news
- resident alien
- Sitting Bull
- slave trade
- Thirty Year War
- unbiased opinion

Although students should not be given a list of figurative terms to memorize, it is important that young students understand that figurative terms are a common type of language used in social studies texts. Then, as figurative language is encountered within social studies books, the terms can be pointed out, added to a word wall, and clarified.

Older students will enjoy researching the meaning of some of these terms. The ones that the teacher chooses to introduce will depend on the age level of the students. Looks Can Be Deceiving is a fun activity that was designed to get kids talking about some of the figurative terms they may encounter in texts.

How It Works

1. Divide the class into small groups. Each group selects an example of figurative language that can be found in social studies. Then, the group must determine the meaning of the phrase. Along with determining the

real meaning, the students must also come up with a couple of other plausible, but incorrect, explanations for the term.

2. On a specified day, each group orally presents their term. Then, after giving the warning that looks can be deceiving, various group members tell a different meaning of the phrase. Each group member may have one to two minutes to convince the audience that he or she is telling the correct definition. Of course, only one of the group members is telling the correct definition. The rest of the class must listen to what the students say and try to determine which of the group members is stating the correct definition.

Many of the figurative language samples would provide a great topic for discussion and debate. This activity requires students to rationalize what works and what does not. If a student decides that he or she thinks one of the meanings does not work, then that student needs to explain why he or she feels that way.

3. The activity is repeated until all of the groups have a chance to share their examples of figurative language.

Additional Ways to Try It Out

After each group presentation and before the secret is revealed, there may also be an informal poll of the audience to see which students believe which presenters. Then, students who agree with specific definitions might meet together to discuss why they believe their chosen answer is the correct one.

At advanced grade levels, students who are listening to each group's presentation may also be allowed to ask questions of individual members of the group regarding the definitions provided. This will require the students presenting to know quite a bit about the correct meaning of their word.

Speed Sharing

Speed Sharing is very similar to the popular cultural event speed dating. Students are provided with a very limited amount of time to express their opinions to another person and to listen to their partner's views before the bell rings. When the bell rings, everyone must switch partners.

This strategy helps students understand diverse viewpoints, see the bigger picture, and look beyond isolated facts in social studies. Students

must be prepared to explain their opinions and hear others' opinions on the same topic.

How It Works

1. Select a topic related to social studies and introduce it to the students. Explain to them that they must take a side on the issue and be prepared to articulate their views and opinions.

2. Students research the topic so that they know a great deal about it and are prepared to express their views and support their ideas. This strategy can motivate students to read and view other materials to gain ideas to support their opinions. As part of this step, students should write their view in one sentence at the top of a sheet of paper. Then, they can list ideas they find in texts that help them support their views.

Each student should come up with 5 to 10 supportive statements for his or her view. Students can list the source for where they found each idea. As part of the research, they should not be concerned if they find ideas that are in support of differing views. Students need to realize that people have different viewpoints on issues. To develop strong arguments for their own opinions, it is necessary to see and understand how others may feel about the topic.

3. Once the students have determined their opinions and written down supportive statements, it is time for the speed sharing to begin. Take the desks and place them in two rows facing each other. If possible, leave a small gap between each pair of desks facing each other so that it is easier for student pairs to hear each other without listening to what all of the other students have to say on the topic. Sometimes it can get noisy with all of the students expressing their opinions at the same time.

4. Explain to the students the guidelines for Speed Sharing. They will have five minutes total for both partners to share their views. Therefore, it works best if each partner takes a minute to express his or her view, then the other partner shares his or her side. The remaining few minutes can be used by the partners to ask questions and seek clarification on the topic. When the bell rings, everyone must stop sharing.

5. While one row of students stays seated, the other half of the class moves one seat over each time the bell rings so that everyone has a new partner

for each speed sharing time period. The student who was sitting at the far end will now move to the empty chair at the other end.

6. The process is then repeated until every student in the half of the class that switches desks is back with his or her first partner. Then, students can orally discuss how the process worked. Did the information they heard influence their views? If so, how did this change the way they shared their opinions with future partners? Did they find their views changing as they listened to the ideas shared by other students? Was it difficult or easy to support their beliefs, and was that directly related to the research they did prior to the activity?

Additional Ways to Try It Out

One modification involves not having students continuously shift to a new partner every five minutes. After the third time the bell rings, students can be instructed to stay in their seat instead of moving on. All of the students can take this opportunity to reassess the list they developed. Are there additional ideas they might have heard from others that can be used to support their views? Do they need to think through and be able to elaborate on one of the ideas they wrote on their list? It may be valuable to take a clean sheet of paper and restate their views and their supportive statements part way through the sharing so that their new notes better serve the purpose. As the students listen to more and more opinions, it will influence their thoughts on a particular topic.

Likewise, the pairs could have a slightly longer time to discuss, so students can jot down great ideas they are gaining from other students. It is important to realize that not every student they sit across from in this activity will have an opposing opinion for this strategy to be effective. However, it is important that the topic be controversial enough that there are some students who see both sides of the issue.

Finally, the students can use their original views and supportive statements to write a brief paper stating their opinions prior to this activity. Then, at the end of Speed Sharing, they can write a second opinion paper. Students can analyze the impact made from hearing diverse viewpoints on the topic. Even if their views did not change by the end of the activity, they may have realized that some points need to be more clearly articulated because of questions other students asked during Speed Sharing. This might also be a good time for students to reexamine texts on the topic so that they can find further support for their opinions.

REFLECTING BACK AND LOOKING FORWARD

While all aspects of literacy development are important, nobody can deny the importance of being able to orally articulate one's thoughts. Oral language is the basis from which other types of literacy develop. It is difficult, if not impossible, to recognize words in print, be able to use them in writing, and be able to create visuals involving specialized terms unless the terms are part of one's oral language.

Furthermore, it is not enough for students to read well, write well, and create and view visuals unless they can orally communicate their knowledge to others. In this chapter, oral language is used as a tool to help students develop the skills necessary to broaden their math, science, and social studies understandings. Many of the activities focus on key terminology and helping students make those terms part of their speaking vocabulary. Other activities are designed to help students articulate opinions, comprehend cause-and-effect relationships, and understand figurative language in social studies. All of the activities target oral language development related to the specific disciplinary literacy skills needed for math, science, and social studies text.

CHAPTER 5

Creating Content Connections Through Writing to Learn

L et's think about the way we view content area learning and writing to meet the goal of developing students who are competent communicators. Writing, in and of itself, is also often considered to be a product. Students write wonderful essays on topics related to content areas, and then rubrics or another type of assessment are used to judge the writing quality of the product. As elementary educators, we help students understand that developing a deep grasp of science, math, and social studies concepts is valued, but we can also strengthen their comprehension of content information through writing. We must rethink how we view both writing and content area learning to develop students who have a strong grasp of content area material and can communicate that understanding to others.

We all know that students learn to write by writing, and writing takes time. We also know that time is one aspect of the day of which we never seem to have enough. How can we help students develop content area knowledge and give them practice writing? We do that through activities involving writing to learn. According to Knipper and Duggan (2006), "Writing to learn engages students, extends thinking, deepens understanding, and energizes the meaning-making process" (p. 462). This type of writing engages students with content area terminology, allows them to determine exactly what they do and do not understand about math, science, and social studies material, and helps them share this information with others. Therefore, students are enhancing their communication skills while developing a better grasp of content area material.

DISCUSSION POINT

Think about the types of writing activities that your elementary students participate in. Are the majority of them targeting learning to write or writing to learn? How might literacy skills be reinforced while students are gaining content-level knowledge?

What Does This Mean for the Content Areas?

The ability to communicate content area information in writing is necessary for students' entire lives. Students do not write to learn only in content area subjects. It is a necessary skill that they will use in the future. As our students leave the traditional educational system to work in the world as scientists, teachers, mathematicians, computer technicians, engineers, and newscasters, the ability to understand content area concepts and communicate their knowledge will be necessary. They must manipulate and think about content area knowledge to articulate it to their audience. As elementary teachers, we can assist students in this journey through writing to read by laying the foundation for the writing skills they will need later in life. Students' writing is also enhanced by the incorporation of quality informative books throughout the content areas. Hansen (2001) has found that using such texts not only exposes students to great books but also helps them gain ideas for their own writing.

Although it is possible for students to passively read material related to math, science, or social studies, writing requires that they become actively involved in their learning. Writing engages their senses and requires them to think about the terms they see and articulate their thoughts. Research strongly supports writing as essential for students to process concepts. Holliday, Yore, and Alvermann (1994) believe "writing should glue thinking to paper" (p. 885). They strongly believe that students must actively engage in writing about their scientific learning and read what they write. In the field of mathematics, Bell and Bell (1985) conducted a study with ninth graders and found that those students who wrote to solve mathematical problems were much more successful. Likewise, a more recent study completed by Steele (2005) supports the use of writing when seventh-grade students solve algebraic problems. She stresses that writing helps students access their schema and actively engage in the activity.

Writing to learn has also been a focus of the science community. Between 2000 and 2003, a large-scale study was completed by the National Science Foundation that involved fourth- through seventh-grade teachers. According to Miller and Calfee (2004), "Few activities can achieve what writing can in science" (p. 20). Writing not only allows students to better determine which content area concepts they understand and which ones they are still struggling to grasp but also allows teachers to assess students' knowledge: "Writing makes thinking visible" (Miller & Calfee,

2004, p. 20). According to surveys of program participants, teachers believe that reading and writing instruction need to be content area based. Although writing to learn is often associated with upper elementary ages, it can be shifted to the lower grade levels as well.

DISCUSSION POINT

Ask students to discuss the type of writing activities they participate in outside of school. What types of writing are they engaged with when not in the classroom? What types of writing do they think they will need to use when they are older? Ask them what it means to write to learn.

Although students often write for the teacher, that is not enough. They must learn to write for a variety of people and a variety of reasons to be able to transfer their writing skills to various situations beyond the classroom. Wollman-Bonilla (2001) have found that students as young as first grade can understand the idea of audience. To be scientifically literate, students must understand how to write for various purposes and use different forms. In social studies, students can develop disciplinary literacy skills through a variety of writing experiences. Providing students with opportunities to examine various texts and write based on the knowledge gained is a valuable skill (Stahl & Shanahan, 2004). In order for students to develop disciplinary literacy skills, it is essential that they write to learn.

Math

Although many of us already ask students to explain their mathematical thinking when they answer math problems, let's expand the way we tie writing into mathematics. The activities discussed in this section provide additional opportunities for students to write about mathematical concepts and problems. ABC Books and "In Translation" Strips are two ways to tie writing into the mathematics classroom. ABC Books can help students learn technical terms that may be difficult for them, and "In Translation" Strips helps students read symbols and translate them into words. Students have to be able to explain the mathematical process in order to solve a problem through words. The Logic Puzzles activity requires students to determine and clearly articulate through writing how to best solve mathematical puzzles.

ABC Books

Although ABC books, or picture dictionaries, may seem to be a very basic idea for elementary teachers, these books are often associated only with the early childhood grades. Teachers often have young students create books containing terms that may not be familiar to them. Students will often list a term, copy its meaning from a text, and include a picture representation. In this way, the books can be individualized so that students create a book that meets their specific needs. However, a middle school math teacher and former student of mine has her sixth-grade students create the texts from scratch. The purpose of these books is to get students engaged with the math terms, foster an interest in the content area topic and concepts, strengthen vocabulary knowledge, and extend student learning beyond the classroom walls. *G Is for Googol: A Math Alphabet Book* by David Schwartz (1998) and *Math Dictionary: The Easy, Simple, Fun Guide to Help Math Phobics Become Math Lovers* by Eula Ewing Monroe (2006) are two books that might be shared as examples.

ABC books require a minimal amount of preparation and materials, can easily be modified to add or replace words, and serve as an excellent way for students to develop knowledge of specialized vocabulary and symbols. Students must also be able to translate words into symbols and vice versa. ABC Books is a strategy that can truly be used with a range of grade levels.

How It Works

1. Students begin by cutting a sheet of paper in half and then folding one half of that paper so that it serves as the front and back cover of the book. Then, they cut lined paper into four and insert the lined pages into the book.

2. Two hole punches can then be made on the folded side of the booklet. Next, students tie their books together with string or ring clips to allow for easy insertion of additional pages. Another option that might be considered is spiral-bound note cards.

3. Students can then decorate their covers with "Math Dictionary," "ABC Book," or any title they choose.

4. As new mathematical terms are introduced in class, students add them to their books. By the end of the class day, the goal is for students to add the definitions of their words. Also, they can include an example for

each of their new terms. This example might be a math example or a sentence. A sixth-grade ABC book created for geometry may contain the following words:

- circumference
- complementary angles
- cylinder
- diameter
- factor
- line
- perimeter
- pi
- prism
- proportion
- radius
- rate
- rotational
- scale
- similar shapes
- supplementary angles
- surface area
- symmetry
- unit

Additional Ways to Try It Out

Consider allowing students to use their ABC books for quizzes. Many teachers I have worked with find that by allowing students to use the booklets for quizzes, students are motivated to keep their ABC books up to date and add new words that they find challenging. Working in the books can help reinforce the terms. Students are writing the terms, giving examples, and having opportunities in the future to revisit the math terms as necessary.

"In Translation" Strips

Often, younger students are asked to sequence the steps for completing an activity. In fact, how-to writing is commonly assessed on national tests. This type of sequential writing can easily be tied to mathematical problems. It can also, as this activity demonstrates, help students develop disciplinary literacy skills, such as translating symbols to words and vice versa. Although students may complete this mathematical activity alone, there are benefits to allowing students to work together in pairs or small groups so that they can share ideas and help each other successfully complete a sometimes difficult process.

How It Works

1. Write a math problem at the top of a sheet of paper.

2. Write the steps for solving the problem underneath it, but do not number them.

3. Cut the individual steps apart. To ensure that your cuts will not give away the order of the steps, this may be easiest with a paper cutter.

4. Give a group of students the steps and ask the group to tape the steps on a sheet of paper in order, with space to write between each step. For example, a packet might consist of the following pieces of paper:

$2x + 10 = 30$

$x = 10$

$2x = 20$

The students would then take the three slips of paper and put them in the correct order:

$2x + 10 = 30$

$2x = 20$

$x = 10$

5. Students must then write out in words how to get from one step to the next and write out each step:

$2x + 10 = 30$

Two times the variable plus ten equals thirty.

Subtract ten from both sides of the equation.

$2x = 20$

Now, two times the variable equals twenty.

Divide both sides by two.

$x = 10$

The variable x equals ten.

Additional Ways to Try It Out

This strategy can easily be modified. Students might be given the sequential steps necessary to solve a mathematical equation but with a mistake somewhere in the steps provided. Students must then write

a paragraph explaining where the mistake was made and how it can be fixed.

Another idea is to give students an equation and allow them to write the steps for solving the equation in both numbers and complete sentences.

Logic Puzzles

Logic puzzles are a great way to exercise the brain and can help build disciplinary skills. Logic puzzles are tricky and reinforce the necessity for students to closely read and reread mathematical material. Also, there are a wide variety of mathematical mind teasers available for the elementary level. Through their completion, students can receive reinforcement of mathematical vocabulary, further develop their ability to translate symbols to words and words to symbols, and even get a better understanding of graphs and charts.

How It Works

1. Introduce the idea of math logic by sharing *Math-terpieces: The Art of Problem-Solving* by Greg Tang (2003) or *Math Curse* by Jon Scieszka (1995). *Math Curse* is a humorous look at problem solving, and it all begins when Mrs. Fibonacci warns the class that almost everything involves a math problem. Students will enjoy listening to and discussing the book as they try to solve some of the problems within it. *Math-terpieces* is the fifth book written by the best-selling author Tang and is arranged around 12 famous masterpieces. Through problems written in rhyme, students are encouraged to develop strategies to solve math problems related to each piece of artwork. Both Tang's and Scieszka's books will get students interested in the world of problem solving.

2. Explain to students the steps to solving math puzzles. They must do each of the following:

- Determine the math problem.
- Decide the best strategy to use for answering the problem.
- Solve the math problem.
- Reread the math problem and check to see if the answer makes sense.

3. Talk about some of the strategies that might help students solve logic puzzles. Students might be able to use and manipulate simple objects to help them solve the problems. They also may find out that making a table or chart can help them. Other times, they may want to look for a pattern or another method. There are often many ways to solve problems, but students want to figure out which way works best for each specific problem. Problem solving teaches students to be strategic when determining the answer to math problems.

4. Introduce some math logic problems. There are many books written on the topic. The following list contains some books that elementary students might enjoy:

- *The Everything Kids' Math Puzzles Book: Brain Teasers, Games, and Activities for Hours of Fun* by Meg Clemens, Glenn Clemens, and Sean Clemens (2003)
- *40 Fabulous Math Mysteries Kids Can't Resist: Fun-Filled Reproducible Mystery Stories That Build Essential Math Problem-Solving Skills* by Martin Lee and Marcia Miller (2001)
- *Get It Together: Math Problems for Groups, Grades 4–12* by Tim Erickson (2005)
- *Math Rules! 1st–2nd* by Barbara VandeCreek (2001; grades 3–4 and 5–6 also available)
- *Primary Grade Challenge Math* by Edward Zaccaro (2003)

In addition, the book *Draw Plus Math: Enhance Math Learning Through Art Activities* by Freddie Levin (2010) contains 20 drawing lessons that focus on numbers and counting, sets of groups, patterns, sorting, data analysis, and graphs, among other mathematical concepts. Although it is not necessarily a book of logic puzzles, many of the lessons involve logic to some extent or can be extended with logic questions. For example, a lesson on sorting begins with a page with illustrations of many bugs. The student is asked many literal-level questions about counting the bugs. The reader must count the number of bugs with stripes, the ones that are long and thin, and those shaped like a triangle. The next page encourages the reader to draw more bugs in three easy steps and then asks, "How many ways can you SORT the bugs in your drawing?" (p. 41). On another page, students draw rabbits with shapes and then are

encouraged to make patterns by color and by color and size. The lesson ends with telling students to make a pattern with color and groups and then asking if there are any other rabbit patterns that could be made. Questions and activities like these encourage students to think and develop the best strategy for answering logic puzzles.

5. As a class or in small groups, have students try to solve the problems. Remind them of the four steps for solving problems.

6. Ask students to write the steps they followed to solve the problem. What were the steps taken to determine the correct answer? What method worked for the students? Did they need to use objects, draw pictures, or look for patterns?

7. Each group of students should explain their answer and the strategy they used and share what they wrote.

8. As a class, write on a sheet of chart paper the different strategies that students used to solve the problems. This chart can be consulted and ideas added as students use their free time to tackle math logic problems on their own or with a partner. If the list gets too lengthy, determine categories of suggestions that can be grouped together. For example, using pieces of paper, using Legos, and using sticks might all be grouped together under the category "Use Objects." A second draft of the class list can be made when the strategies brainstormed gets to be extensive.

Additional Ways to Try It Out

This activity can also be modified. Groups might each select a math problem to complete. The students in the group then write out a detailed explanation of how they solved the problem. Each of the groups exchanges the problem they created and their written explanation with another group. Each group examines the problem and solution provided by their peers. The students' goal is to read the solution to see if it clearly explains how to solve the problem. Does it work? Could it be written more clearly? The goal is to help students more clearly articulate their mathematical reasoning in writing.

Upper elementary students can create math logic problems for their peers. Before they give the problem to their classmates, they should determine the answer. Then, after other students solve the problem and share their written solution, the creators of the problem can check to see if their peers came up with the same solution and agree on the best strategy

for solving the problem. While multiple groups may get the same answer, groups that attained it through different strategies should share the written description of how they came up with the answer so that the class can determine the best strategy for solving the math problem.

Science

Found Poetry, RAFT, and Student-Created Informational Books are three strategies that can help students develop the disciplinary literacy skills they need to understand scientific content area material. These activities not only strengthen students' scientific knowledge but also help improve their writing skills, and the ability to communicate scientific knowledge through writing is a skill that becomes even more important as students progress through the grades. Found Poetry encourages writing while requiring students to examine a variety of texts. RAFT (Santa, 1988) is a great activity for reinforcing the importance of audience in scientific writing and also introducing the idea that science information can be presented in a variety of formats. Student-Created Informational Books can provide experiences for even the youngest of students to demonstrate their knowledge of the linguistic features they see in informative books.

Found Poetry
. . . .

Found poetry involves rearranging words, phrases, and even sentences that are found in other sources to create a poem (Fletcher, 2002). Phrases or sentences gleaned from songs, textbooks, trade books, websites, and other sources are combined to create the poetry. The poet can even add other phrases or sentences to help the flow of the poem. Examples of found poetry can be seen in recently published books for adults, and you may want to talk about how these poems were created when introducing Found Poetry to students. For instance, *Dancing on the Pedals: The Found Poetry of Phil Liggett, the Voice of Cycling* by Phil Liggett and Doug Donaldson (2005) was created from Liggett's broadcasts of the Tour de France, and *O Holy Cow! The Selected Verse of Phil Rizzuto* by Phil Rizzuto (2008) is based on his broadcasts of the New York Yankees' baseball games. These two books contain lines from broadcasts that are combined in a meaningful way.

How It Works

1. Explain found poetry to the students by sharing an example, such as the "Thunderstorms" poem included with this activity (see the "A Look Inside One Classroom" section), but be sure to remove the underlining. Explain that found poems involve phrases or sentences from published sources as well as lines written by the person creating the poem. Talk about each of the lines in the poem. Ask the students to identify which lines came from the trade book *Storms* by Seymour Simon (1989; underlined portions in the sample are from this book).

2. Small groups of students may then be given a copy of the "Thunderstorms" poem. The groups can be provided additional published materials on storms to see if the students can modify the poem and include more sources. Provide picture books, brochures, song lyrics, movies, advertisements, or a variety of other sources. Using diverse texts not only encourages students to be creative and stretch their imaginations as they create these poems, but it also provides opportunities for students to see scientific material discussed in a variety of ways.

3. Encourage students to include phrases and sentences from other sources and also add their own phrases.

4. Ask each group to share their found poem.

5. Now it is time for groups to create their own original found poem. Select a recently studied scientific topic and allow students to work in their small groups to create the poem. Specify the minimal number of sources you want them to use.

A Look Inside One Classroom

A fourth-grade teacher wanted to have her students create found poems about electricity because they were studying the topic in science. As an example, the following found poem about thunderstorms was shared with the students:

Thunderstorms

I hate thunderstorms.
The plink plink of the rain coming down.
In twenty minutes, a single thunderstorm can drop 125 million gallons of water.
I look up and can't believe the sky!
In minutes, the cloud may grow 40,000 or more feet high.
I want to run because they scare me. However I tell myself

From farther away, thunder sounds like a growling sound.
Grrrrrrr...That's what I hear
However, I know it <u>can be heard even twenty miles away on a quiet day.</u>
I remember what mom says...just use caution.
But still, I hate thunderstorms.

As the class read through the sample poem, the teacher noted that the author of the poem used parts of Simon's popular book *Storms* to create the poem. After reading through the picture book, the author of the poem wrote it on thunderstorms and included a number of facts learned about the topic from Simon's text. The teacher explained to the students that all of the underlined sentences were pulled directly from the trade book, with minor edits, and the other sentences were added to create the poem.

The class immediately noticed that repetition was used because the first line of the poem was repeated in the last line. The teacher stated that this was a poetic element that the students might want to use in their own poems. Finally, since students had already learned about the poetic element of shape in a prior poetry lesson, the teacher encouraged them to use that element in the found poetry they created.

As the students prepared to write, the fourth-grade teacher provided the following guidelines for their poems:

> Create a poem using words that you find in the various electricity-related materials provided. These texts include science textbook pages, songs about electricity, activities completed with electricity, and trade books on the topic. There is not a specific format for this type of poetry. Choose words you want to include and also add words or phrases of your own. You may also want to include the element of shape.

The teacher chose to incorporate a wide variety of texts in this lesson. Students were already familiar with their science textbook. However, the teacher also introduced several trade books that came along with their science series. The teacher shared *It's Electric!* by Anna Prokos (2006), *Discovery of Electricity* by Stephen Feinstein (2008), and other books related to electricity. She distributed copies of electricity-related activities from a science activity book published by the AIMS Education Foundation, *Electrical Connections: Activities Integrating Math and Science* (2005). The last book she introduced was Joanna Cole's (1997) *The Magic School Bus and the Electric Field Trip*. Then, the Rockbots song "Electricity" (see www.songsforteaching.com) was played for the students, and a copy of the

lyrics was provided for them to read as well. Once all the materials were introduced, the students were able to select a partner or choose to work on their own to create their poetry. Each group created a rough draft and a final copy of their poem.

Ashley and Lauren chose to incorporate the element of repetition into their poem like the sample poem shared. Also, they chose to surround their poem with the shape of a lightbulb:

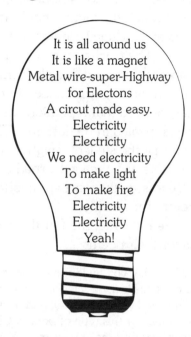

It is all around us
It is like a magnet
Metal wire-super-Highway
for Electons
A circut made easy.
Electricity
Electricity
We need electricity
To make light
To make fire
Electricity
Electricity
Yeah!

Likewise, Isaac, Steve, and Adam incorporated the poetic element of repetition by using the phrase "Move it Move it!" to provide emphasis in various parts of their found poem:

Move it Move it!
Most things need power to move
Move it Move it!
Electricity is the most powerful thing to
Move it Move it!
Positive, negative charges
Move it Move it!
Conductors, Insulaters
Move it Move it!
We need Electricity to
Move it Move it!

The students did a great job of writing found poetry and incorporating poetic elements in their writing, and the teacher did an excellent job of ensuring success with these students. First of all, students were given plenty of time to think about the topic and create their poetry. They were introduced to found poetry in a previous lesson so that it was not an entirely new topic when it came time to write their poems. Also, the teacher provided scaffolding to help the students with their writing. She shared a sample poem to demonstrate how a found poem might be created on a different science topic, storms. Furthermore, the teacher provided a wide variety of sources that added to the students' creativity. Finally, she gave them a choice of whether they would prefer to work with a partner, a small group, or individually to create their poems. The time and effort put into creating the found poems produced some excellent results.

Additional Ways to Try It Out

Like any lesson, modifications may be made based on the teacher and student needs. The teacher may choose to have students identify the sources of their phrases and words by color-coding lines to reflect the source from which the phrases originated. For example, one color may be used for any phrases or lines the student creates. Then, a different color may be used for any phrases or sentences found in trade books, and a third color could be used for song lyrics. Not only will students enjoy how the colors add to the appearance of the poetry, but also the teachers and students will be able to see what sources were used. This is also a great time to help students understand that there are two types of found poetry. One type is referred to as treated, because the author has made dramatic changes in the information, and the other type is called untreated, because the information used is in almost the same form as its original source.

When students are first creating this type of poetry, the teacher may decide to use only a couple of sources, but as the students become more comfortable with including text from sources with their own words, the teacher may provide a variety of texts. Finally, students can be offered the opportunity to find outside sources related to the topic for their found poems. Students can be encouraged to use as many diverse types of texts as possible as they create their found poetry.

RAFT

· ·

Dear Principal,

Hey, What's up? I won't be in today. Got the flu. It must have been due to the wild party I went to this weekend. Who would have thought a swim in my bikini for the Polar Bear Party would get me so sick? Catch you later!

Love,
Meg

Have you ever felt ill and left a memo like the above for your principal to find upon arrival at work in the morning? Chances are, probably not, or you would not be in the educational field today. As adults, we have learned about appropriate writing and the importance of taking into consideration the audience who will read the writing, the best format for presenting the information, and the topic we want to share. We know that we cannot just jot our ideas on paper, but instead we must think through to whom we are writing and also what purpose the writing should serve.

Think about the types of writing we engage in as adults. E-mail messages are a popular way to share information, and some people still send letters and notes if the recipient does not have access to a computer. Messages can be to grandparents we rarely get to see, friends we met on trips who we want to maintain contact with, and companies regarding warranty issues with items. Along with letters or e-mails, many teachers write recipes, menus, grocery lists, morning announcements for students to read over the intercom, reminders on sticky notes, directions, memos to the principal or superintendent, notes to volunteers who help in the classroom, and many other types of writing.

All of these types require us to consider several things. First of all, we think about our role as the writer. Are we writing as a friend, as an employee, or as someone else? The relationship of the person receiving the message and the person writing it is important to take into consideration. Who is our audience and how do we want to influence the audience or share the information? Who will receive our written words? What type of document are we writing? Are we going to write a lengthy letter, a very brief note, or a bulleted list? Finally, we must think about our topic as we write. How can we best share the information?

Students must learn that writing can be modified to serve a variety of purposes. In science, it is especially important to know how to write for multiple purposes. There are many different types of scientific writing that

must be learned. Students must be able to take factual science lab notes, write articles related to scientific information, and understand the difference between writing that informs and writing that persuades. They also must know when each type of writing should be used. RAFT (role, audience, format, and topic) is a strategy that can be used with elementary students to develop this knowledge.

How It Works

1. Explain to students that there are four main areas to consider when they write.

> • **Role**—This refers to the students' role with the writing. Are they writing as an expert, as someone who has strong opinions on the scientific material, or as someone wanting more information? What is the purpose of the writing? Are they writing to inform? If so, what information will they include? They would probably want to keep the writing factual so that the reader understands the gist of the text. If they are writing to persuade, they may want to selectively pick statistics related to a topic to share with the reader so that they can encourage the reader to react in a specific manner.
>
> • **Audience**—Who will receive the writing? Ask students to think about how their writing differs depending on whether they are writing to a family member or a friend. Would they use the same tone and write about the same information to their grandparents as they would to a friend they met on vacation last year?
>
> • **Format**—What type of writing are they creating? Are they writing structured notes on scientific reading with the intent of studying them later, notes detailing exactly what occurred during a scientific experiment, or an article persuading friends to recycle?
>
> • **Topic**—What scientific topic do they want to talk about in the writing?

2. After discussing each of these four characteristics of writing, it is time for the students to complete some scientific writing. As a class, decide on one idea for each aspect of RAFT. Then, as an entire class, complete a writing sample on a smartboard or large sheet of paper. As the entire writing sample is read aloud with the class, refer back to the role, audience, format, and topic selected prior to writing. Did the sample adequately address each of the elements of RAFT?

3. Provide the students with a list of possible roles, audiences, functions, and topics. Another option is to allow students to brainstorm a list of possibilities for each of the four elements. If students are writing about a specific science unit that they are currently studying, they can be provided with the topic but encouraged to choose the other three aspects of RAFT. As part of this stage, brainstorm how writing might vary with different audiences, roles, and forms? How would writing to the president about the scientific information be different from writing about the same information to a new student at school? How would the writing be different if they are writing to persuade or inform?

4. After selecting the role, audience, format, and topic, allow students time to work in groups to complete a written text. It is important for them to write down each of the four elements that are chosen for the writing to ensure that they maintain their focus.

5. After the writing is finished, have the students recheck their writing to see if they feel that they adequately addressed each of the elements. Then, the students can share their written products.

A Look Inside One Classroom

One third-grade teacher decided to tie this strategy to Earth Day. One day prior to the event, in the early spring, the students had been busy collecting litter from the recess field. This led to a class discussion of the source of the litter. The teacher explained that other students and people came onto the field on the weekends to play and often left litter without thinking about the problems it caused.

He directed the focus of the conversation back to the topic of habitats, which the students had recently been studying. He suggested they write to the litterbugs who were on the recess field when school was not in session to let them know the effect their habits had on the habitat.

The teacher introduced the topic of RAFT and provided the following guidelines to the students:

Role: Principal

Audience: People littering

Format: Letter

Topic: Explain feelings about the litter. Include three facts about the litter's effect on plant and animal habitats.

Students were also directed back to their science text book so that they could review information on habitats to include in their letters. They could also use facts about habitats that they read in other sources or heard in the media.

It is evident that the students took their role seriously with this assignment, and many were quite emotional in their writing. The topic was relevant to them, and many took their role as principal very seriously. One student, Edward, stated, "My school and I have been wondering why yoll have been causeing crullity to the world. Thar are animals and plants habitats bieng disestrod and rund." After that, he talks about many problems caused with the littering, including references to what can happen to humans because of the litter: "Now litter hurts us to like if theres a broken beer botile, and you step on it buy accsedint it could stab you." He ends with a plea to the litter bugs: "Lastley could yoll quit killing the envierment!!!"

Most students discussed specific damage caused by the litterbugs, including the fact that germs were left from the litterbugs smoking on the playground and dropping their cigarettes. Other students mentioned their concern about the six-pack rings that can get stuck around animals' necks and the fact that animals might not know the litter is not food and could harm them. Students used quite a few of the vocabulary terms that they had learned about habitats, and one student, Liza, expressed concern that "the garbage fills the humus rich soil with dangerous chemicals." She also stated, "The animals help spread seeds and if the seeds are coverd in garbage the animals cannot spread the seads because they cannot see the seeds."

Although the students had a range of writing abilities, they all did an excellent job of incorporating factual information into their letters, considering their audience and their role to the audience, and writing in a letter format. The following is a sample letter written by a third grader. While she took a gentler approach than some students and asked the litterbugs to stop, she did a great job at explaining the damage that the litterbugs were doing to the habitat and demonstrated knowledge of scientific information:

Dear Litter Bugs,

I'm the principal of Mount Pleasant Elementary School. I've heard that you've been littering and dumping the trashcans over the weekend. I would like to ask you to please stop. It is bad for the environment. Could you please stop littering

because if trash gets stuck on a plant, they can't get the sunlight. That would not let the plants grow because they need sunlight. Also small animals like squirrels, chimp-munks, and birds could get trapped in bags. They would not get the things they need and die. As you know the soil is rich in humus. Litter can get in the soil and hurt the worms and soil. Some animals hibernate during the winter. They need energy to do that before they hibernate. Litter can stop them from getting that. If a fast piece of litter fell to the ground, a bird might go down and peck at it. Pieces of it could get in their mouth. In case of that, they could get sick. Coniferous manufacture cones. Some animals need cones. Litter could get ontop of were it's growing and stop it. Could you please stop littering. It perturbs the children when they play. The children also, feel bad about litter. I detest litter. Please try to stop littering. Think about the children and animals.

Thank you.

Eleanor Thornhill

Additional Ways to Try It Out

RAFT is a versatile writing strategy that requires students to think about four key aspects of their writing. Through the use of this strategy, we can reinforce science content and teach students to write for a variety of audiences and purposes. Once students are familiar with RAFT, they can also analyze other types of scientific writing to determine the role, audience, format, and topic for their pieces.

Create small groups and give each group a piece of published writing. See if the students can determine the RAFT for the piece. Each group of students can share their piece of writing and the RAFT they believe the author had in mind when writing it. Each group can assign a new role, audience, format, and topic to another small group of students. Then, each group must revise the written product they reviewed to meet the new RAFT elements.

Student-Created Informational Books

Recent research involving second- and third-grade students conducted by Purcell-Gates, Duke, and Martineau (2007) reveals that students' ability to comprehend and create informational and procedural texts in science is directly related to the degree to which they are involved with authentic literacy events. Students need extensive experience creating meaningful artifacts about relevant content area concepts for an actual audience. Creating informative books allows students to realize that they

are knowledgeable about content and that knowledge can be shared with others through effective written communication.

Creating informational books is an easy way for even the youngest of students to create their own texts based on authors' quality nonfiction texts they read. Even though students may not use all of the features seen in trade books in their own books, the activities associated with creating the books will familiarize them with many linguistic features. Thinking about the most appropriate linguistic features for their own books and having the opportunity to practice using many of them is important. After those experiences, students will realize how to use linguistic elements to enhance their own comprehension of science texts.

How It Works

1. Begin by discussing with students informative books that they have read in class or enjoyed at home. Talk about the content and anything they remember about the books. As a group, review what makes a book informative instead of fictional.

2. Ask students to work in small groups and sort the texts in the classroom library into fiction and nonfiction texts. Then, have students take a closer look at the books that they consider informative.

3. Next, have the students look through the informative books and note specific linguistic features in the texts. Students working in groups can develop a list of features they find. Teachers can also take this time to point out other linguistic features that students might not notice, which might include visuals, underlining, fonts, definitions, and maybe even questions at the end of the book or additional activities.

4. Now it is time for the students to create their own "all about…" informative text on a topic related to social studies that they have been studying. In these texts, encourage students to incorporate as many linguistic features as necessary. They can work in flexible groups according to interest in researching the topic.

A Look Inside One Classroom

A first-grade class was studying habitats and the mammals, reptiles, amphibians, birds, and insects that live in those habitats. The whole class made posters for each habitat, and each student found two facts on their favorite living thing to attach to the posters. After that activity, students

formed groups based on their interests to create "all about…" books for each habitat. The following are some of the topics focused on in the student-created books:

- Ocean: Great white sharks, dolphins, and sea horses
- Pond: Turtles and dragonflies
- Desert: Rattlesnakes and coyotes
- Grasslands: Zebras, lions, elephants, giraffes, and cheetahs
- Rainforest: Bats, toucans, butterflies, and jaguars

The class had previously sorted the books in their classroom library according to linguistic features. Working in groups, the students went through the books in the library and put sticky notes on examples of figures, charts, captions, and fact boxes. Students then discussed different features and shared samples with the class that they found in the books. After that, the teacher went through the books and chose the very best examples for different features often found in "all about…" books and removed the other sticky notes. Therefore, there was a separate bin of trade books containing excellent examples of a table of contents, an index, a glossary, fact boxes, diagrams, and other linguistic features.

Each day, the students spent time working on their books. As part of this time, the teacher would teach a minilesson on different features often found in "all about…" informative books. For example, as the class was hatching chicks, the teacher explained glossaries and talked about how the glossary of a book written on chicks might include the word *pip*, which is the part of the nose used to help the chick get out of the shell. On another day, there was a lesson on creating fact boxes, in which students might show unique facts that do not fit in with the text. One student writing about ladybugs was amazed at the fact that they can bite, and that was a fact he wanted to put in his book for readers, even though it did not really fit anywhere in the text he was writing. The class talked about how a fact box might be a good way to include interesting facts. Students were able to decide which linguistic features they wanted to include in their individual books. As needed, they could also look in the bins for published children's books that demonstrated excellent examples of the linguistic features that the students were creating for their books.

Figure 4 shows pages from two books created by first graders. Figure 4A is a page from Parker's book about ants, and Figure 4B is from

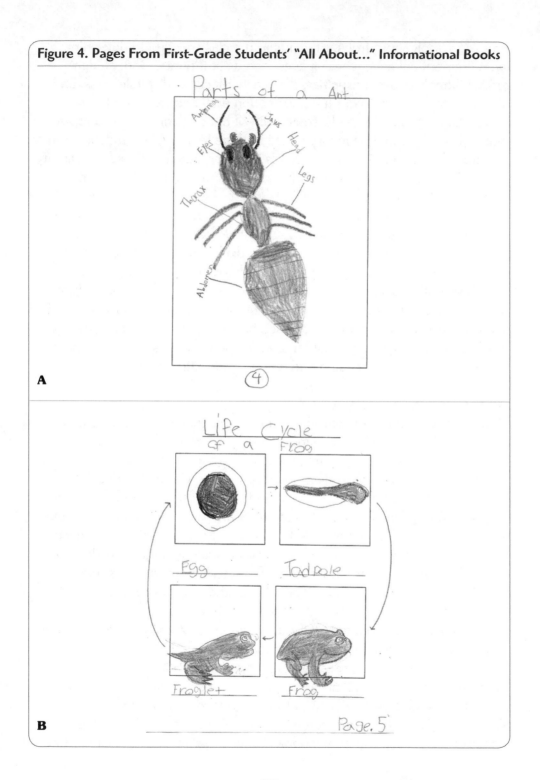

A

B

Pressley's book about frogs. Students in the class needed to determine what their animal eats, where it lives, and what it hunts. Both students read children's books, participated in teacher-facilitated minilessons, and also used technology to get the information they needed to write their books. During some of the lessons, each of the students had a laptop so that technology could be incorporated into the lesson. The students used a research website that is free to schools in the county and those with library cards. There, the students could click on pictures and have information read to them about different animals. The students had categories to explore and questions to answer and included that information in their written pages.

This activity was an excellent way to reinforce the types of linguistic features that the students will need to be able to read in science texts. The students learned that not all informational books have all of the features, but when writing a text, the author has to determine which features best convey important information that the author wants the reader to learn. The students also had an opportunity to see how published authors represent those features in books, pursue an area of science that is of interest to them, and actively engage in reading and writing informational texts.

Additional Ways to Try It Out

Many elementary schools participate in a book buddies program that matches older students with younger ones. As part of these programs, the older students visit the younger students during a specified time and share a book. This can be taken one step further. Older students can create books that reinforce content area information for younger students. Brigham Young University conducted the Earth Science Storybook Project (Lusk, Bickmore, Christiansen, & Sudweeks, 2006) in which preservice elementary teachers, who were mentored by geology faculty, worked to create earth science storybooks to be used by elementary teachers in the field. The project revealed many benefits. Although everyone benefited from the experience, the preservice teachers improved their attitudes toward science, developed a better understanding of content area concepts, and felt more competent to teach the material.

Just like the project coordinators in the aforementioned study, we want our elementary students to develop a firm grasp of content area information and develop positive attitudes toward this information. We also seek to help build content area communication skills. Therefore, elementary students can create books for younger audiences that reinforce

science, social studies, and even mathematical information. To do this, the older students will have to first familiarize themselves with the scientific material that the younger students are learning and the prior knowledge the younger students have on the topic. This information can be gained by interviewing the teacher of the younger students. The teacher can also visit the classroom of the soon-to-be authors and share his or her students' interests and suggest topics that will make good books for their classroom library. Since schools spiral the curriculum, the older students may already have a fairly well-developed understanding of the material at the lower grade levels. However, by reviewing texts on similar topics, they can see how other authors talk about the concepts, gain ideas for their books, and develop their reading and writing skills. Then, it is time to begin writing the informative books.

Teachers may also choose to have their students create informative books electronically. An electronic book is similar to a physical text but in digital form. Students can add sound, animation, and other special effects as desired. Research shows that these texts can be effective with young students (Lefever-Davis & Pearman, 2005). Also, the electronic books have proven to help struggling readers develop literacy skills (Rhodes & Milby, 2007).

Before students create their own informative e-books, teachers will want to share several examples with the class or let the students explore some websites where e-books are accessible. The following websites are suggestions:

International Children's Digital Library (en.childrenslibrary.org/). This website offers a teacher training manual, which explains how digital libraries might be used with students in a classroom. According to the website, the library was initially created by an interdisciplinary team at the University of Maryland in cooperation with the Internet Archive. Also, College Park Kidsteam, which includes children ages 7–11 working with adults in the lab, helps develop and evaluate materials for the website. The site, which began in 2002, has approximately 4,000 books in more than 50 languages. It contains only traditional text e-books, so all of the books have been published and recognized in the country where they were published. On this website, it is possible to conduct an advanced search of the books and limit the search to make-believe or true texts.

However, at this time, it is evident that many of the books are fiction. There are some that are informative, but many of the linguistic features

we see today in informative books are absent. The books are often older and lack a lot of the visual appeal found in modern-day informative books. However, there is value in the website. Students can develop an understanding of e-books and see a variety of examples in the library. This website may serve to introduce students to e-books, and students may also analyze the "true" books and create e-books on similar topics that use many of the linguistic features found in today's printed books that make the texts more readable.

Starfall (www.starfall.com). This website has many bright and colorful e-books for the youngest of readers. It targets kindergartners and was originally created in 2002 to help students learn to read with phonics. Although the repetition of phonic elements may seem stilted, students can see how different e-books are created.

Storyline Online (www.storylineonline.net/). This website contains many familiar favorites published by well-known authors. *Thank You, Mr. Falker* by Patricia Polacco (1998), *Stellaluna* by Janell Cannon (1997), and *Wilfrid Gordon McDonald Partridge* by Mem Fox (1989) are just a few stories that can be found on this website. However, it appears that all of the books listed at the present time are fictional.

Talking Book Library (www.talkingbooklibrary.net/Matrix.htm). After looking at samples of electronic books available and analyzing the effects used in the texts, students can go to this website and read e-books written by teachers and other educators. There are many modern, colorful books that share fictional stories, but there are also books that teach concepts related to math, science, and social studies. Teachers can even create and submit texts to this website for possible inclusion on the website.

Although downloading electronic books from the Internet and printing them is usually not allowed, it is easy for teachers to share e-books with entire classes via a projector. While working in small groups, students can create their own electronic books. First, they must select a social studies topic. They can then research the topic through multiple informative texts, the Internet, and other sources and determine the information they want to share with their audience. To do this, they need to determine their audience. Are the viewers going to be students in the same grade? Will it be shared with younger students to build background knowledge? Can it

be shown to parents to explain the information they are learning in social studies? Taking into consideration their audience, students can then begin their research. Then, the class can view the presentations and share ideas that might make the books more reader friendly. Also, ideas for improving the books can be shared. After modifications are made, students can then use their e-books with the intended audience. As long as teachers are using electronic books for classroom use and in a noncommercial manner, no copyright laws will be violated.

Social Studies

When looking at the type of social studies writing often seen in the elementary grades, one sees that topic summaries and journal entries are common. However, poetry writing is a type of writing that students often do not associate with social studies, and yet it affords students an opportunity to develop skills that can lead to disciplinary literacy in social studies. In order for students to create any of the types of poetry discussed in the section that follows, students will need to be able to read and analyze a wide variety of documents. Through comparing the information that students find in texts, they can select the information they want to share in their poems. Students enjoy writing these types of poetry and have a purpose for reading and locating information.

Unlike math and science, the difficulty level of general words found in social studies text is often quite high (Shanahan & Shanahan, 2008), and poetry, because of its brevity, requires writers to choose their words selectively. This is an excellent time to help students build their social studies vocabulary. Because poems contain fewer words than many other types of writing, students should select powerful or specific words for their poems' content. Writing poetry provides students with additional opportunities to use those specialized terms in writing.

In each of the following activities, students can develop social studies knowledge through a variety of writing experiences. The first type of poetry writing discussed is biopoems, which follow a specific formula. While completing the lines of the poem, students have the opportunity to share a wealth of knowledge about a specific person. "If I Were..." Poetry and Poems for Multiple Voices help students understand differing viewpoints. While students must put themselves in the place of someone else to create an "if I were..." poem, they must think about two different

viewpoints on a person, place, or event to create a poem for multiple voices. Additionally, providing students with opportunities to examine various texts and write based on the knowledge gained is a valuable skill (Stahl & Shanahan, 2004). Biopoems, "If I Were..." Poems, and Poems for Multiple Voices are all activities that can help even the youngest of readers think about information they read in various sources.

Biopoems

A biopoem is an 11-line poem written about a person. To create a biopoem, students must have quite a bit of knowledge on the person's background, experiences, and beliefs. Students can read a variety of texts to find the information necessary to describe the person.

How It Works

1. Explain to students that they will be creating a poem on a famous person. They may then form small groups based on their interests. It is easy to tie this type of poetry into any social studies topic studied.

2. After the small groups have each chosen the person on whom they want to focus, have them locate a variety of resources that contain information on that person.

3. Students can then read through the shorter texts and skim through the lengthier ones to get an understanding of the person they will write about in their poems. They can place sticky notes next to interesting facts they find in traditional texts and make note of websites where they find information.

4. Provide students time to discuss in their group five interesting facts that they learned about their famous person. By doing this, students are learning a great deal of information about the person. Even though all of that information will not be included in their poem, by reading and talking about the material, they will build their social studies vocabulary.

5. Share the following formula for a biopoem and explain each of the lines:

Line 1: First name of this person

Line 2. Four traits of this person

Line 3. "Relative of…"

Line 4. "Lover of…" (three things)

Line 5. "Who feels…" (three things)

Line 6. "Who needs…" (three things)

Line 7. "Who fears…" (three things)

Line 8. "Who gives…" (three things)

Line 9. "Who would like to see…" (three things)

Line 10. "Resident of…"

Line 11. Last name of this person

Explain that all of the lines may not contain information that is directly stated in the text. Often, students have been taught about question–answer relationships (Rafael, 1986). After students think about these relationships, they will realize that some lines in the biopoem formula can easily be completed because the answers to the "questions" are right there in the formula. Examples would be the first line and the last two lines: What is the person's first name? Where is this person a resident? What is the person's last name? However, many of the other lines will require the student to think and search or use information from the book with what they know. In these instances, students need to infer the information needed. For example, determining a person's fears and needs may require students to infer information from the material read.

6. Provide students with time to work in small groups to create their biopoems.

7. After all students are done, have them orally share their poems. Students should also note the sources they used to gain the information. This ensures that students consulted a variety of resources.

A Look Inside One Classroom

One sixth-grade teacher had her students create biopoems about famous African Americans, using websites to gain information. All of the students were directed to the websites A Legacy of Black Talent (afgen.com/profiles .html) and African-American Pioneers (afgen.com/pioneer.html). As the sixth graders looked through the websites, they completed a sheet that required them to find information on various people discussed on the website. Afterward, students were directed to select one person from one

of the websites and research that person in depth. Then, the students were each asked to write a biopoem on the famous person.

With this activity, the teacher introduced a number of famous African Americans to all of her students and also provided the element of choice. The students enjoyed having the opportunity to choose one person to study. While a few of the students researched some of the more familiar African Americans, such as Harriet Tubman, Jesse Jackson, and Rosa Parks, many chose people who are less famous, such as Benjamin Hooks, Sarah Breedlove Walker, Dr. Susan Smith McKinney Steward, Ida B. Wells, and Elizabeth Taylor Greenfield. It is evident from the poems that the students learned information about each of the famous people. In the poem on Elizabeth Taylor Greenfield, it is clear that the student knows that Greenfield sang, was adopted by her master, wanted to see the end of slavery, and lived in Mississippi. In another student's poem, details and inferences about Ida B. Wells were listed:

Ida
Believer, hardworking, helpful, inspiring
Relative of her mom and dad
Lover of her family, women's rights, the cure of yellow fever
Who feels brilliant, pretty, young
Who needs money, love, and a cure
Who fears death, no money, mens beliefs
Who gives women hope, persurverince, strength
Who would like to see men treat woman like equals, the cure to yellow fever, her
   family together
Resident of Tennessee
Wells

At first, the student who wrote this poem had the same concern as other classmates. The students were unsure what to write for the lines where they had to share what the person feels, shares, needs, and fears. The teacher took this opportunity to talk with the students about making inferences and encouraged them to support inferences with the factual information that they read on the websites. The teacher did an excellent job of tying in technology and encouraging higher level thinking skills. To extend the lesson, all students then wrote essays to summarize the information they learned on the famous African Americans and created coins showing their accomplishments. The benefit of Biopoems is that

the writer has the opportunity to put a great deal of information in a very limited amount of writing.

"If I Were..." Poetry

"If I were..." poetry allows students to look at life from a perspective other than their own (Koch, 2000). Perhaps the easiest way for students to create this poetic form is to allow them to write as if they are a famous person or think about what life might be like if they lived during a specific time period. Therefore, this type of poetry is very easy to tie into social studies.

How It Works

1. As with the Biopoems activity, students can form groups, each based on their interest in a famous person. They then locate resources on that person.

2. Introduce the idea of viewpoint. Have students ever heard the saying, "walk a mile in my shoes"? What does it mean to put yourself in someone else's shoes? Younger students may stick with very literal facts about famous people. If necessary, the teacher may choose to have younger students write a sample poem as an entire class as if they were the principal, the president, or another recognizable person. Older students should be able to write the lines of the poem as if they are really seeing life from another's perspective.

3. Explain that "If I were..." poetry is a type of formula poem. Lines do not rhyme, and each line begins with the same phrase, "If I were...."

4. Provide time for students to write their poems. Because of the nature of this type of poetry, students may try to write a poem with many lines, but encourage them to select a limited number of lines. Perhaps after a rough draft is created, students might be instructed to choose the five or 10 best lines that tell about the person. Students need to focus on quality of lines and not quantity.

5. Allow students to share their poems. Take time to compare information that different groups of students may have written about for the same person. Provide students with a chance to explain why they chose to include the information they shared in their poems.

A Look Inside One Classroom

One second-grade class was learning about Mary McLeod Bethune, and the teacher had just finished sharing Eloise Greenfield's (1977) *Mary McLeod Bethune*. Jacob, a student in the class, wrote the following poem based on the information that he had learned about Bethune. To follow the poetic format, he began each line with "If I were Mrs. Bethune."

If I Were Mary McLeod Bethune

If I were Mrs. Bethune, I would be the only one in my family to go to school.
If I were Mrs. Bethune, I would have started the first hospital for blacks.
If I were Mrs. Bethune, I would have started an elementry school named Bethune-
  Cookman College.
If I were Mrs. Bethune, I would be buried on my school grounds.
If I were Mrs. Bethune I would Live in Mayesvile, South Carolina.

To write the poem, Jacob had to have knowledge about Bethune's life, and his poem illustrates that he knows many facts about her. Jacob knows the city of her birth, that she had a college named after her, and many other important facts about her life.

In another classroom, a fifth-grade teacher also chose to use this form of poetry to reinforce information related to the topic of immigration. She read aloud parts of the book *If Your Name Was Changed at Ellis Island* by Ellen Levine (1993). The class discussed conditions that immigrants dealt with based on information they learned from the book and in class. She then asked students to put themselves in another person's shoes. They each created individual poems about immigrants, beginning each line with "If I were an immigrant...."

This type of poetry allows students to develop a better understanding of perspective as they seek to write from another viewpoint. Experiences such as this can be discussed and related to other social studies texts that students read.

Poems for Multiple Voices

Poetry for multiple voices is a poetic form that can be challenging for students because of its unfamiliar format (Tompkins, 2009). Lines of the poem represent two or more viewpoints on a topic. Therefore, the written format is important in order to ensure that the reader knows which lines represent whose view. It often helps to read some sample

poems. Many teachers are familiar with Paul Fleischman's *Joyful Noise: Poems for Two Voices* (1988) and *I Am Phoenix: Poems for Two Voices* (1985), both of which are related to nature and comprised of short poems that can be read by two people. There are also other books that can help students understand how multiple voices can read a poem. Fleischman (2000) authored a book for readers entitled *Big Talk: Poems for Four Voices*, which is written so that either four groups or four individuals can read each poem. To make the format easier to understand, he color-coded the lines so that students know when to read each line. Many teachers of very young students will also want to share some of Mary Ann Hoberman's books, such as *You Read to Me, I'll Read to You: Very Short Stories to Read Together* (2001), which uses color-coding similar to Fleischman's book. Hoberman also wrote a book of scary stories, *You Read to Me, I'll Read to You: Very Short Scary Tales to Read Together* (2007) and a book in which students will see some of their favorite book characters, *You Read to Me, I'll Read to You: Very Short Fairy Tales to Read Together* (2004).

How It Works

1. Explain to students that they will be creating a poem showing two or more perspectives on a topic. Share some examples of poems for multiple voices from some of the previously mentioned texts.

2. Give students a topic such as the U.S. presidential election. Then, talk about how two very different groups might view it differently. What two groups might have different perspectives on this topic? For a topic such as this, most students will say the Democrats and the Republicans.

3. On a smartboard, write the title of the poem in the middle of the board. In this example, the title will be "The United States Presidential Election." Then, write the word *Democrats* at the top of one side of the board and *Republicans* at the top of the other side. Discuss what both of these political groups agree on about the specific topic, and list these phrases down the middle of the board. Students might list ideas such as the following:

- People vote during the election.
- It only occurs every four years.
- It determines the next leader of the United States.

4. Ask students for some opinions or facts that are specific to the Democrats about the presidential election. When an idea is given, ask the students for a matching idea that represents the Republican side. List all of the ideas under the appropriate columns. The beginning of the poem on the presidential election may look like this:

The United States Presidential Election

Democrats

                                                         Republicans

                  People vote during the election

Donkeys

                                                        Elephants

                 The election is important

The liberals will win

                                                  The conservatives will win

                It only happens every four years

5. Continue adding lines until the poem is finished.

6. Divide the students into two groups. Explain that all of the students will read aloud the middle column. However, one group of students will read the lines in the Democrats column, and the other group will read the lines in the Republicans column.

A Look Inside One Classroom

A fourth-grade teacher used this type of poetry to develop social studies knowledge. She began by sharing a few of Fleischman's poems in *Joyful Noise: Poems for Two Voices*. Several students modeled reading the poems. The teacher then talked about how this type of poetry can be excellent for sharing two very different viewpoints and told the students that they would be using this poetic form to share two viewpoints of the American Revolution. One voice would be a patriot soldier during the war, while the second voice would be an African American who joined the war to gain his freedom from slavery. As a class, the students brainstormed the thoughts, feelings, and beliefs of the two viewpoints. They then looked at their social studies textbook and several social studies trade books, such as *American Revolution* by Stuart Murray (2005), *Everybody's Revolution: A New Look at the People Who Won America's Freedom* by Thomas Fleming (2006), and *Samuel's Choice* by Richard Berleth (1990), to gather additional ideas. The students selected which side they wanted to write about, and the class divided into two groups and moved to their respective sides of the classroom.

To understand this difficult concept, the teacher thought it would help to have the students physically move into two groups. One group would represent the soldier's view, and the other group would represent the African American's perspective. The following poem was created by the class:

Joining Forces: A Poem for Two Voices

Fighting for freedom

Give me liberty or give me death

Fighting for a free life

Joining forces

Honored

Shocked

No more British control

No more slave owner control

Willing to fight

Breaking away from England

Breaking away from slavery

We will join together or die

We won't be defeated

For the colonists

For my family

While writing all of the poetic forms discussed in this chapter will help students develop disciplinary literacy skills in social studies, there is also a great deal of value in rereading and analyzing classmates' poems. By analyzing what peers write, students will review social studies content and draw on their own understanding of the material (Boyer, 2006).

REFLECTING BACK AND LOOKING FORWARD

Quality writing activities take time, and there is no way around that. However, writing to learn helps students improve not only their writing skills but also their content area knowledge. Therefore, the activities discussed in this chapter save time by targeting both areas. The purpose of any writing activity is communication. Students need meaningful writing activities to communicate specific math, science, and social studies ideas. Students' writing in the content areas is designed to make their thinking visible, get their ideas on paper, and communicate information. Students need to write well so that others can understand the writing.

Writing is a process, and students need to celebrate the small improvements they see in their writing along the way. As the world is becoming more and more technologically oriented, the importance of writing is even greater. Many of the technological activities that students enjoy require them to write to share their ideas. As technology continues to play an even larger role in their lives, this will become even more evident. Each of the activities discussed within this chapter is designed to build the disciplinary writing skills necessary for developing math, science, and social studies knowledge.

Creating Meaningful Visuals and Developing Viewing Skills in the Content Areas

Viewing and visual representation skills have typically been relegated to a very low status in our educational system. From the time children are able to stick their fingers in pudding or finger paint, many of them cannot wait to draw. From an early age, they also want to use chalk, crayons, and other materials to convey information and ideas. Adults value these forms of expression when children are very young and quickly find places of honor to display these visuals for all to see.

Viewing is also a common activity from the time children are born. When it comes to viewing, young children enjoy looking at illustrations and photographs and are naturally drawn to visual images. Furthermore, children spend a great deal of time in front of televisions and computer screens viewing visual images. However, even with all of this viewing experience, it does not mean that children can or know how to critically view information.

DISCUSSION POINT

Ask students to describe the types of viewing experiences they participate in outside of the classroom. Why do they participate in these activities? What do they think they are gaining from them? Are any of these experiences similar to the visual literacy skills that students use in math, science, or social studies? Do students see any way that they can use these experiences to help them better understand content area material?

As they grow and become immersed in the school culture, many students realize that visuals are not a highly valued part of the school culture. Often, the educational curriculum has an irrational loyalty to

reading and writing (Flood & Lapp, 1997). Although traditional texts are extremely important, there are many other types of texts that students can read that have a great deal of value. The benefits of viewing and visually representing information have been shown for many years (Ausburn & Ausburn, 1978), but these skills still play a very small role in our classroom lessons. Students all learn differently, and as Gardner (1983) emphasizes, visual-spatial learners can thrive when information is presented in a manner that builds on that strength.

In elementary school, it does not take students long to realize that they should strive to read books that do not have a lot of pictures in them to be viewed as good readers by their peers and adults. Therefore, publishers seek to market high-interest, low-readability children's books for struggling readers that look as if they are not typical picture books. Furthermore, many teachers in older grades tend to shift away from incorporating picture books into the classroom because the perception of picture books is that they are for younger children. Instead of sharing picture books, it is more common to see short segments of a chapter book read aloud or shared with the class. Likewise, when students want to draw, it is often necessary for them to wait until they have completed their "real" work and have leftover time. They may be asked to draw a picture that goes along with a story they wrote if they have extra time.

DISCUSSION POINT

Think about how you were taught in the elementary grades. What role did visuals play in your learning? Did teachers draw your attention to visuals in text? Were you taught to understand the visuals you viewed? Did the emphasis on them vary depending on the content area? How will these experiences affect how you teach students to view and create visuals?

What Does This Mean for the Content Areas?

Viewing and visually representing information not only tap into students' interests, but drawing has also been shown to actually help students understand content material. Anning (1999) believes that drawing to learn needs more emphasis in the classroom and that teachers should encourage it as a way to help students solve problems. She believes that as early as the

primary grades, students should learn that there are many different "genres of drawing" (p. 170) that serve different purposes across the different content areas. In math, there are often charts and graphs that display data. Although it is not unusual for science texts to contain labeled illustrations, social studies texts include videos, maps, timelines, and other visuals. Students must not only understand how to view visuals in math, science, and social studies but also know how to create them.

Tompkins (2009) continues to stress that just as with the more common forms of communication, such as writing and speaking, the ability to visually represent information requires students to take into consideration audience, purpose, and form. In our educational system, national standards in math, science, and social studies focus on these important viewing and visual representation skills that are expected of students in the elementary classroom. For instance, principles and practices for school mathematics includes representation as one of the process standards (NCTM, 2000). Likewise, technology is listed as one of the eight categories in the National Science Education Standards (NRC, 1996), and the National Curriculum Standards for Social Studies (NCSS, 2010) stress the importance of students understanding the relationship between society, science, and technology. When examining state standards for Texas, Florida, and California, it is also evident that there is a growing focus on visual representation. Students throughout the United States must not only solve mathematical problems through drawing but also record scientific observations through visuals and create visuals such as charts, maps, and graphs in order to successfully meet social studies standards. Clearly, current standards encourage alternative ways to present information.

TRY IT OUT

Think about your own teaching in math, science, and social studies. Divide a sheet of paper into three columns, one for each content area. List in each column the visuals you recently presented to students. Think about how the students' attention was focused on the visuals. Did they think about the author's intent with the visual and why that type of visual (e.g., photo, illustration, chart) might have been included? Now, look ahead at the material students will be learning soon. What visuals will you be sharing? Decide how you can help students see the value of visuals and the important role they play in connection with the text.

There is a great deal of benefit to linking visuals with mathematics. Crespo and Kyriakides (2007) believe that teachers can use students' mathematical drawings to gain an understanding of students' mathematical knowledge. Through a discussion of these student-created illustrations, it is possible to gain a better understanding of students' thought processes regarding math problems. The discussion and drawings can provide insight into students' mathematical thinking.

Research conducted by Van Meter (2001) with fifth-grade students suggests that drawing can also help students gain scientific knowledge. Those students who drew illustrations spent more time on task than those who only read the science material and viewed the illustrations provided with it. Furthermore, in another study, fourth- and fifth-grade students who drew pictures had a statistically significant better conceptual understanding of scientific concepts than those who only wrote in a science log (Edens & Potter, 2003). Drawing pictures required the students to take the content they were learning through printed words and use it to create illustrations. This is an example of transmediation, which involves taking information in one symbol system and encoding it into another system (Leland & Harste, 1994). This encoding enhances students' learning as they better understand the material.

Encouraging students to create visuals and helping them understand visual representations have always been important because of the natural interest that students bring to the classroom. Furthermore, there are benefits for current students. If visual literacy does not play a more prevalent role in classrooms, then students will be at a disadvantage when they must live and work in a technologically rich world. Research by Avgerinou (2009) shows that students spend more hours engaged with technology than they spend in school. Visual images play a large role in that technology. Students must be visually intelligent and know how to critically view images, or they will forever be at the mercy of the people creating them. Even the youngest of learners must be prepared for the digital texts that they will be bombarded with later in life.

Instead of marginalizing visuals, we must embrace viewing and visually representing information and make it a valued part of our curricula to develop disciplinary literacy skills. Think about the type of visuals that adults often create and the viewing opportunities in which they participate. Much of the text we read as adults is short, as discussed in Chapter 3, and yet a great deal of that text contains visuals. Utility bills, laboratory results

of blood tests, travel directions, and newspaper articles often contain visuals in the form of charts, graphs, or diagrams. These types of viewing experiences do not even begin to address the types of visuals and viewing opportunities that many adults have as part of their employment. As technology and the Internet play a larger role in our lives, there are even greater expectations for adults to be savvy viewers. Although the texts will change as technology becomes more and more prevalent, we can still help prepare students for visual images that they may encounter as adults.

Students must learn that just as authors can slant text to show a specific opinion, creators of visuals can use them in a manner to influence the viewer. This can be true whether the creator is sharing results from a science experiment, views on a topic related to social studies, or data from research. Considine, Horton, and Moorman (2009) point out that being immersed in media does not guarantee that students comprehend it or are aware of the creators' intents. According to Conley (2008), students are bombarded by images, "and they influence how people view reality" (p. 133). By incorporating more visual literacy into the classroom, teachers not only build students' lifelong skills but also make their learning relevant to the world beyond the classroom. As Flynt and Brozo (2010) state, "the digitally connected world is here and now" (p. 526), so we can no longer wait to incorporate visual literacy into the content classroom.

In each section of this chapter, ideas and activities are shared to help elementary students develop visual literacy skills in math, science, and social studies. As students create a variety of visuals and develop a better understanding of content information through transmediation, they will gain disciplinary literacy skills and the knowledge they need to be successful in the content areas.

Math

Students will develop graphs to explain numerical information, design comic strips to reinforce how to solve problems, and create presentations with technology to teach concepts to their classmates. It is not only important that students be able to create and view mathematical visuals to develop disciplinary literacy skills, but also, by participating in these activities, they will reinforce other skills that they will need throughout school and life. Students will work collaboratively, improve oral skills as they articulate their plans and thoughts with peers, and learn how to create

and share information through technology. Each strategy can be modified and used with a variety of grade levels. Fashion Doll Fall requires that students explain their learning through words and visuals. Student-Created Smartboard Lessons incorporates technology and allows students to teach their peers through slides. Creative Comics brings a familiar type of text to the content area of math.

Fashion Doll Fall

Although many people may think of dolls as appealing to girls only, this activity will make many teachers rethink that belief. Regardless of gender, dolls can be used as part of an engaging activity with students at a variety of grades. This activity engages students in hands-on mathematics while helping them create visuals that explain their findings. Many high school teachers have used a version of this activity with science and math, but this modified version can easily be used with students at the elementary grade levels. Further modification can be made according to the mathematical skill level of participating students.

Through this activity, students create graphs to share results of the activity with others. This requires an ability to read graphs and charts, which is necessary to develop mathematical disciplinary literacy. Students are also expected to take information that they have recorded visually and translate it into words to describe their findings. Furthermore, students must orally articulate the results of their experiments. Then, to complete the final mission report, students must be able to explain in words what occurred and develop visuals to accompany the text.

Fashion Doll Fall has three major components. There are two parts to the overall mission and a final mission report that must be submitted in order for the students to successfully complete the activity. Therefore, the activity may be completed over a period of days.

How It Works

1. Gather a box of small dolls. Then, divide the students into small groups. Each group will be assigned a doll or may choose one from a selection of dolls.

2. Explain to the students that they are about to embark on a mission that involves their fashion dolls and must become engineers. As engineers, they will use their mathematical knowledge and hands-on materials to

solve a problem. Do any of the students know how math and dolls can go together? Introduce the Fashion Doll Fall activity by reading aloud a letter similar to the following:

Dear Students,

You have a challenge set before you. Your fashion doll has just turned 50, and she has become a mature and wiser woman. She is educated, well traveled, held several jobs, and brought joy to millions of people across the world. Your doll has done more than most adults twice her age have, and she has accomplished it without gaining a single wrinkle or gray hair. However, she is bored, because for a fashion doll, she thinks she has seen and done it all. There is one thing in life, though, that she still wants to experience. This is where you come in. She wants to bungee jump!

With your help, and working in teams, your doll will succeed in her mission to bring a little pizzazz back into her humdrum life. Good luck, young bungee engineers!

Sincerely yours,
Mission Supervisor

3. Students are then divided into small groups, and each group is provided with the mission materials. Each group receives rubber bands, a tape measure, computer paper, pencils, ruled paper, graph paper, and masking tape.

4. After discussing the safe handling of mission materials, especially rubber bands, it is time to give students the following directions:

Mission Stage 1 Directions

a. Attach a rubber band to your doll's feet in any manner you would like. Then, make a short bungee cord by attaching more rubber bands to the first one.

b. Attach your computer paper to the wall as high as you can reach.

c. Mark a jumping point on your computer paper from which to drop the doll and place her at the "jumping point." Hold the end of the bungee cord next to her at the jumping point. Then, let your doll fall headfirst from the jumping point. Use your tape measure to measure the distance she falls on the first plunge.

d. Repeat each jump at the same height three times and then calculate the average distance. Record the number of rubber bands and the distance she falls on a graph similar to the one provided in Figure 5. Add two more rubber bands to the bungee cord and repeat the experiment until all seven rows are completed in the table. You may need to move to a higher place as your bungee cord becomes longer.

e. On a sheet of paper, plot the data points from your table on a graph. Double-check your table and graph to make sure the information is accurate.

Figure 5. Data Collection Table

Units of x	Trial 1	Trial 2	Trial 3	Average (y)	Points to Plot	
					x	y

f. Exchange your graph with another team. That team should write five well-written sentences describing the information on the graph. Then, that team should give your team back the graph with the statements. Check the statements to determine if they are accurate. If not, then work together as a team so that the sentences accurately reflect the information on your graph.

5. After students are done, groups should share the table and sentences with the mission supervisor (teacher) before continuing on to the Mission Stage 2 Directions.

6. Students are now entering into the final stage of the dolls' bungee jump experiences. Explain that it is now time for the final bungee jump. Give students the location for the jump. This may be from the top of a file cabinet, a banister, or another high object. Read aloud the next set of mission directions:

Mission Stage 2 Directions

a. Use the information your group has collected so far to estimate the number of rubber bands necessary to give your doll the greatest thrill in this bungee jump. She should come as close as possible to the ground without hitting her head!

b. Once all groups have completed step a, it is time for each group's doll to compete. Each team's data should be recorded in a table on the smartboard.

7. Each doll competes, results are compared, and the winning group is announced.

8. It is time for each group to write a final mission report. Read the following scenario:

> As brilliant new student engineers, newspaper reporters are eager to share the story of the fashion doll fall with others. Describe in your mission report exactly what occurred during the mission stages. Can you explain what occurred during the mission? Can you explain any problems your team encountered? What worked really well for your team? What would you recommend future budding engineers do differently? Don't forget that newspaper reporters love visuals! Take the final class data table and create a graph that can be part of your mission report. Incorporate that graph into your story!

9. Groups then orally share their stories, compare their summaries, and explain why they chose the visuals they created to accompany their stories.

Additional Ways to Try It Out

Toys are a natural attention getter for many students and can help motivate them to engage in content area lessons. This activity can easily be modified to use other toys and gather other types of data. Teachers may choose to use race cars instead of dolls and measure the distance the race cars travel. This type of activity is especially valuable because students are not only viewing visuals but also creating them. The ability to take the information seen in charts and graphs and put that information into words and vice versa is a necessary skill for disciplinary knowledge.

Technology can be incorporated into this lesson or any lesson that involves creating graphs by visiting the National Center for Education Statistics Kids' Zone webpage Create a Graph: Classic (www.nces.ed.gov/nceskids/graphing/classic/). At that website, students have the opportunity to create five different types of graphs: bar, line, area, x/y, and pie. Also, students can select the font, background and grid colors, location of legend, and whether it will be a two-dimensional, three-dimensional, or shadow graph.

Fashion Doll Fall can easily help students develop a number of disciplinary literacy skills. Through all parts of the mission, students not only refine their language skills but also learn mathematical concepts. Students learn to represent information through visuals, develop technical vocabulary, and develop collaborative skills as they work together with their peers.

Student-Created Smartboard Lessons

Students are digital natives, whereas many adults are digital immigrants (Prensky, 2005). As natives, students have been immersed in digital information since they were very young. Digital immigrants, or those who are newer to technology, tend to be more cautious with the use of technology because they are concerned that they might do something wrong. Anyone who has worked with students, who are digital natives, can see that they have no fear of pushing the wrong button or making mistakes with technology. Students are eager to interact with technology to see what they can do.

Therefore, smartboard lessons can be created by very young students and are a great way to engage them with technology and math. Because the complexity of slides can vary greatly, all students can achieve success with this activity. Younger students can complete simple shows, while those with more technological knowledge can add extras such as sound and movement. Creating smartboard lessons is a great way for students to build technological skills and think through a mathematical lesson they create. Mathematicians must be able to read symbols and translate them into words and vice versa, understand the steps necessary to solve problems, and be familiar with specialized mathematical vocabulary. All of these skills can be developed through the creation of mathematical smartboard lessons.

How It Works

1. Explain to students that in order to teach anything, they must have a strong understanding of the material. In this activity, they will become teachers. Their assignment is to teach a mathematical process to their classmates.

2. Allow students to work in pairs. Explain that they must not only use visuals to help explain their work but also show an understanding of key terms related to the mathematical operation.

3. Specific expectations for the lessons will vary depending on the age level of the students and the complexity of the mathematical problem, but the following are suggestions that might be expected:

- The lesson should be interactive and use manipulatives for visual understanding (e.g., base 10 blocks, counters, money, candy pieces).
- The lesson should contain at least five slides, including a title slide.
- The lesson should be colorful and creative.

4. Encourage each pair to practice their lesson after it is created so that they feel they are fully prepared to share it.

5. Now it is time to share their creations. As they orally share with their peers and explain their slides, they develop their mathematical knowledge by reinforcing knowledge of the mathematical operation. Furthermore, students develop their technological skills as they create slides for their classmates to view.

A Look Inside One Classroom

Two fourth-grade boys completed this activity with division. The slides they created are shown in Figure 6. The two boys took their audience into consideration, and they used a bright color on each slide and a variety of fonts to capture their peers' interest. The pair also made the presentation interactive by having students move the stars on the second slide into one of two ovals. To reinforce technical vocabulary that must be known to talk about division, the slide 3 asks users to look under boxes to see the names for four different parts of the division process. When the boxes are removed, the words "quotient," "dividend," "divisor," and "remainder" are revealed. The steps to complete the problem are listed down the left side of the slide. First, viewers are told to divide the dividend by the divisor. Then, the viewer multiplies the answer by the divisor. Finally, the user subtracts that number from the dividend and then brings down the leftover amount. Therefore, the answer is 7 with a remainder of 1. Viewers then have a chance to test their knowledge by correctly matching the term with the mathematical symbol on slide 4. As the slideshow progresses, viewer demands get progressively more difficult as students are required to use all of the parts of a problem shown on slide 5 to create a division problem. On the final slide, students complete one more problem.

While this activity can help students develop the skills necessary to view and visually represent mathematical problems, there are obviously other gains. It is interesting how the two students used many linguistic features commonly found in informative texts in the creation of their technological presentation. The fourth graders not only incorporated a variety of visuals but also explored the use of a number of fonts and colors. Also, many of the slides had the main idea centered as a heading at the top. These are all linguistic features that one often encounters with informative text.

Figure 6. Fourth-Grade Students' PowerPoint Slideshow on Division

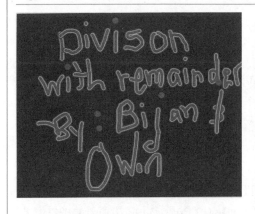
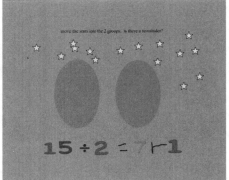
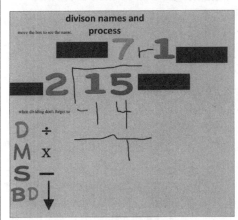
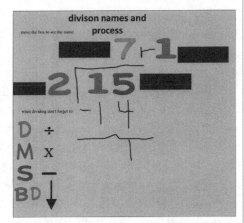
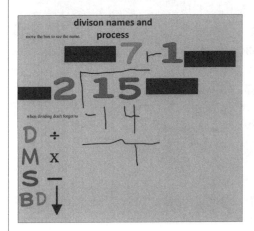
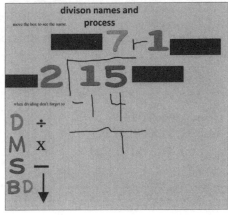

Furthermore, not all of the slides are read left to write as is often seen in traditional texts. Slide 3 made this readily apparent, with the steps of the problem listed vertically down the left side. Because a great deal of technological information is not read left to right, this presentation is consistent with the reading demands that one might encounter in various media. It is important to take the opportunity to point out that reading content area texts often requires readers to move beyond left-to-right reading. Visual aids are often inserted into texts and require readers to realize the visuals' importance and navigate both visuals and written text.

Additional Ways to Try It Out

This strategy can be modified in a variety of ways. Teachers can easily adapt this lesson to incorporate any of the mathematical operations: addition, subtraction, multiplication, or division. It is important to remember that students are creating visuals to teach classmates about a mathematical concept. By working in pairs, they gain even more mathematical and technological knowledge. Then, through orally sharing their presentation and answering questions that others may have, they further refine their knowledge. As students view the creations, they also see the variety of ways that authors might choose to illustrate a mathematical operation.

Even if a classroom is not technologically equipped with a smartboard, this activity can still be used with other materials. Students can use posterboard and other types of materials in lieu of the smartboard to create a public local text that can be shared with classmates. If done in this manner, students will want to divide the board or paper into five or more illustrations that will chronologically represent the steps for completing a math problem.

Creative Comics

"Far Side," "Garfield," "Charlie Brown,".… They all bring back fond memories and probably a few laughs as we remember reading them or possibly still enjoy them. What is it about comic strips that make them so enjoyable? Perhaps it is the fact we can read them in a brief period of time and are entertained at the same time. Maybe they remind us of the cartoons we enjoyed as children on the television. Comics have

transcended time, and even though it may be more difficult to get students to seek out traditional printed books to read because of all of the other types of text available, comic strips are a type of text that will capture their interest. Also, comic strips are a natural tie-in to technology, a way to connect out-of-school experiences with in-school learning, and an opportunity to provide another way to share information through text and visuals.

Students have a strong interest in comic strips outside of the classroom. They watch cartoons on television and might even read comic books. Comics are not the typical type of text that students read in school. Therefore, they enjoy this different form of writing in class. Comics often have text bubbles that provide a limited amount of space to write dialogue. Students must be able to capture the essence of what they want to say in a succinct manner. Other forms of comic strips may require captions, in which the author writes the main idea for each frame. Most comic strips involve two or more characters engaging in conversation on a topic, so the words are written in a dialogue format similar to plays and other types of text that students might read.

How It Works

1. Decide on the information that students should gain from the comic-strip creation. Should they teach others about solving word problems? Maybe the goal is to explain a math process.

2. Bring in some popular comic strips that students enjoy outside of class. Discuss the common features seen. Comics contain text bubbles, limited words, illustrations, frames, and captions and are not written left to right across each frame. These are all ideas that may be brainstormed.

3. Explain to students that they will be creating math comic strips. Let them know the purpose behind the comic strips that they will create.

4. Students can work in pairs or by themselves. If technology is available, students might go to ReadWriteThink's Comic Creator webpage (www .readwritethink.org/files/resources/interactives/comic/) to create their cartoons. Otherwise, they may choose to create the individual frames on index cards and put the frames in order on a large sheet of paper.

5. Have students share their creations. Ask them to explain why they created their comic strips the way they did and allow other students to give input on the finished creations.

A Look Inside One Classroom

One fifth-grade teacher decided to have her students create math comic strips at the end of the school year, so the students could review the math processes that they had learned that year. As an example, the teacher shared a comic strip that she had created about multiplication. The character in her comic strip explained how to multiply a double-digit number by another number. While the character had thought bubbles showing the math steps, captions were also used to explain the step-by-step process.

The teacher began by telling the students that they should pick one math process taught that year and draft out the process in no more than six steps. Then, students were to explain in comic-strip format how that process works. They were directed to follow the step-by-step instructions provided on the Comic Creator webpage. The site is free and allows students to select the title, subtitle, and number of panels for the template.

Then, students were to select from a variety of people, props, and backgrounds for each panel. There are a number of text bubble choices that students can make, and then they can write their dialogue in the balloons. Many of the fifth graders chose to focus on multiplication or division for their mathematical comic strips, but one student decided to create a comic strip explaining how to convert decimals into percentages (see Figure 7). In the student's comic strip, one caveman is trying to figure out the math problem. The talking rock gives the caveman hints, such as rounding a number from the thousandths place to become a two-digit number, and then moving the decimal to the right two places to make it a percentage. In some ways, the comic strip this student created parallels a familiar plot in traditional tales in which good wins over evil. The good character in the comic, Flugabaloo, succeeds in the end, and the dinosaur, who offers no mathematical help, disappears. The caveman needs assistance, and the dinosaur seems to take great pleasure in trying to bother him. When the caveman is able to solve the problem with the help of the talking rock, the dinosaur lets the caveman know that he can have his body back, and poof, the caveman turns into a modern-day man, and the dinosaur is gone.

Additional Ways to Try It Out

Comic strips can be created by students in a variety of grade levels. Creating them can also be a great activity for older peers to teach younger students. Another activity would be for the finished comic strip creators to

Figure 7. Fifth-Grade Student's Comic Strip on Converting Decimals Into Percentages

make a photocopy of their cartoon strips, number the frames in order on the back, and then cut apart the individual frames. Can their classmates successfully put the comic strip frames in the correct order so that the steps make sense? Is the writing clear so that the expectations for each step make sense to the reader?

Through using texts as diverse as comic strips, we create connections with the types of texts that students encounter outside the classroom. Along with expressing their mathematical knowledge, students learn to express themselves in a succinct manner. Many other types of writing that they do outside of class also require that information be conveyed in

a limited number of words. Making these connections between texts is a necessary and important activity in any elementary classroom.

Science

Students can develop an understanding of technical scientific vocabulary through student-created visuals. With Sniglets, students create visuals that reinforce their understanding of commonly used morphemes they see in scientific terms. Along with building visual representation skills as students strengthen their vocabulary, students must understand that visuals can convey information about scientific concepts. Creating a museum display related to a scientific topic for the Eyes on Science Museum Exhibit activity can do just that. The activities within this section will not only help students learn to present information visually and be more savvy viewers but also help build students' scientific vocabulary and their understanding of scientific text.

Sniglets

Sniglets are not new, but they are a creative way to help students expand their scientific vocabulary and prepare them for the technical vocabulary that they will encounter in the future. Comedian Rich Hall created sniglets in the 1980s. Sniglets are words that are not in the dictionary but should be. For years, people enjoyed the humor in sniglets, and the term became well known. In fact, sniglets were so popular that Hall wrote several books of sniglets purely for enjoyment purposes. However, there is more than enjoyment that can be gained from the creation of these funny words. In the educational world, Sniglets be used as a classroom activity to build morphemic knowledge.

Morphemes are the smallest unit of meaning. Root words and affixes are morphemes. While long words such as *Mississippi* and *elephant* are morphemes, the letter *s* is also a morpheme when it means more than one and is attached onto the end of a word. Some morphemes, such as root words, can have meaning by themselves and are known as free morphemes. Other morphemes, such as affixes, only have meaning when attached to another morpheme and are called bound morphemes. Both types of morphemes are important when creating words and understanding vocabulary. In fact, research supports having students analyze morphemes

in words in fourth grade and above (White, Power, & White, 1989). However, instead of asking students to memorize long lists of morphemes, it is important to actively involve students in using morphemic clues to determine the meaning of unfamiliar words they encounter (White, Sowell, & Yanagihara, 1989).

Sniglets require students to manipulate morphemes and take a closer look at morphemes within existing words. As students use morphemes to create new words, they get additional exposure to common scientific morphemes. This repeated exposure will help students remember the meanings of morphemes and expand students' scientific vocabulary. Science text contains a great deal of technical vocabulary, so this activity increases students' vocabulary because they can use their morphemic knowledge to read unknown words in scientific text they encounter in the future. Creating sniglets is a motivational way for students to learn the meaning of different morphemes so that they can use their creativity to make up new words. In turn, they remember the morphemes because they not only manipulate them in words but also write the definitions, draw visuals, and write sentences using their new words.

How It Works

1. Many students find it interesting to see long words. Write "pneumonoultramicroscopicsilicovolcanoconiosis" on a smartboard, large sheet of paper, or wall chart. Ask students to brainstorm the definition of the word. Explain that determining the definition of this word is actually similar to solving a puzzle. This word, similar to others that they may encounter in science texts, is created from a number of morphemes. Explain that morphemes are a unit of meaning. As a class, help students break the word down into eight morphemes (*pneumono-*, *ultra-*, *micro-*, *scopic-*, *silico-*, *volcano-*, *coni-*, *-osis*). Allow small groups to try to find the meaning of each morpheme. When students are done, they can put the parts together to come up with the definition of the word. The term uses a number of science morphemes and actually means an illness of the lungs caused by the inhalation of small dust particles.

2. Now talk about other words that students often encounter that contain morphemes. *Hydro-* is a common morpheme that they may read. Similar to many morphemes, the last letter in *hydro-* may vary and be an *o* or an *a*. Have they seen *hydr-* in words? Students, depending on their

age, may share terms such as *fire hydrant*, *dehydrate*, and *hydrogen*. Also, words such as *unicycle*, *bicycle*, and *tricycle* all have the common morpheme *-cycle*. There are also words that explain certain fears, such as *claustrophobia*, *acrophobia*, and even *triskaidekaphobia*, which is the fear of the number 13. The morpheme *-phobia* means fear. It is also important to talk about common affixes such as *re-*, *de-*, *pre-*, *-ing*, *-ive*, and others that are suffixes and prefixes found in many words. What do those affixes mean when attached to other morphemes?

3. It is now time to look closer at morphemes often seen in science texts. Students can find lists of morphemes on the Internet or look in science texts to determine if they can find any morphemes that they have seen in many words and try to determine the meaning of the morphemes. The morphemes shown in Table 3 are commonly seen in scientific words, along with their definitions. The list is not comprehensive. Students can add to it based on the words they encounter in science texts. Although some morphemes may not be encountered until older grades, those morphemes can be used to challenge more capable students. However, it might be more educational and interesting to let students find their own morphemes, and then the student-created list can be checked to see if there are others that might be added. There will be additional morphemes in texts at various grade levels, and not all of these morphemes will be seen in all science books, but it is a good list to help students start thinking about morphemes.

4. Students then combine individual morphemes to create new scientific words that are not in the dictionary but should be, that is, sniglets. The important point to emphasize is that sniglets are not real words but made-up words created by combining morphemes. The students then write the definitions for their sniglets, use them in sentences, and draw pictures to go with the new words.

5. Student-created sniglets are shared with the rest of the class. After the sniglet is read, other students can analyze the word to see if they can determine its meaning based on the morphemes that make it up. Students can examine how the word was formed and which morphemes were used. A sniglet is a humorous word, but it should also make sense given the morphemes in the word.

6. Later, students can look on the Internet, at videos, or in other print sources for additional examples of the morphemes.

Table 3. Morphemes Commonly Seen in Scientific Words

anthr-/andr- (man)	ecto- (outer)	macro- (large)	post- (after)
aqua- (water)	-ed (past)	-mania (madness)	pre- (before)
astr- (star)	electro- (electricity)	mar- (sea)	pro- (forward)
auto- (self)	endo- (within)	meta- (change)	proto- (first)
bi- (two)	eu- (well, good)	-meter (measure)	pseudo- (false)
biblio- (book)	ex- (out)	micro- (small)	psycho- (mind)
bio- (life)	-flect/flex- (bend)	mis- (wrong)	quad- (four)
cardio- (heart)	-form (shape)	multi- (many)	re- (again, back)
chemo- (chemical)	frag-/fract- (break)	-ology (study of)	scop- (see)
chlor- (green)	geo- (earth)	ortho- (straight)	-scribe (write)
chron- (time)	hydro- (water)	paleo- (old, ancient)	-sect (cut)
-cide (kill)	hyper- (too much)	-ped/-pod (foot)	sub- (under)
co- (with)	hypo- (not enough)	-phobia (fear)	super- (above)
-cycle (repeating event)	-ify/-ize (make)	phono- (sound)	tele- (far away)
de- (down)	-ing (action, process)	photo- (light)	trans- (across)
di- (two)	-iosis (disorder)	poly- (many)	tri- (three)
eco- (habitat)	-logy (science, body of knowledge)	port- (carry)	uni- (one)

A Look Inside One Classroom

One fifth-grade teacher asked her class to create sniglets in an effort to expand their scientific vocabulary. She gave her students a list of 30 morphemes that she had found in their science text. As a class, they discussed which ones were often seen as prefixes, suffixes, and roots of words. Through manipulating morphemes, students created a variety of sniglets. Each student was given a sheet of paper on which to write a sniglet, give its definition, use the word in a sentence, and draw an illustration of it. Figure 8 is an example of a fifth-grade student's sniglet, *pseudoanthropphobia*, or the fear of false humans. Through the creation of the picture, the student showed that she understands the meaning of three morphemes that she may have encountered in scientific text. Drawing reinforces her understanding of the morphemes as she illustrates the meaning of the sniglet.

Figure 8. Fifth-Grade Student's Sniglet

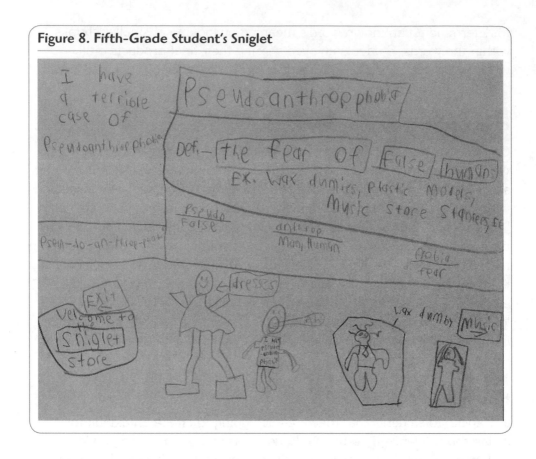

Another student, Chaunyce, used three morphemes to come up with her sniglet. She used the morphemes *thermo-* (hot), *hydro-* (water), and *-phobia* (fear) to create the sniglet *thermohydrophobia*. Then, she drew a picture of water and defined her sniglet as a fear of hot water. To use her singlet in a sentence, she wrote, "My cousin haves a severe case of thermohydrophobia." Kashonna created *pseudobioticology*, the study of false organisms, for her sniglet. She showed a picture of a flying turtle and wrote, "Pseudobioticology would be a fun job but every thing you study would be fake." Finally, Qumari, another fifth-grade student, came up with *hydromarphobia*, which is an exaggerated fear of the sea.

By creating sniglets, these fifth-grade students played with words and developed attitudes toward unknown terms. Instead of being overwhelmed when presented with unknown, polysyllabic terms that they may encounter in scientific text, this activity gave students the confidence they need to try

to determine an unknown word's meaning by looking at smaller chunks within the words. Students enjoyed sharing their final products orally with classmates.

Eyes on Science Museum Exhibit

Children's museums often contain a lot of bright displays that teach the viewer about the material displayed. These museums rarely have more than short texts accompanying the displays, but they convey a lot of information with very little text. Now students are going to work in groups to create an "eyes on science" museum exhibit based on a scientific topic that they have been studying. Students need to visualize scientific material and be able to read pictures, graphs, charts, diagrams, and other visuals to be scientifically literate. The ability to go back and forth between text and visuals takes experience. The purpose of creating the exhibit is to help students learn the importance of visuals and help them create visuals that convey information. Students will also benefit as they have a chance to view what others have created.

How It Works

1. Explain to students that they are each going to create an exhibit for a classroom science museum. Although museums sometimes provide audiotapes to explain exhibits or guides to give tours, this one has none. The students, as museum curators, must create their entire exhibits with visuals that convey important information about each item.

2. Talk about how visuals are used to convey information in informative texts. For example, if upper elementary students are studying the solar system, they might begin by looking at the visuals in books and discuss the information conveyed.

   Planet Hunter: Geoff Marcy and the Search for Other Earths by Vicki Oransky Wittenstein (2010) uses a wide variety of visuals and linguistic features to help the reader gain as much as possible from the informative text. Even though the book is geared for fifth-grade students and higher, there are many aspects of it that could be enjoyed by younger students. Small sections of the book could be shared without reading the book in its entirety. The book also has a lot of personal information on Marcy, which will make him seem very real to young students. This

information includes his struggles with math, what he learned from parents and teachers, and how he used to climb out his bedroom window at night to look at the planets.

The class can look through the text and discuss all of the different features that make the information easier to understand. There are bright orange boxes with special headings that provide background information on other planet hunters. The author also uses photographs of important people, events, places, and even artifacts. The book includes diagrams of the solar system and the layers of a planet. Additionally, there is a glossary and a list of other texts, including websites, that pertain to the book.

3. Tell students the topic of the museum. It should be a topic that they have recently studied, and the museum exhibit can be used as a culminating activity for a science unit. Students must work in groups to create a specific number of exhibits for the museum. Each exhibit should contain a visual that conveys information on the topic.

In keeping with the topic of the solar system, each group might be told to create an exhibit containing a display of a famous person associated with the study of the solar system, two displays pertaining to specific planets they have learned about, and a fourth display on some other aspect of the solar system that they want to visually represent. With this example, small groups of students can brainstorm how they can share information about famous people through visuals. Perhaps they will use photographs they find on the Internet and then create a timeline for significant events in the people's lives. The students might decide to create a papier-mâché planet and then use individual pieces of paper to attach facts to the planet. In addition, students can use posterboard or create PowerPoint slides to show graphs or charts containing information about the planets. Students want to convey important information through visuals so that viewers can walk away after viewing the exhibit with a better knowledge of the topic.

4. Serve as a facilitator by listening and providing suggestions to the small groups of students as they work to plan their displays.

5. On the designated day, students will display their exhibit in an assigned area. Then, classmates will have an opportunity to walk through the exhibits to see what information they can gain from each one. Other classes or even parents might want to see the students' creations. The idea is not to spend an inordinate amount of time or money on any exhibits. However, students should carefully consider the best way to share

information with a viewer. A great deal of important information can be conveyed with very few words.

6. Afterward, discuss the characteristics of a good visual. Why are visuals important when students read and look at texts? Are there certain ways to represent information visually that may be better than others? As a viewer, what is your role in looking at visuals? What types of questions should people viewing a visual ask themselves?

As students play with words, they realize that unknown words are not something to dread and conquer. Students not only learn to take risks in determining word meanings but also expand their vocabulary. Teaching students that they can successfully decode unknown words will help them remove the mental block they feel when encountering new words and help ensure student success with informative reading.

Social Studies

The first two activities shared in this section help students grasp the main idea of social studies content and visually represent that information to others so that they can understand it. While the Newsletters activity requires students to represent important information in a succinct manner, the Herringbone strategy requires students to state the who, what, when, where, why, and how of a passage. This structured form of note-taking focuses attention on the key points in a text. Finally, Body Biographies engages students in looking at a topic from multiple perspectives. Through the visual creation of a famous person, students can gain a better understanding of the key figure and realize the importance of considering diverse viewpoints in text.

Newsletters

Students can also use their knowledge of the linguistic features they find in informative books to create brief, one-page newsletters depicting famous people, places, or events they are studying in social studies. Students can use fonts, headings, color, diagrams, charts, and other features that they have seen in text. Because space is limited in newsletters, students must use visuals to convey information about their topics. Although this activity

may be difficult for younger students to complete on their own, they could complete it as a whole-class activity.

How It Works

1. Briefly review the linguistic features often seen in informative texts. Students might look at a variety of trade books, websites, or other types of text. Ask them to work in groups to brainstorm a list of linguistic features they find in the texts.

2. As a class, discuss the features that the students listed. Why might authors choose to use color, special fonts, diagrams, charts, and other linguistic features? Some authors may use the features to draw attention to certain material or because of space limitations.

3. Look at newsletters or fliers that the students might have seen. These may discuss coming events in the community, descriptions of places, or other information. Discuss the commonalities of these pieces of text. The purpose is to help students understand the importance of using very few words to convey ideas.

4. Explain that students will be working with partners to create a one-page newsletter discussing a famous person, place, or event that they have studied. They must think about the topic of their newsletter and also discuss the most important points that they think should be discussed. Then, they will need to find visuals to help convey the information.

5. Remind the students that the use of visuals will help them deal with space limitations, enable them to convey additional information in an eye-catching format, and provide them with opportunities to use linguistic features such as size, color, and font to make the text more readable.

6. Now it is time to create their products. You may choose to provide students with a template showing the types of information that you want recorded in the newsletters. Be sure to emphasize that the students must choose their visuals and words carefully because of space restrictions.

7. Allow students to share their newsletters with the rest of the class. Then, display them in the classroom as a form of local text.

A Look Inside One Classroom

One third-grade teacher decided to have her students create newsletters based on famous explorers they had been studying. The students used

a variety of sources to gather the necessary information for their texts, such as *The First Americans: Prehistory–1600* by Joy Hakim (2007). Also, webpages such as Explorers on the KidsKonnect.com website (www.kidskonnect.com/subject-index/16-history/265-explorers.html) and Explorers on the Web on the CyberSleuth Kids website (cybersleuth-kids .com/sleuth/History/Explorers/index.htm) were reviewed.

After reviewing a sample newsletter created by the teacher on Christopher Columbus, students discussed the types of features in the newsletter and the information it contained. The students were provided a template to use, but they had the opportunity to change color scheme and formatting. Explorers researched were based on the third-grade social studies standards, and each student worked with a partner to create a newsletter. Figure 9 is the first page of a newsletter created by two students. The students selected a title explaining the explorer's search and used color for two main headings on the page. Six questions they thought the reader might want answered were then organized under those headings. Symbols, flags, and a cartoon illustration representing the state of Florida were used to provide additional information to the text contained in the newsletter.

After the class created the newsletters, each pair of students orally shared an overview of their newsletter. They talked about the information included and the manner in which they organized it. As time permitted later, students had the opportunity to read the other students' newsletters.

Additional Ways to Try It Out

Some classrooms already create newsletters detailing weekly events. If your class does this, allow students to analyze and talk about the linguistic features they find in those newsletters. Students can determine if there are ways that the newsletter may be improved. Perhaps they can consider some of these ideas as they create their own social studies newsletters. Creating newsletters is not a new activity, but relating the activity to social studies content ensures that students are developing disciplinary literacy skills.

Herringbone

One of the skills required to develop disciplinary literacy in social studies is the ability to understand key events in history. This involves knowing the who, what, where, when, how, and why for important events. Historians

Figure 9. First Page of Two Third-Grade Students' Newsletter on Ponce de León

Juan Ponce de Leon

1492

HIS SEARCH FOR THE FOUNTAIN OF YOUTH

All about Juan Ponce de Leon

What country did he sail for?

The Fountain of Youth in Florida, U.S.A

Where was he born?

Spain, Europe

When was he born? When did he die? How old was he?

Born: 1460
Death: 1521
Years of age:61

Volume 1, Issue 1

How he died

He died from a poison spear thrown at him on February of 1521.

When and where he visited

Why did he leave his country?
To search for the Fountain of Youth

What did he hope to find?
The Fountain of Youth

Did he find what he was looking for?
No because the Fountain of Youth does not exist.

must also be able to make connections between events and infer cause and effect to fully understand what preceded an event and what will follow. The Herringbone strategy encourages students to show that information in a visual form (Tierney, Readence, & Dishner, 1990; see the Herringbone Diagram reproducible on page 221 in the Appendix). According to Barton and Sawyer (2003), visuals aids such as these enhance student understanding of text because they provide memorable images of information.

How It Works

1. Ask students to read a chunk of informative text about a famous person or key event.

2. Discuss with the class the type of information needed to fully understand an event in history. As they read, students need to ask themselves who did what, where and when it occurred, how it occurred, and why.

3. Put the Herringbone Diagram reproducible on the smartboard. As a class, complete each part of the herringbone. Some passages may not have information for each of the six key questions asked, but students should fill in as much information as they know.

4. Ask a student to take all of the information on the herringbone sheet and see if they can state it in one or two summary sentences.

5. After students have completed this activity, allow them to work in groups to try the strategy with other types of social studies text.

Additional Ways to Try It Out

Students can also use the completed Herringbone Diagram sheet to discuss the event and its relationship to other events in history. Do the students have any ideas about what led to this event? They will have to work backward in their minds from the event they read about and diagrammed on the reproducible. Students may have read information prior to the current passage, which can help provide them with ideas. Students can also think ahead. What do they think will happen as a result of the current event they put on the Herringbone Diagram sheet?

History also requires people to "be able to make connections between first events and second events and third events" (Shanahan & Shanahan, 2008, p. 56). The Herringbone strategy can also be used in this manner. Students can create several herringbone diagrams for a chunk of text. Then,

as a class, the students can try to sequence the diagrams correctly and explain the connections between each. What will happen next? Can students guess the effect of the third event? What caused the chain of events?

Body Biographies

What thoughts, feelings, views, and prior experiences make up who people are? Are there certain concerns, beliefs, and ideas that make people unique? All of these things can be illustrated visually in body biographies. This strategy is a lot of fun for teachers and students of all ages. Students get to use their creativity to develop a body biography of a significant person in history. By doing so, they can discuss key events in social studies and develop a better understanding of how and why events occurred. Students also have the opportunity to analyze a variety of documents as they determine which symbols to use for their finished products. Finally, the field of social studies requires students to better understand perspectives and views. Students, through the completion of body biographies, will understand how viewpoints can vary.

A body biography is a multimedia creation about a person. Body biographies were originally created by Underwood (1987) and designed to be autobiographical. Many people have shown their use with secondary English language arts classes (e.g., Boyd, 2003; Smagorinsky & O'Donnell-Allen, 1998), but body biographies can be especially valuable for developing disciplinary knowledge in social studies. Although many texts share examples created by older students, elementary students can do a wonderful job creating body biographies.

These biographies can depict a famous person in social studies so that students develop a better understanding of the context within which the person lived, worked, and made history. Because historical events do not exist in isolation, the students will also gain information about the time period, events that had a significant effect on the character, and the influence of the character on others. This helps students look at the overall picture and realize the connections of significant events. Body biographies are a creative method for students to visually represent a person and their understanding of the context within which he or she existed. Students must think about pivotal events, the person's relationships with others, and significant places that might have all influenced the creation of that person's

viewpoints. If students work in small groups, the additional benefit is that students work collaboratively to determine important qualities of the person that should be represented and select the best way to represent those traits.

How It Works

1. Ask students, or groups of students, to draw the basic outline of a person on a large sheet of paper. If the sheet is large enough, they can trace around a student to get the basic shape. However, if that is not possible, they may draw the outline of a person on a legal-size sheet of plain white paper. Both methods work well because students only need space to create symbols for key items.

2. Next, have the students determine the famous historical figure they want to illustrate. The class may brainstorm a list of people. By providing students with an element of choice, better results are achieved.

3. Explain that through the use of a variety of texts and materials, students must show important traits of the person. To depict the historical figure, students will need to reread material previously shared in class, look on the Internet, watch videos and films, or read trade books. This activity motivates students to learn all that they can about a person so that they can create a multidimensional representation. As students look at texts, encourage them to jot down any key ideas that may want to represent. These should be items that had a significant influence on the person or were important to the historical figure.

4. After the students complete their lists, explain that there are many ways that they may choose to represent the information. By discussing in their groups, students can determine the best way to represent these important ideas. According to Readence and colleagues (2004), students will want to consider color, placement of symbols, and materials used as they develop their creations.

Color can be used for effect. Perhaps a large red line through a phrase will emphasize that the words represent something that the person would never consider. Concepts or thoughts that made the person very emotional might also be shown in warm colors. People, events, ideas, or thoughts that make the person feel happy may be shown in a different color. Students can think about how they can use color to emphasize information.

Students will also want to think about the placement of symbols. People, places, and items that occupy a place in the character's heart might

be shown there, and thoughts that occupy the character's mind, such as worries and concerns, might be shown on top of the head. If items pertain to the hands, that may be a good location for those symbols.

Materials play a huge role in the successful creation of body biographies, and many students are quite creative with symbols. Students are not limited to just writing and drawing on the paper. They may choose to add small objects created from a variety of materials to represent items important to the person. Also, brief bits of text, such as quotes that students repeatedly saw emphasized in texts researched and lines from poems or songs that remind them of the person, might be included. Magazine pictures, clip art from the Internet, and newspapers can also provide materials for the body biographies.

Some students have used letters cut out from a variety of sources to show specific phrases. One student showed the character's name through a wide variety of letters cut and glued on the paper and stated that it was done in that manner to show the person represented was very creative. The goal is not to have students write paragraphs on the paper but instead symbolically depict through a variety of media that which is important to the person.

A Look Inside One Classroom

A fourth-grade teacher wanted her students to show two perspectives on a significant event. Students were in the process of finishing a unit related to leaders of the U.S. Civil War. The students were allowed to determine whether they wanted to depict Abraham Lincoln, who wanted to end slavery and preserve the union, or Robert E. Lee, who had the difficult decision of which side to fight on in the Civil War: the Union or the Confederacy. Lincoln struggled with the desire to end slavery, but at the same time, he did not want to split the country apart. He wanted to allow slavery in those states that already had it. Lee attended West Point in Pennsylvania and spent more than 30 years in the U.S. Army, but he was loyal to his home state of Virginia. Both leaders clearly had internal struggles because of conflicting beliefs that they had to contend with in their decisions.

The class was then divided into small groups of four or five students each. Those who chose Lincoln read *Abraham Lincoln: Expanding and Preserving the Union* by Christi Parker (2008), while the students reviewing Lee were each given a copy of *Robert E. Lee: Expanding and*

Preserving the Union by Wendy Conklin (2008). These texts contain many linguistic features found in informative text, such as a table of contents, colored fonts, and a glossary. Also, the visuals include photos, illustrations, copies of newspaper articles, and maps. Books such as these can help reinforce the type of reading that students will need to understand as they progress through life.

After reading their texts, groups of students brainstormed ideas from the text that supported each perspective on the leader, and a member of each group wrote down the ideas. Each group was given a sheet of butcher paper, and students traced the outline of one group member on the paper and divided the outline in half. Students were asked to think of creative ways to represent the brainstormed ideas graphically without using a lot of words. The students also created a key for their body biography on a separate sheet of lined paper. The key contained a pencil drawing of the symbol and a sentence or two stating what the symbols represented. After the class finished their body biographies, the life-size outlines were hung in the hallway, and students shared their ideas with classmates.

Students came up with many ideas. One group created a body biography of Lincoln, as shown in Figure 10. After tracing one of the group member's outline on the sheet of paper, the students drew a line vertically down the middle of the body and used the left half to represent Lincoln's desire to end slavery and the right half to show his desire to keep the Union together. The students came up with many symbols to use on their body biography. As a group, they drew a stick figure and then glued Popsicle sticks horizontally and vertically across the figure in the shape of a square. The drawing was placed near Lincoln's head on the half of the body representing his desire to end slavery. The students noted that the image reflected Lincoln's memories of pens at slave auctions, which bothered him his entire life. One of the group's ideas shown on the other half of the body biography is a group of people with a piece of yarn glued around them in a lasso shape. The students explained that this represented the idea that Lincoln wanted to keep the country together and wanted the southern states to rejoin the Union.

On many of the Lee body biographies created, students photocopied pictures of New York and Virginia to show the inner struggle he felt regarding all of his friends in the Union. He loved his home state of Virginia and felt immense loyalty to it. However, his time spent at West Point in New York was also important to him.

Figure 10. A Fourth-Grade Student Group's Body Biography for Abraham Lincoln

It was interesting to note that many students used terms from the two books' glossaries in their supporting statements for the symbols. Therefore, they built their vocabulary by seeing the words, writing them, and reading the sentences on their sheets.

Additional Ways to Try It Out

Students can take the basic body biography one step further and show two views on one person. They can show how a person views himself or herself versus how others view the person. Students may believe a leader felt like he was doing things for all the right reasons, but yet the people during the time period clearly did not view the person in the same manner. Another idea is to show how a person changes over time by depicting how significant historical events and encounters with others transformed a famous person. For both of these ideas, students can divide the outline in half and show the person before (on the left half) and after (on the right half). It is also possible to state a specific time period and ask students to select two people who played a pivotal role in that period. Both of those people can be represented on one body biography, with one on the left and the other on the right. Students may also enjoy guessing the famous figure depicted in the body biography by analyzing the symbols used.

All of the stages of the body biography creation process have value. Students experience transmediation when they take information gained through reading words and represent it through symbols. Many students who struggle with expressing themselves in words feel success with activities such as this, and this success can foster positive attitudes toward content area material. Also, sharing body biography creations is vital. Through this oral sharing, students can develop a deeper understanding of the content material. Students may not have considered the influence of certain people and events on the life of the character, and through a discussion of the symbols that classmates used and the meaning held by them, all of the students will benefit. After the discussion, groups may even choose to add other symbols onto their body biographies.

REFLECTING BACK AND LOOKING FORWARD

Visuals play a very important role in adults' daily lives and also play a pivotal role in students' middle and high school content area learning.

Therefore, it is imperative that young students learn not only to create meaningful visuals but also critically view those they see. By helping elementary-level students do this, teachers capitalize on students' natural interests and the out-of-school experiences they bring to the classroom.

Each content area has specific disciplinary knowledge and skills that students must master to be viewed as literate. To adopt the disciplinary knowledge and skills, students are required to develop a sophisticated understanding of visual literacy. By integrating visuals and viewing experiences into math, science, and social studies lessons at even the youngest of grade levels, elementary students will be better prepared to deal with the literacy demands that they will encounter later in life.

In this chapter, a variety of ideas were recommended to help students develop their visual literacy skills. In order for students to understand math, science, and social studies content and develop the necessary visual literacy skills to be successful on into adulthood, it is imperative that the foundation begin in the earliest of grades.

Reproducibles

CONTENT AREA TRADE BOOK EVALUATION

Scoring: 1 = does not meet expectations; 3 = meets expectations; 5 = exceeds expectations.

Book/Author	Accuracy of Content	Cohesion of Ideas	Organization and Layout	Specialized Vocabulary	Student Considerations	Teacher Goals
	Outstanding Features:					
	Outstanding Features:					
	Outstanding Features:					
	Outstanding Features:					

Content Counts! Developing Disciplinary Literacy Skills, K–6 by Jennifer L. Altieri.
© 2011 by the International Reading Association. May be copied for classroom use.

FLIP ASSESSMENT SHEET

We FLIP Over Text!

Look at the text. Give a score from 1 (*low*) to 10 (*high*) in each category. Then, give the text an overall FLIP score. The hints give you ideas to think about when looking at text. Hints are just food for your brain!

F = **Friendly** (Hint: Table of contents, italicized words, underlined words, bold words, graphs, photos, charts, timelines, illustrations, glossary, index)

☹   1 2 3 4 5 6 7 8 9 10   ☺

L = **Language** (Hint: Word difficulty and length, sentence length, paragraph and text length)

☹   1 2 3 4 5 6 7 8 9 10   ☺

I = **Interest** (Hint: When I skim the text, do I want to read more?)

☹   1 2 3 4 5 6 7 8 9 10   ☺

P = **Prior Knowledge** (Hint: Do I know enough about this topic to understand the text?)

☹   1 2 3 4 5 6 7 8 9 10   ☺

Overall FLIP Score

☹   1 2 3 4 5 6 7 8 9 10   ☺

I FLIP over this text because:

_____

_____

_____

_____

LIFT-THE-FLAP FLIP ASSESSMENT SHEET

F	L	I	P	FLIP
Is the text *friendly*?	Look at *language*! Look at the words and sentences!	Is it *interesting*? Do I want to read more?	Do I have *prior knowledge*? What do I know about the topic?	**Text title and author:** _____ _____ by _____ **Is this a good text for me?** Yes No

COMPASS FOR NAVIGATING WORDS IN TEXT

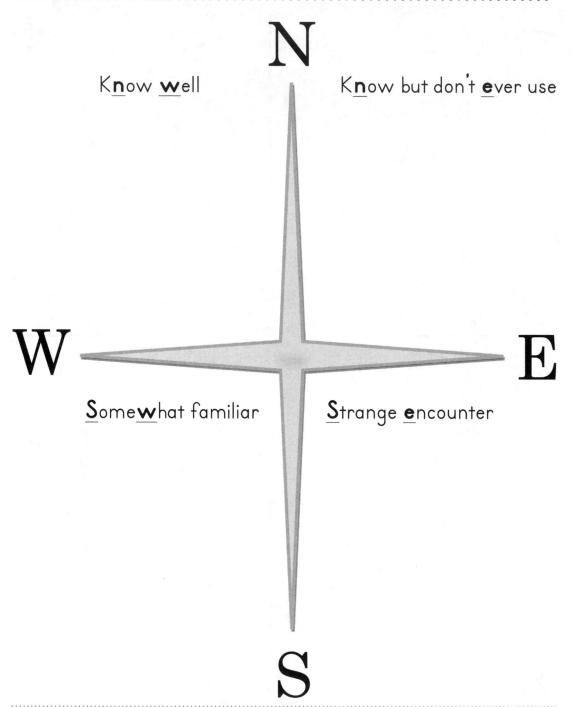

N

Know **well**   K**n**ow but don't **e**ver use

W   E

Some**w**hat familiar   **S**trange **en**counter

S

WORD PROBLEM CODE BREAKER

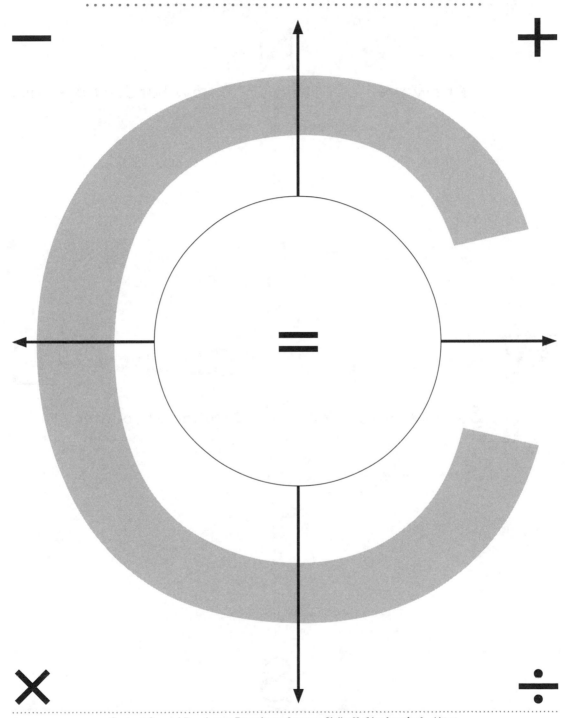

STOPLIGHT STRATEGY FOR
SOLVING WORD PROBLEMS

Get ready to think and solve word problems. Word problems are like puzzles waiting to be solved. Go!

 1. Read the word problem.

2. State the problem that you must solve in a complete sentence:

_____

 Proceed with caution. The next part of the trip can be tricky.

3. Determine what information in the problem is important or unimportant.

 4. Take the important information in the word problem and write out the steps needed to complete it:

_____

_____

_____

_____

 Let's keep going on to the next step because the destination is in sight.

5. Look at the steps and determine the answer:

_____

 6. Answer two important questions:

• Does the answer make sense?

• How do we know that the answer is reasonable?

VISUAL EXPERT ROLE SHEET

Name: _____   Text: _____

Pages to Read: _____   Next Group Meeting: _____

Congratulations! You are a visual expert. With your extensive experience viewing images (e.g., television, computer, movies), it is time to share your opinion on the visuals in this text. After reading through the text, determine if there are additional visuals that might add value to the text. Are there graphs, tables, figures, or other visuals that might make the text easier to understand or more interesting to read? On a sheet of paper, create a couple of visual aids not found in the text that might improve the text. Write on the back of the paper where you would place the visuals in the text.

Also, analyze any visuals already included in the text. Why are they valuable or not valuable? Could they be improved or modified? If you think they could be improved, explain on the form below and create a better version on another sheet of paper.

When you are done, it is time to share your visual expertise with your teammates. Be sure to bring your sheets of paper with newly created visuals and any modified samples of the visuals already in the text to the next group meeting!

Visuals in the Text

Page	Valuable or Not Valuable?	Suggestions

MAD SCIENTIST ROLE SHEET

Name: _____ Text: _____

Pages to Read: _____ Next Group Meeting: _____

Think about mad scientists who you may have seen in the media and in books. Mad scientists are obsessed with their topics. They think about science all the time.

You are now a mad scientist! After reading the assigned text, think about other information that you might locate on this topic or even the author. Seek out other informative books, Internet articles, videos, or poems related to the topic, and you might even interview people who are experts on the topic. What other sources can you consult to add information to the topic? The sky is the limit! Be creative and keep your eyes open for any type of brochures, websites, experts, and so forth that might add information for you to share with your group.

Don't forget to write down the sources and page numbers with a couple of sentences about why you think the source is important. Staple another sheet of paper if you need more room for your brilliant ideas.

Source	Page	Important Information Gained From This Source

TIME MACHINE TRAVELER ROLE SHEET

Name: _____   Text: _____

Pages to Read: _____   Next Group Meeting: _____

With your X-ray vision and navigational skills, you have been selected from a large number of applicants to fly a time machine into the future so that you can see how the material you are learning today might be important to everyone in the future. Then, you will report back on your mission to let others without access to a time machine know what you have found.

Before you begin, think about the world today. How does the information in the text apply to the world around us? Why is it important or significant?

Now, don your helmet and fly into the future. Although you can't go there physically, your mind has the amazing capability to see what it will be like in the future. Read, view, and talk to others about the future. Determine why the material is relevant and applicable to the future. Then, be prepared to share your wisdom with your teammates!

Before Your Time Machine Flight
Briefly explain how the material in the text applies to the world around us right now:

_____

_____

_____

After the Time Machine Flight
Briefly explain how the material applies to the future and cite any sources that gave you ideas.

Suggestions	Source

SCIENCE NEWSCASTER ROLE SHEET

Name: _____ Text: _____

Pages to Read: _____ Next Group Meeting: _____

Have you ever watched television and had your program interrupted because of a breaking news alert? The newscasters only do that when news is urgent and they want their viewing audience to know information right away. Newscasters must be able to give an overview of a lot of information in a limited period of time.

    The local news station has found out about your ability to summarize a great deal of material in a very brief period of time, and they are confident that you realize that all of the key points must be shared with your audience. Your new job as a newscaster is to create a "Breaking News Alert!" story about the text you just read. First, jot down key ideas you want to share in the space below. Then, on another sheet of paper, combine those ideas to create a 30-second news story about the information. Don't forget to practice your news story so that you know the information before sharing it with your teammates. Good luck with your job as a science newscaster!

Key Points to Share in the Newscast

1. _____

_____

2. _____

_____

3. _____

_____

4. _____

_____

5. _____

_____

WORD MAGICIAN ROLE SHEET

Name: _____ Text: _____

Pages to Read: _____ Next Group Meeting: _____

Abracadabra! You are a word magician, and your expertise with words is known around the world. You can take a simple word and do so many things with it.

Look in the text for interesting words that you think others should know. List the word and the page number where it is located, draw an illustration to remember the word, and write a sentence using it, other forms of the word, and the definition. (Carefully locate the correct definition, since many words have multiple meanings.)

Use another sheet of paper for additional words. Be prepared to show the results of your word magic with others in the group the next time you meet.

Word _____   **Page** _____   **Sentence** _____

Other Forms _____   _____   _____   _____

Definition _____

Illustration

_____
| |
| |
| |
| |
| |
|_____|

Word _____   **Page** _____   **Sentence** _____

Other Forms _____   _____   _____   _____

Definition _____

Illustration

_____
| |
| |
| |
| |
| |
|_____|

ARTIST DOCUMENT ANALYSIS

Have you ever noticed that good artists have a keen eye for analyzing the world around them? Analyzing documents (texts, photographs, maps, charts, artifacts, and motion pictures) requires detective-like attention to detail. Below is a chart to help you become an ARTIST!

Audience	
Reason why it was written: to persuade, entertain, inform, or other (explain)	
Type of document: newspaper, letter, map, photograph, report, cartoon, press release, advertisement, motion picture, or other (explain)	
Important details: emotional words, facts, quotes, headings, fonts, bold or italicized text, questions to the author, or other (include at least three)—Do they show bias?	
Source: Who is the author or creator? Who is the publisher?	
Time of creation: Does this tell us anything?	

I-CHART

Topic:	Question 1:	Question 2:	Question 3:	Other Important Information Learned
What do we think we know?				
Textbook: _____ _____				
Nonfiction Trade Book 1: _____ _____				
Nonfiction Trade Book 2: _____ _____				
Website: _____ _____				
Summary				

Note. Adapted from "Critical Reading/Thinking Across the Curriculum: Using I-Charts to Support Learning," by J.V. Hoffman, 1992, *Language Arts, 69*(2), p. 124.

Content Counts! Developing Disciplinary Literacy Skills, K–6 by Jennifer L. Altieri.
© 2011 by the International Reading Association. May be copied for classroom use.

HERRINGBONE DIAGRAM

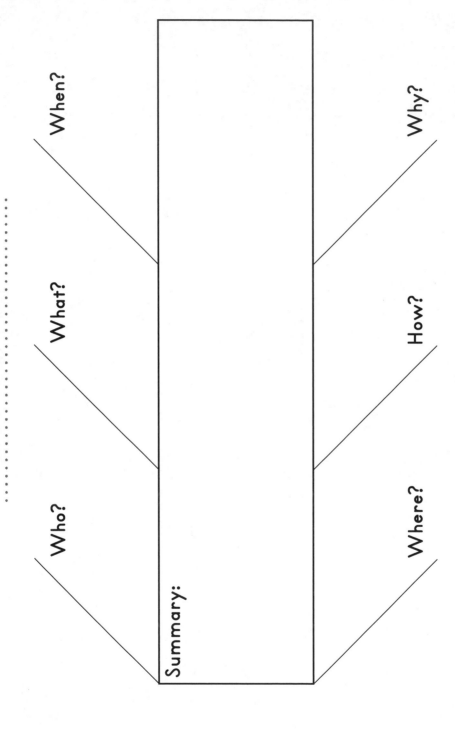

Who?

What?

When?

Summary:

Where?

How?

Why?

Note. From *Reading Strategies and Practices: A Compendium* (3rd ed.), by R.J. Tierney, J.E. Readence, & E.K. Dishner, 1990, Boston: Allyn & Bacon. Reprinted with permission.

Content Counts! Developing Disciplinary Literacy Skills, K–6 by Jennifer L. Altieri. © 2011 by the International Reading Association. May be copied for classroom use.

REFERENCES

Altieri, J.L. (2005). Creating poetry: Reinforcing mathematical concepts. *Teaching Children Mathematics, 12*(1), 18–23.

Altieri, J.L. (2010). *Literacy + math = creative connections in the elementary classroom.* Newark, DE: International Reading Association.

Alvermann, D.E. (2001a). Reading adolescents' reading identities: Looking back to see ahead. *Journal of Adolescent & Adult Literacy, 44*(8), 676–690.

Alvermann, D.E. (2001b). *Effective literacy instruction for adolescents.* Executive summary and paper commissioned by the National Reading Conference. Chicago: National Reading Conference.

American Association for the Advancement of Science. (2002). Middle grades science textbooks: A benchmarks-based evaluation. *AAAS Project 2061.* Retrieved January 10, 2009, from www.project2061.org/publications/textbook/mgsci/report/about.htm

Anning, A. (1999). Learning to draw and drawing to learn. *International Journal of Art & Design Education, 18*(2), 163–172. doi:10.1111/1468-5949.00170

Armbruster, B.B. (1984). The problem of "inconsiderate text." In G.G. Duffy, L.R. Roehler, & J. Mason (Eds.), *Comprehension instruction: Perspectives and suggestions* (pp. 202–217). New York: Longman.

Armbruster, B.B., & Anderson, T.H. (1988). On selecting "considerate" content area textbooks. *Remedial and Special Education, 9*(1), 47–52. doi:10.1177/074193258800900109

Atkinson, T.S., Matusevich, M.N., & Huber, L. (2009). Making science trade book choices for elementary classrooms. *The Reading Teacher, 62*(6), 484–497. doi:10.1598/RT.62.6.3

Ausburn, L.J., & Ausburn, F.B. (1978). Visual literacy: Background, theory and practice. *Programmed Learning and Educational Technology, 15*(4), 291–297.

Avery, C. (2003). Nonfiction books: Naturals for the primary level. In R.A. Bamford & J.V. Kristo (Eds.), *Making facts come alive: Choosing and using nonfiction literature K–8* (2nd ed., pp. 235–246). Norwood, MA: Christopher-Gordon.

Avgerinou, M.D. (2009). Re-viewing visual literacy in the "bain d'images" era. *TechTrends, 53*(2), 28–34. doi:10.1007/s11528-009-0264-z

Baldi, S., Jin, Y., Skemer, M., Green, P.J., & Herget, D. (2007). *Highlights from PISA 2006: Performance of U.S. 15-year-old students in science and mathematics literacy in an international context* (NCES 2008–016). Washington, DC: National Center for Education Statistics, Institute of Education Sciences, U.S. Department of Education.

Bamford, R.A., & Kristo, J.V. (2000). A decade of nonfiction: Ten books with unique features. *Journal of Children's Literature, 26*(2), 50–54.

Bamford, R.A., Kristo, J.V., & Lyon, A. (2002). Facing facts: Nonfiction in the primary classroom. *The New England Reading Association Journal, 38*(2), 8–15.

Barr, R., Blachowicz, C.L.Z., & Wogman-Sadow, M. (1995). *Reading diagnosis for teachers: An instructional approach* (3rd ed.). White Plains, NY: Longman.

Barton, J., & Sawyer, D.M. (2003). Our students are ready for this: Comprehension instruction in the elementary school. *The Reading Teacher, 57*(4), 334–347.

Bell, E.S., & Bell, R.N. (1985). Writing and mathematical problem solving: Arguments in favor of synthesis. *School Science and Mathematics, 85*(3), 210–221. doi:10.1111/j.1949-8594.1985.tb09614.x

Blachowicz, C.L.Z. (1986). Making connections: Alternatives to the vocabulary notebook. *Journal of Reading, 29*(7), 643–649.

Blachowicz, C.L.Z., Sullivan, D.M., & Cieply, C. (2001). Fluency snapshots: A quick screening tool for your classroom. *Reading Psychology, 22*(2), 95–109.

Boyd, F.B. (2003). Experiencing things not seen: Educative events centered on a study of *Shabanu. Journal of Adolescent & Adult Literacy, 46*(6), 460–474.

Boyer, T.L. (2006). Writing to learn in social studies. *The Social Studies, 97*(4), 158–160. doi:10.3200/TSSS.97.4.158-160

Brassell, D. (2006). Inspiring young scientists with great books. *The Reading Teacher, 60*(4), 336–342. doi:10.1598/RT.60.4.3

California Department of Education. (2000). *History–social science content standards for California public schools, kindergarten through grade twelve.* Sacramento: Author.

Calkins, L., Montgomery, K., & Santman, D. (with Falk, B.). (1998). *A teacher's guide to standardized reading tests: Knowledge is power.* Portsmouth, NH: Heinemann.

Carr, E.M., & Ogle, D. (1987). K-W-L plus: A strategy for comprehension and summarization. *Journal of Reading, 30*(7), 626–631.

Caswell, L.J., & Duke, N.K. (1998). Non-narrative as a catalyst for literacy development. *Language Arts, 75*(2), 108–117.

Chall, J.S., Jacobs, V.A., & Baldwin, L.E. (1990). *The reading crisis: Why poor children fall behind.* Cambridge, MA: Harvard University Press.

Chall, J.S., Snow, C., Barnes, W., Chandler, J., Goodman, I., Hemphill, L., et al. (1982). *Families and literacy: The contribution of out-of-school experiences to children's acquisition of literacy: A final report to the National Institute of Education.* Cambridge, MA: Harvard Graduate School of Education. (ERIC Document Reproduction Service No. ED234345)

Cho, H., & Kahle, J.B. (1984). A study of the relationship between concept emphasis in high school biology textbooks and achievement levels. *Journal of Research in Science Teaching, 21*(7), 725–733. doi:10.1002/tea.3660210706

Collard, S.B., III. (2003). Using science books to teach literacy—and save the planet. *The Reading Teacher, 57*(3), 280–283.

Conley, M.W. (2008). *Content area literacy: Learners in context.* Boston: Allyn & Bacon.

Connor, C.M., Kaya, S., Luck, M., Toste, J.R., Canto, A., Rice, D., et al. (2010). Content area literacy: Individualizing student instruction in second-grade science. *The Reading Teacher, 63*(6), 474–485. doi:10.1598/RT.63.6.4

Considine, D., Horton, J., & Moorman, G. (2009). Teaching and reaching the millennial generation through media literacy. *Journal of Adolescent & Adult Literacy, 52*(6), 471–481. doi:10.1598/JAAL.52.6.2

Crespo, S.M., & Kyriakides, A.O. (2007). To draw or not to draw: Exploring children's drawings for solving mathematics problems. *Teaching Children Mathematics, 14*(2), 118–125.

Cullinan, B.E. (1989). *Literature and the child* (2nd ed.). San Diego, CA: Harcourt Brace Jovanovich.

Cunningham, J.W. (1982). Generating interactions between schemata and text. In J.A. Niles & L.A. Harris (Eds.), *New inquiries in reading research and instruction: 31st yearbook of the National Reading Conference* (pp. 42–47). Rochester, NY: National Reading Conference.

Daisey, P. (1994). The value of trade books in secondary science and mathematics instruction: A rationale. *School Science and Mathematics*, *94*(3), 130–137. doi:10.1111/j.1949-8594.1994.tb15639.x

Daisey, P., & José-Kampfner, C. (2002). The power of story to expand possible selves for Latina middle school students. *Journal of Adolescent & Adult Literacy*, *45*(7), 578–587.

Daniels, H. (2002). *Literature circles: Voice and choice in book clubs and reading groups* (2nd ed.). Portland, ME: Stenhouse.

Dimino, J.A. (2007). Bridging the gap between research and practice. *Journal of Learning Disabilities*, *40*(2), 183–189. doi:10.1177/00222194070400020901

Donovan, C.A., & Smolkin, L.B. (2001). Genre and other factors influencing teachers' book selections for science instruction. *Reading Research Quarterly*, *36*(4), 412–440. doi:10.1598/RRQ.36.4.4

Donovan, C.A., & Smolkin, L.B. (2002). Considering genre, content, and visual features in the selection of trade books for science instruction. *The Reading Teacher*, *55*(6), 502–520.

Donovan, C.A., Smolkin, L.B., & Lomax, R.G. (2000). Beyond the independent-level text: Considering the reader–text match in first graders' self-selections during recreational reading. *Reading Psychology*, *21*(4), 309–333. doi:10.1080/027027100750061949

Duke, N.K. (2000). 3.6 minutes per day: The scarcity of informational texts in first grade. *Reading Research Quarterly*, *35*(2), 202–224. doi:10.1598/RRQ.35.2.1

Duke, N.K. (2004). The case for informational text. *Educational Leadership*, *61*(6), 40–44.

Duke, N.K., & Bennett-Armistead, V.S. (2003). *Reading and writing informational text in the primary grades: Research-based practices*. New York: Scholastic.

Duke, N.K., & Tower, C. (2004). Nonfiction texts for young readers. In J.V. Hoffman & D.L. Schallert (Eds.), *The texts in elementary classrooms* (pp. 111–128). Mahwah, NJ: Erlbaum.

Dunn, M.A. (2000). Closing the book on social studies: Four classroom teachers go beyond the text. *The Social Studies*, *91*(3), 132–136. doi:10.1080/00377990009602456

Edens, K.M., & Potter, E. (2003). Using descriptive drawings as a conceptual change strategy in elementary science. *School Science and Mathematics*, *103*(3), 135–144. doi:10.1111/j.1949-8594.2003.tb18230.x

Eeds, M., & Cockrum, W.A. (1985). Teaching word meanings by expanding schemata vs. dictionary work vs. reading in context. *Journal of Reading*, *28*(6), 492–497.

Fello, S.E., Paquette, K.R., & Jalongo, M.R. (2006). Talking drawings: Improving intermediate students' comprehension of expository science text. *Childhood Education*, *83*(2), 80–86.

Finn, P.J. (1999). *Literacy with an attitude: Educating working-class children in their own self-interest*. Albany: State University of New York Press.

Fletcher, R. (2002). *Poetry matters: Writing a poem from the inside out*. New York: HarperTrophy.

Flood, J., & Lapp, D. (1997). Broadening conceptualizations of literacy: The visual and communicative arts. *The Reading Teacher*, *51*(4), 342–344.

Flynt, E.S., & Brozo, W. (2010). Visual literacy and the content classroom: A question of now, not when. *The Reading Teacher*, *63*(6), 526–528. doi:10.1598/RT.63.6.11

Fresch, S.L. (1995). Self-selections of early literacy learners. *The Reading Teacher*, *49*(3), 220–227.

Fry, E. (1977). Fry's readability graph: Clarifications, validity, and extension to level 17. *Journal of Reading, 21*(3), 242–252.

Fuhler, C.J. (1992). The integration of trade books into the social studies curriculum. *Middle School Journal, 24*(2), 63–66.

Gardner, H. (1983). *Frames of mind: The theory of multiple intelligences.* New York: Basic.

Gernon, A., & Grisham, D.L. (2002). Expository texts in the intermediate grades: What teachers teach. *California Reader, 35*(2), 11–20.

Giblin, J.C. (2000). More than just the facts: A hundred years of children's nonfiction. *The Horn Book, 76*(4), 413–424.

Gill, S.R. (2009). What teachers need to know about the "new" nonfiction. *The Reading Teacher, 63*(4), 260–267. doi:10.1598/RT.63.4.1

Greenwood, S. (2004). Content matters: Building vocabulary and conceptual understanding in the subject areas. *Middle School Journal, 35*(3), 27–34.

Guthrie, J.T., Schafer, W.D., & Huang, C. (2001). Benefits of opportunity to read and balanced instruction on the NAEP. *The Journal of Educational Research, 94*(3), 145–162. doi:10.1080/00220670109599912

Guthrie, J.T., Schafer, W.D., Von Secker, C., & Alban, T. (2000). Contributions of instructional practices to reading achievement in a statewide improvement program. *The Journal of Educational Research, 93*(4), 211–225 doi:10.1080/00220670009598710

Guthrie, J.T., Wigfield, A., Humenick, N.M., Perencevich, K.C., Taboada, A., & Barbosa, P. (2006). Influences of stimulating tasks on reading motivation and comprehension. *The Journal of Educational Research, 99*(4), 232–246. doi:10.3200/JOER.99.4.232-246

Gutstein, E., Lipman, P., Hernandez, P., & de los Reyes, R. (1997). Culturally relevant mathematics teaching in a Mexican American context. *Journal for Research in Mathematics Education, 28*(6), 709–737.

Hakuta, K., Butler, Y.G., & Witt, D. (2000). *How long does it take English learners to attain proficiency?* (Policy Report 2000–1). Santa Barbara: Linguistic Minority Research Institute, University of California. Retrieved January 13, 2011, from escholarship.org/uc/item/13w7m06g

Hand, B., & Prain, V. (2002). Teachers implementing writing-to-learn strategies in junior secondary science: A case study. *Science Education, 86*(6), 737–755. doi:10.1002/sce.10016

Hansen, J. (2001). *When writers read* (2nd ed.). Portsmouth, NH: Heinemann.

Hapgood, S., & Palincsar, A.S. (2006). Where literacy and science intersect. *Educational Leadership, 64*(4), 56–60.

Harlen, W. (1997). Primary teachers' understanding in science and its impact in the classroom. *Research in Science Education, 27*(3), 323–337.

Harvey, S., & Goudvis, A. (2007). *Strategies that work: Teaching comprehension for understanding and engagement* (2nd ed.). Portland, ME: Stenhouse.

Hasbrouck, J.E., & Tindal, G. (1992). Curriculum-based oral reading fluency norms for students in grades 2 through 5. *Teaching Exceptional Children, 24*(3), 41–44.

Haury, D.L., & Rillero, P. (1994). *Perspectives of hands-on science teaching.* Columbus, OH: ERIC Clearinghouse for Science, Mathematics, and Environmental Education. Retrieved January 13, 2011, from www.ncrel.org/sdrs/areas/issues/content/cntareas/science/eric/eric-1.htm

Heath, S.B. (1983). *Ways with words: Language, life, and work in communities and classrooms*. New York: Cambridge University Press.

Heisey, N., & Kucan, L. (2010). Introducing science concepts to primary students through read-alouds: Interactions and multiple texts make the difference. *The Reading Teacher, 63*(8), 666–676. doi:10.1598/RT.63.8.5

Henke, R.R., Chen, X., & Goldman, G. (1999a). What happens in classrooms? Instructional practices in elementary and secondary schools, 1994–95. *Education Statistics Quarterly, 1*(2), 7–13.

Henke, R.R., Chen, X., & Goldman, G. (1999b). *What happens in classrooms? Instructional practices in elementary and secondary schools, 1994–95* (NCES 1999-348). Washington, DC: National Center for Education Statistics, U.S. Department of Education.

Heubach, K.M. (1995, December). *Integrating literature into a fourth-grade social studies curriculum: The effects on student learning and attitude*. Paper presented at the annual meeting of the National Reading Conference, New Orleans, LA.

Hilke, E.V. (1999). *Children's literature and the K–4 social studies standards*. Bloomington, IN: Phi Delta Kappa Educational Foundation.

Hoffman, J.V. (1992). Critical reading/thinking across the curriculum: Using I-charts to support learning. *Language Arts, 69*(2), 121–127.

Holliday, W.G., Yore, L.D., & Alvermann, D.E. (1994). The reading–science learning–writing connection: Breakthroughs, barriers, and promises. *Journal of Research in Science Teaching, 31*(9), 877–893.

Hoover-Dempsey, K.V., & Sandler, H.M. (1997). Why do parents become involved in their children's education? *Review of Educational Research, 67*(1), 3–42.

Huck, C.S., Hepler, S., Hickman, J., & Kiefer, B.Z. (2001). *Children's literature in the elementary school* (7th ed.). New York: McGraw-Hill.

Hunsader, P.D. (2004). Mathematics trade books: Establishing their value and assessing their quality. *The Reading Teacher, 57*(7), 618–629.

Ikpeze, C.H., & Boyd, F.B. (2007). Web-based inquiry learning: Facilitating thoughtful literacy with WebQuests. *The Reading Teacher, 60*(7), 644–654. doi:10.1598/RT.60.7.5

Jalongo, M.R. (2006). *Early childhood language arts* (4th ed.). Boston: Allyn & Bacon.

Janzen, J. (2008). Teaching English language learners in the content areas. *Review of Educational Research, 78*(4), 1010–1038. doi:10.3102/0034654308325580

Jones, R.C., & Thomas, T.G. (2006). Leave no discipline behind. *The Reading Teacher, 60*(1), 58–64. doi:10.1598/RT.60.1.6

Kamberelis, G. (1999). Genre development and learning: Children writing stories, science reports, and poems. *Research in the Teaching of English, 33*(4), 403–460.

Kamil, M.L., Kim, H.S., & Lane, D. (2004). Electronic text in the classroom. In J.V. Hoffman & D.L. Schallert (Eds.), *The texts in elementary classrooms* (pp. 139–153). Mahwah, NJ: Erlbaum.

Kiefer, B.Z. (with Hepler, S., & Hickman, J.). (2007). *Charlotte Huck's children's literature* (9th ed.). New York: McGraw-Hill.

Kleiner, A. & Farris, E. (2002). *Internet access in U.S. public schools and classrooms: 1994–2001* (NCES 2002-018). Washington, DC: National Center for Education Statistics, Institute of Education Sciences, U.S. Department of Education. Retrieved January 13, 2011, from www.nces.ed.gov/pubsearch/pubsinfo.asp?pubid=2002018

Knipper, K.J., & Duggan, T.J. (2006). Writing to learn across the curriculum: Tools for comprehension in content area classes. *The Reading Teacher, 59*(5), 462–470. doi:10.1598/RT.59.5.5

Koch, K. (2000). *Wishes, lies, and dreams: Teaching children to write poetry.* New York: HarperCollins.

Kristeva, J. (1984). *Revolution in poetic language.* New York: Columbia University Press.

Laine, C.H., Bullock, T.L., & Ford, K.L. (1998). In search of content area reading instruction: The role of science classrooms. *Educational Research Quarterly, 21*(3), 3–19.

Lamme, L.L., & Ledbetter, L. (1990). Libraries: The heart of whole language. *Language Arts, 67*(7), 735–741.

Lefever-Davis, S., & Pearman, C. (2005). Early readers and electronic texts: CD-ROM storybook features that influence reading behaviors. *The Reading Teacher, 58*(5), 446–454. doi:10.1598/RT.58.5.4

Leinhardt, G., & Young, K.M. (1996). Two texts, three readers: Distance and expertise in reading history. *Cognition and Instruction, 14*(4), 441–486. doi:10.1207/s1532690xci1404_2

Leland, C.H., & Harste, J.C. (1994). Multiple ways of knowing: Curriculum in a new key. *Language Arts, 71*(5), 337–345.

Lemke, J.L. (1989). Making text talk. *Theory Into Practice, 28*(2), 136–141. doi:10.1080/00405848909543392

Leu, D.J., Jr. (2000). Literacy and technology: Deictic consequences for literacy education in an information age. In M.L. Kamil, P.B. Mosenthal, P.D. Pearson, & R. Barr (Eds.), *Handbook of reading research* (Vol. 3, pp. 743–770). Mahwah, NJ: Erlbaum.

Liu, Z. (2005). Reading behavior in the digital environment: Changes in reading behavior over the past ten years. *Journal of Documentation, 61*(6), 700–712. doi:10.1108/00220410510632040

Lusk, M.G., Bickmore, B.R., Christiansen, E.H., & Sudweeks, R.R. (2006). Use of a mentored creative writing project to improve the geology education of preservice elementary teachers. *Journal of Geoscience Education, 54*(1), 31–40.

Lynch-Brown, C., & Tomlinson, C.M. (1999). *Essentials of children's literature* (3rd ed.). Boston: Allyn & Bacon.

Macken, C.T. (2003). What in the world do second graders know about geography? Using picture books to teach geography. *The Social Studies, 94*(2), 63–68. doi:10.1080/00377990309600184

Maloch, B., Hoffman, J.V., & Patterson, E.U. (2004). Local texts: Reading and writing "of the classroom." In J.V. Hoffman & D.L. Schallert (Eds.), *The texts in elementary classrooms* (pp. 129–138). Mahwah, NJ: Erlbaum.

Manderino, M. (2007, November). *Integrating the visual: Student strategies for multiple text synthesis.* Paper presented at the annual meeting of the National Reading Conference, Austin, TX.

Manzo, K.K. (2005). Social studies losing out to reading, math. *Education Week, 24*(27), 1, 16–17.

McCarthey, S.J. (2000). Home–school connections: A review of the literature. *The Journal of Educational Research, 93*(3), 145–153. doi:10.1080/00220670009598703

McConnell, S. (1993). Talking drawings: A strategy for assisting learners. *Journal of Reading, 36*(4), 260–269.

McPherson, K. (2007). New online technologies for new literacy instruction. *Teacher Librarian, 34*(3), 69–71.

Miller, R.G., & Calfee, R.C. (2004). Making thinking visible: A method to encourage science writing in upper elementary grades. *Science and Children, 42*(3), 20–24.

Moore, P.J., & Scevak, J.J. (1997). Learning from texts and visual aids: A developmental perspective. *Journal of Research in Reading, 20*(3), 205–223. doi:10.1111/1467-9817.00033

Morrison, J.A., & Young, T.A. (2008). Using science trade books to support inquiry in the elementary classroom. *Childhood Education, 84*(4), 204–208.

Morrow, L.M., Pressley, M., Smith, J.K., & Smith, M. (1997). The effect of a literature-based program integrated into literacy and science instruction with children from diverse backgrounds. *Reading Research Quarterly, 32*(1), 54–76. doi:10.1598/RRQ.32.1.4

Moss, B. (1991). Children's nonfiction trade books: A complement to content area texts. *The Reading Teacher, 45*(1), 26–32.

Moss, B. (2004). Teaching expository text structures through information trade book retellings. *The Reading Teacher, 57*(8), 710–718.

Moss, B. (2005). Making a case and a place for effective content area literacy instruction in the elementary grades. *The Reading Teacher, 59*(1), 46–55. doi:10.1598/RT.59.1.5

Moyer, P.S. (2000). Communicating mathematically: Children's literature as a natural connection. *The Reading Teacher, 54*(3), 246–255.

National Council for the Social Studies. (2010). *National curriculum standards for social studies: A framework for teaching, learning, and assessment.* Silver Spring, MD: Author.

National Council of Teachers of English. (2008). *The NCTE definition of 21st century literacies* (Position statement). Retrieved March 8, 2011, from www.ncte.org/positions/statements/21stcentdefinition.

National Council of Teachers of Mathematics. (2000). *Principles and standards for school mathematics.* Reston, VA: Author.

National Research Council. (1996). *National science education standards.* Washington, DC: National Academy Press.

Norton, D.E., & Norton, S.E. (2003). *Through the eyes of a child: An introduction to children's literature* (6th ed.). Upper Saddle River, NJ: Prentice Hall.

O'Brien, D. (2001). "At-risk" adolescents: Redefining competence through the multiliteracies of intermediality, visual arts, and representation. *Reading Online, 4*(11). Retrieved January 13, 2011, from www.readingonline.org/newliteracies/lit_index.asp?HREF=obrien/index.html

Padak, N., & Rasinski, T. (2007). Is being wild about Harry enough? Encouraging independent reading at home. *The Reading Teacher, 61*(4), 350–353. doi:10.1598/RT.61.4.9

Palmer, R.G., & Stewart, R.A. (1997). Nonfiction trade books in content area instruction: Realities and potential. *Journal of Adolescent & Adult Literacy, 40*(8), 630–641.

Pappas, C.C. (1993). Is narrative "primary"? Some insights from kindergarteners' pretend readings of stories and information books. *Journal of Reading Behavior, 25*(1), 97–129.

Pappas, C.C. (2006). The information book genre: Its role in integrated science literacy research and practice. *Reading Research Quarterly, 41*(2), 226–250. doi:10.1598/RRQ.41.2.4

Pentimonti, J.M., Zucker, T.A., Justice, L.M., & Kaderavek, J.N. (2010). Informational text use in preschool classroom read-alouds. *The Reading Teacher, 63*(8), 656–665. doi:10.1598/RT.63.8.4

Perie, M., Grigg, W., & Donahue, P. (2005). *The nation's report card: Reading 2005* (NCES 2006-451). Washington, DC: National Center for Education Statistics, Institute of Education Sciences, U.S. Department of Education.

Perkins-Gough, D. (2004). The eroding curriculum. *Educational Leadership, 62*(1), 84–85.

PISA, PIRLS spotlight global trends. (2008). *Reading Today, 25*(4), 1, 4–5.

Plummer, D.M., & Kuhlman, W. (2008). Literacy and science connections in the classroom. *Reading Horizons, 48*(2), 95–110.

Prensky, M. (2005). Listen to the natives. *Educational Leadership, 63*(4), 8–13.

Pressley, M., Rankin, J., & Yokoi, L. (1996). A survey of instructional practices of primary teachers nominated as effective in promoting literacy. *The Elementary School Journal, 96*(4), 363–384.

Purcell-Gates, V., Duke, N.K., & Martineau, J.A. (2007). Learning to read and write genre-specific text: Roles of authentic experience and explicit teaching. *Reading Research Quarterly, 42*(1), 8–45. doi:10.1598/RRQ.42.1.1

The push to improve STEM education. (2008, March 27). *Education Week, 27*(30), 8. Retrieved January 14, 2011, from www.edweek.org/ew/articles/2008/03/27/30intro.h27.html

Rafael, T.E. (1986). Teaching question answer relationships, revisited. *The Reading Teacher, 39*(6), 516–522.

Raygor, A.L. (1977). The Raygor readability estimate: A quick and easy way to determine difficulty. In P.D. Pearson (Ed.), *Reading: Theory, research, and practice: 26th yearbook of the National Reading Conference* (pp. 259–263). Clemson, SC: National Reading Conference.

Readence, J.E., Bean, T.W., & Baldwin, R.S. (2004). *Content area literacy: An integrated approach* (8th ed.). Dubuque, IA: Kendall/Hunt.

Reutzel, D.R., Smith, J.A., & Fawson, P.C. (2005). An evaluation of two approaches for teaching reading comprehension strategies in the primary years using science information texts. *Early Childhood Research Quarterly, 20*(3), 276–305. doi:10.1016/j.ecresq.2005.07.002

Rhodes, J.A., & Milby, T.M. (2007). Teacher-created electronic books: Integrating technology to support readers with disabilities. *The Reading Teacher, 61*(3), 255–259. doi:10.1598/RT.61.3.6

Rice, D.C. (2002). Using trade books in teaching elementary science: Facts and fallacies. *The Reading Teacher, 55*(6), 552–565.

Rogers, M.A.P., & Abell, S.K. (2007). Connecting with other disciplines. *Science and Children, 44*(6), 58–59.

Ross, E.P. (1994). *Using children's literature across the curriculum.* Bloomington, IN: Phi Delta Kappa Educational Foundation.

Routman, R. (2000). *Kids' poems: Teaching first graders to love writing poetry.* New York: Scholastic.

Santa, C.M. (with Havens, L., Nelson, M., Danner, M., Scalf, L., & Scalf, J.). (1988). *Content reading including study systems: Reading, writing and studying across the curriculum.* Dubuque, IA: Kendall/Hunt.

Saul, E.W., & Dieckman, D. (2005). Choosing and using information trade books. *Reading Research Quarterly, 40*(4), 502–513. doi:10.1598/RRQ.40.4.6

Schiro, M. (1997). *Integrating children's literature and mathematics in the classroom: Children as meaning makers, problem solvers, and literary critics.* New York: Teachers College Press.

Schleppegrell, M.J. (2007). The linguistic challenges of mathematics teaching and learning: A research review. *Reading & Writing Quarterly, 23*(2), 139–159. doi:10.1080/10573560601158461

Schmar-Dobler, E. (2003). Reading on the Internet: The link between literacy and technology. *Journal of Adolescent & Adult Literacy, 47*(1), 80–85.

Schumm, J.S., & Mangrum, C.T., II. (1991). FLIP: A framework for content area reading. *Journal of Reading, 35*(2), 120–124.

Shanahan, T., & Barr, R. (1995). Reading recovery: An independent evaluation of the effects of an early instructional intervention for at-risk learners. *Reading Research Quarterly, 30*(4), 958–996.

Shanahan, T., & Shanahan, C. (2008). Teaching disciplinary literacy to adolescents: Rethinking content-area literacy. *Harvard Educational Review, 78*(1), 40–59.

Shockley, B. (1994). Extending the literate community: Home-to-school and school-to-home. *The Reading Teacher, 47*(6), 500–502.

Silva, C., Weinburgh, M., Smith, K.H., Barreto, G., & Gabel, J. (2008). Partnering to develop academic language for English language learners through mathematics and science. *Childhood Education, 85*(2), 107–112.

Smagorinsky, P., & O'Donnell-Allen, C. (1998). Reading as mediated and mediating action: Composing meaning for literature through multimedia interpretive texts. *Reading Research Quarterly, 33*(2), 198–226. doi:10.1598/RRQ.33.2.3

Smith, K.P. (2001). Acknowledging, citing, going beyond: Issues of documentation in nonfiction literature. In M. Zarnowski, R.M. Kerper, & J.M. Jensen (Eds.), *The best in children's nonfiction: Reading, writing, and teaching Orbis Pictus Award books* (pp. 32–41). Urbana, IL: National Council of Teachers of English.

Smith, M.C. (2000). The real-world reading practices of adults. *Journal of Literacy Research, 32*(1), 25–52. doi:10.1080/10862960009548063

Smolkin, L.B., & Donovan, C.A. (2001). The contexts of comprehension: The information book read aloud, comprehension acquisition, and comprehension instruction in a first-grade classroom. *The Elementary School Journal, 102*(2), 97–122.

Stahl, S.A., & Shanahan, C. (2004). Learning to think like a historian: Disciplinary knowledge through critical analysis of multiple documents. In T.L. Jetton & J.A. Dole (Eds.), *Adolescent literacy research and practice* (pp. 94–115). New York: Guilford.

Steele, D. (2005). Using writing to access students' schemata knowledge for algebraic thinking. *School Science and Mathematics, 105*(3), 142–154. doi:10.1111/j.1949-8594.2005.tb18048.x

Stewart, R.A. (1994). A causal connective look at the future of secondary content area literacy. *Contemporary Education, 65*(2), 90–94.

Sudol, P., & King, C.M. (1996). A checklist for choosing nonfiction trade books. *The Reading Teacher, 49*(5), 422–424.

Swafford, J., & Kallus, M. (2002). Content literacy: A journey into the past, present, and future. *Journal of Content Area Reading, 1*(1), 7–21.

Taba, H. (1967). *Teacher's handbook for elementary social studies*. Reading, MA: Addison-Wesley.

Taylor, D., & Dorsey-Gaines, C. (1988). *Growing up literate: Learning from inner-city families*. Portsmouth, NH: Heinemann.

Templeton, T.N., Neel, R.S., & Blood, E. (2008). Meta-analysis of math interventions for students with emotional and behavioral disorders. *Journal of Emotional and Behavioral Disorders, 16*(4), 226–239. doi:10.1177/1063426608321691

Tierney, R.J., Readence, J.E., & Dishner, E.K. (1990). *Reading strategies and practices: A compendium* (3rd ed.). Boston: Allyn & Bacon.

Tompkins, G.E. (2009). *Language arts: Patterns of practice* (7th ed.). Boston: Allyn & Bacon.

Underwood, W. (1987). The body biography: A framework for student writing. *English Journal, 76*(8), 44–48.

Vacca, R.T., & Vacca, J.A.L. (2008). *Content area reading: Literacy and learning across the curriculum* (9th ed.). Boston: Allyn & Bacon.

Van Meter, P. (2001). Drawing construction as a strategy for learning from text. *Journal of Educational Psychology, 93*(1), 129–140. doi:10.1037/0022-0663.93.1.129

VanSledright, B. (2002). Confronting history's interpretive paradox while teaching fifth graders to investigate the past. *American Educational Research Journal, 39*(4), 1089–1115. doi:10.3102/000283120390041089

Varelas, M., Pappas, C., Barry, A., & O'Neill, A. (2001). Examining language to capture scientific understandings: The case of the water cycle. *Science and Children, 38*(7), 26–29.

Venezky, R.L. (2000). The origins of the present-day chasm between adult literacy needs and school literacy instruction. *Scientific Studies of Reading, 4*(1), 19–39. doi:10.1207/S1532799XSSR0401_3

Walker, N.T., & Bean, T.W. (2005). Sociocultural influences in content area teachers' selection and use of multiple texts. *Reading Research and Instruction, 44*(4), 61–77.

Wallace, R.R. (2005). A comparison of students' reading levels and the reading levels of their assigned textbooks. *The Reading Professor, 27*(2), 54–74.

Walpole, S. (1998). Changing texts, changing thinking: Comprehension demands of new science textbooks. *The Reading Teacher, 52*(4), 358–369.

Walter, A. (2006). Happy poems: Children's awareness of audience. *Language Arts, 83*(6), 523–529.

Webster, P.S. (2009). Exploring the literature of fact. *The Reading Teacher, 62*(8), 662–671. doi:10.1598/RT.62.8.4

Weiss, I.R. (1987). *Report of the 1985–86 National Survey of Science and Mathematics Education.* Durham, NC: Research Triangle Institute. (ERIC Document Reproduction Service No. ED292620)

White, T.G., Power, M.A., & White, S. (1989). Morphological analysis: Implications for teaching and understanding vocabulary growth. *Reading Research Quarterly, 24*(3), 283–304.

White, T.G., Sowell, J., & Yanagihara, A. (1989). Teaching elementary students to use word-part clues. *The Reading Teacher, 42*(4), 302–308.

Wigfield, A., Guthrie, J.T., Tonks, S., & Perencevich, K.C. (2004). Children's motivation for reading: Domain specificity and instructional influences. *The Journal of Educational Research, 97*(6), 299–310. doi:10.3200/JOER.97.6.299-310

Williams, B.T. (2008). "Tomorrow will not be like today": Literacy and identity in a world of multiliteracies. *Journal of Adolescent & Adult Literacy, 51*(8), 682–686. doi:10.1598/JAAL.51.8.7

Williams, J.P., Stafford, K.B., Lauer, K.D., Hall, K.M., & Pollini, S. (2009). Embedding reading comprehension training in content-area instruction. *Journal of Educational Psychology, 101*(1), 1–20. doi:10.1037/a0013152

Wineburg, S.S. (1991). Historical problem solving: A study of the cognitive processes used in the evaluation of documentary and pictorial evidence. *Journal of Educational Psychology, 83*(1), 73–87. doi:10.1037/0022-0663.83.1.73

Wollman-Bonilla, J.E. (2001). Can first-grade writers demonstrate audience awareness? *Reading Research Quarterly, 36*(2), 184–201. doi:10.1598/RRQ.36.2.4

Wood, K.D. (2003). New dimensions of content area literacy: Not just for secondary teachers anymore. *California Reader, 36*, 12–17.

Worthy, J., Moorman, M., & Turner, M. (1999). What Johnny likes to read is hard to find in school. *Reading Research Quarterly, 34*(1), 12–27. doi:10.1598/RRQ.34.1.2

Yopp, H.K., & Yopp, R.H. (2003). Ten important words: Identifying the big ideas in informational text. *Journal of Content Area Reading, 2*(1), 7–13.

Yopp, R.H., & Yopp, H.K. (2006). Informational texts as read-alouds at school and home. *Journal of Literacy Research, 38*(1), 37–51. doi:10.1207/s15548430jlr3801_2

Yopp, R.H., & Yopp, H.K. (2007). Ten important words plus: A strategy for building word knowledge. *The Reading Teacher, 61*(2), 157–160. doi:10.1598/RT.61.2.5

Young, T.A., & Vardell, S. (1993). Weaving Readers Theatre and nonfiction into the curriculum. *The Reading Teacher, 46*(5), 396–406.

LITERATURE CITED

Agee, J. (2002). *Who ordered the jumbo shrimp? And other oxymorons.* New York: Sunburst.

AIMS Education Foundation. (2005). *Electrical connections: Activities integrating math and science.* Fresno, CA: Author.

Arnold, C. (2007). *Super swimmers: Whales, dolphins, and other mammals of the sea.* Watertown, MA: Charlesbridge.

Ball, J. (2005). *Go figure! A totally cool book about numbers.* New York: DK.

Berleth, R. (1990). *Samuel's choice.* Morton Grove, IL: Albert Whitman.

Bill, T. (2010). *Pika: Life in the rocks.* Honesdale, PA: Boyds Mills.

Bishop, N. (2007). *Spiders.* New York: Scholastic.

Brennan-Nelson, D. (2003). *My momma likes to say.* Chelsea, MI: Sleeping Bear.

Brennan-Nelson, D. (2004). *My teacher likes to say.* Chelsea, MI: Sleeping Bear.

Brennan-Nelson, D. (2007). *My grandma likes to say.* Chelsea, MI: Sleeping Bear.

Brennan-Nelson, D. (2009). *My daddy likes to say.* Chelsea, MI: Sleeping Bear.

Campbell, S.C. (2008). *Wolfsnail: A backyard predator.* Honesdale, PA: Boyds Mills.

Campbell, S.C. (2010). *Growing patterns: Fibonacci numbers in nature.* Honesdale, PA: Boyds Mills.

Cannon, J. (1997). *Stellaluna* (Oversize ed.). New York: Harcourt Brace.

Carle, E. (2009). *The very hungry caterpillar* (40th anniv. pop-up ed.). New York: Philomel.

Clemens, M., Clemens, G., & Clemens, S. (2003). *The everything kids' math puzzles book: Brain teasers, games, and activities for hours of fun.* Avon, MA: Adams Media.

Cole, J. (1997). *The magic school bus and the electric field trip.* New York: Scholastic.

Conklin, W. (2008). *Robert E. Lee: Expanding and preserving the union.* Huntington Beach, CA: Shell Education.

Crump, M. (2010). *Mysteries of the Komodo dragon: The biggest, deadliest lizard gives up its secrets.* Honesdale, PA: Boyds Mills.

DeGross, M. (1998). *Donovan's word jar.* New York: Amistad.

dePaola, T. (2004). *Adelita: A Mexican Cinderella story.* New York: Puffin.

Dotlich, R.K. (2006). *What is science?* New York: Henry Holt.

Erickson, T. (2005). *Get it together: Math problems for groups, grades 4–12* (11th ed.). Berkeley, CA: EQUALS/Lawrence Hall of Science.

Feinstein, S. (2008). *Discovery of electricity*. New York: Macmillan McGraw-Hill.

Fleischman, P. (1985). *I am phoenix: Poems for two voices*. New York: HarperTrophy.

Fleischman, P. (1988). *Joyful noise: Poems for two voices*. New York: HarperTrophy.

Fleischman, P. (2000). *Big talk: Poems for four voices*. Cambridge, MA: Candlewick.

Fleming, T. (2006). *Everybody's revolution: A new look at the people who won America's freedom*. New York: Scholastic.

Fox, M. (1989). *Wilfrid Gordon McDonald Partridge*. La Jolla, CA: Kane/Miller.

Franco, B. (2009). *Pond circle*. New York: Margaret K. McElderry.

Gibbons, G. (1999). *Sea turtles*. Pine Plains, NY: Live Oak Media.

Greenfield, E. (1977). *Mary McLeod Bethune*. New York: HarperCollins.

Gwynne, F. (1988). *The king who rained*. New York: Aladdin.

Gwynne, F. (1976). *A chocolate moose for dinner*. New York: Aladdin.

Hakim, J. (2007). *The first Americans: Prehistory–1600* (Rev. 3rd. ed.). New York: Oxford University Press.

Halfmann, J. (2007). *Little Skink's tail*. Mt. Pleasant, SC: Sylvan Dell.

Hansen, A.S. (2010). *Bugs and bugsicles: Insects in the winter*. Honesdale, PA: Boyds Mills.

Hoberman, M.A. (2001). *You read to me, I'll read to you: Very short stories to read together*. New York: Little, Brown.

Hoberman, M.A. (2004). *You read to me, I'll read to you: Very short fairy tales to read together*. New York: Little, Brown.

Hoberman, M.A. (2007). *You read to me, I'll read to you: Very short scary tales to read together*. New York: Little, Brown.

Hulme, J.N. (2005). *Wild Fibonacci: Nature's secret code revealed*. Berkeley, CA: Tricycle.

Jenkins, S. (2004). *Actual size*. Boston: Houghton Mifflin.

Kirby, P.F. (2009). *What bluebirds do*. Honesdale, PA: Boyds Mills.

Lee, M., & Miller, M. (2001). *40 fabulous math mysteries kids can't resist: Fun-filled reproducible mystery stories that build essential math problem-solving skills*. New York: Scholastic.

Leedy, L., & Street, P. (2003). *There's a frog in my throat! 440 animal sayings a little bird told me*. New York: Holiday House.

Levin, F. (2010). *Draw plus math: Enhance math learning through art activities*. Vancouver, WA: Peel.

Levine, E. (1993). *If your name was changed at Ellis Island*. New York: Scholastic.

Lewis, J.P. (2007a). *Arithme-tickle: An even number of odd riddle-rhymes*. New York: Harcourt.

Lewis, J.P. (2007b). *Scien-trickery: Riddles in science*. New York: Harcourt.

Liggett, P., & Donaldson, D. (2005). *Dancing on the pedals: The found poetry of Phil Liggett, the voice of cycling*. Halcottsville, NY: Breakaway.

Mariconda, B. (2008). *Sort it out!* Mt. Pleasant, SC: Sylvan Dell.

Mitchell, J.S. (2000). *Tractor-trailer trucker: A powerful truck book*. Berkeley, CA: Tricycle.

Mitchell, J.S. (2001). *Crashed, smashed, and mashed: A trip to junkyard heaven*. Berkeley, CA: Tricycle.

Mitchell, S.K. (2007). *The rainforest grew all around*. Mt. Pleasant, SC: Sylvan Dell.

Monroe, E.E. (2006). *Math dictionary: The easy, simple, fun guide to help math phobics become math lovers*. Honesdale, PA: Boyds Mills.

Monroe, M.A. (2007). *Turtle summer: A journal for my daughter.* Mt. Pleasant, SC: Sylvan Dell.

Murray, S. (2005). *American Revolution*. New York: DK.

Parker, C.E. (2008). *Abraham Lincoln: Expanding and preserving the union*. Huntington Beach, CA: Shell Education.

Peterson, C. (2010). *Seed, soil, sun: Earth's recipe for food*. Honesdale, PA: Boyds Mills.

Polacco, P. (1998). *Thank you, Mr. Falker*. New York: Philomel.

Pringle, L. (2010). *Cicadas! Strange and wonderful*. Honesdale, PA: Boyds Mills.

Prokos, A. (2006). *It's electric!* New York: Macmillan McGraw-Hill.

Rizzuto, P. (2008). *O holy cow! The selected verse of Phil Rizzuto* (Expanded ed.; T. Peyer & H. Seely, Eds.). New York: HarperCollins.

Schwartz, D.M. (1998). *G is for googol: A math alphabet book*. Berkeley, CA: Tricycle.

Schwartz, D.M., & Schy, Y. (2010). *What in the wild? Mysteries of nature concealed… and revealed*. Berkeley, CA: Tricycle.

Scieszka, J. (1995). *Math curse*. New York: Viking.

Sidman, J. (2005). *Song of the water boatman: And other pond poems*. New York: Houghton Mifflin.

Simon, S. (1989). *Storms*. New York: Mulberry.

Stewart, M. (2009). *Under the snow*. Atlanta, GA: Peachtree.

Swinburne, S.R. (2006). *Wings of light: The migration of the yellow butterfly*. Honesdale, PA: Boyds Mills.

Tang, G. (2003). *Math-terpieces: The art of problem-solving*. New York: Scholastic.

Terban, M. (1983). *In a pickle, and other funny idioms*. New York: Clarion.

VandeCreek, B. (2001). *Math rules! 1st–2nd*. Marion, IL: Pieces of Learning.

Wittenstein, V.O. (2010). *Planet hunter: Geoff Marcy and the search for other Earths*. Honesdale, PA: Boyds Mills.

Yolen, J. (2009). *A mirror to nature: Poems about reflection*. Honesdale, PA: Wordsong.

Zaccaro, E. (2003). *Primary grade challenge math*. Bellevue, IA: Hickory Grove.

INDEX

Note. Page numbers followed by *f*, *t*, and *r* indicate figures, tables, and reproducibles, respectively.